From Fabian's Bay
to
Fabian Way

The Development of Kilvey, St. Thomas, Danygraig, and Port Tennant in Victorian Swansea

Jeff Stewart MBA CMgr FCMI MIC

Print ISBN 978-0-9576791-5-3

Published by

Llyfrau Cambria Books, Wales, United Kingdom.

Cambria Books is the imprint of

Cambria Publishing Ltd.

Discover our other books at: www.cambriabooks.co.uk

Dedications

Dedicated with love to my mother Pat Stewart, to my late father Ken Stewart, and to my wife Jan for always being there whenever I needed you to be.

Cover image credit.

'*View of Swansea and railway bridge*'. by: Newman and Co.; [ca. 1850] Glamorganshire Top. B8/10 B220 (PB02529). By permission of Llyfrgell Genedlaethol Cymru/The National Library of Wales

CONTENTS

Foreword

The past of the town of Swansea has been quite well documented, but sixty years ago, Norman Lewis Thomas correctly identified the crucial importance of its "districts and villages". These have been less well served. Interesting publications exist, but this is the first fully-fledged history of any one of the communities which ringed the town and were crucial to its growth. It is not surprising that it is the story of the Eastside.

The growth of copper smelting in the lower Swansea Valley was the source of Swansea's prosperity. with at least nine large and moderate-sized smelters in Hafod, Landore, Morriston, and east of the river. It led to the conversion of the Town Reach of the Tawe into the North Dock, often called 'The Float' which opened in 1852. This necessitated a "New Cut" to take the river water, and this put an end to the Tirlandwr farmland on the edge of the Eastside. In 1881 the first of Swansea's modern docks was opened seaward of St. Thomas, and by 1920 two more had followed.

John Lewis was elected a councillor for the area in 1876 and it was said of him that he "soon believed it would be Swansea near St. Thomas". This sense of identity generated pride in the community across St. Thomas, Danygraig, Port Tennant, and Kilvey, and took in Pentreguinea and Foxhole – the Eastside.

This is an account of a very significant area, the people of which have shown a great interest in their past. It takes you back to the 12th Century and explores a great mass of themes across the centuries. The author is to be congratulated on his long labours.

Let us hope he spurs people from other parts of Swansea into action.

Gerald Gabb

Introduction

Fourteen years after the end of the Second World War my parents Ken and Pat Stewart, like many young newlyweds of that time were 'living in rooms', specifically the middle bedroom upstairs and the corresponding downstairs middle room with attached lean-to kitchen of Johnny and Florrie 'Tottie' Mahoney's terraced house at 142 Danygraig Road, the house where I was born in July 1959.

Our years living at the Mahoney's house is a time remembered with love and laughter. Johnny and Tottie were real characters and were like an extra set of grandparents to me, so much so that a few years later, I ran away from home intending to move back to the Mahoney's house, only to get a clip around the ear from Tottie, who marched me straight back home again. I still have vivid memories of my days there, playing with friends in and around Pant St, Tymawr St, Ysgol St and Danygraig Road, eating 'chocolate blobs' and 'oysters' from Joe Romano's ice-cream van, and drinking Mrs Scott's homemade ginger beer, sold from her house just a few steps away across the road from the Mahoney's.

My parents saved hard for a deposit on a mortgage for their own home and in 1964, a few months after I had started attending Danygraig Infants School my family, which now also included my two younger brothers, moved to our new house in Margaret St directly across the street from my Nana Crowley's house. Danygraig School was a wonderful place, and as I moved from Infants to Juniors, I made friendships that have lasted a lifetime, but at the age of eleven, I left to go to Cefn Hengoed Secondary Comprehensive School in Winch Wen, where I would make many new friends from areas that up to that time I had barely heard of.

Every morning, hundreds of children from our side of Kilvey Hill were transported in Morris Bros. buses to attend school on the other side of the hill and then back home again every afternoon, and it was during these twice-daily trips to and from Cefn Hengoed that I first noticed the incredible camaraderie amongst us all, whilst at the same time, I also became aware of just how isolated 'our Eastside' was from the rest of Swansea. A barren Kilvey Hill loomed over us to the north, to the east was the Crymlyn Bog guarded by Tir John Power Station and the Carbon Black, a bustling and noisy Swansea Docks with its coal hoists and shipping was below us to the south, and to the west, the River Tawe ebbed and flowed and separating us from the town, the New Cut Bridge offering the only route in or out.

Many years have passed since my initial no doubt romanticized thoughts of an isolated Eastside, but after returning to Swansea after almost thirty years of living and working overseas those thoughts linger still, and whilst the area has continued to physically change, generations of families are content to remain Eastsiders, and many of the children I grew up with now have grandchildren and great-grandchildren of their own who are still living in the area.

This book, whilst not intended to be a comprehensive study, is my effort at plotting the history of 'our side of Kilvey Hill', as the part played by the Eastside and its residents has often been overlooked in the many books dealing with the growth and development of Swansea's history.

Whenever the subject of Swansea's industrial past is raised, for most people it is the copper industry that inevitably springs to mind, but whilst it could be argued that the industries on the west side of the Tawe were central to this, it was the Eastside of Swansea, more than any other area, that carried the town's growth on its back, and yet it hardly if ever, gets a mention.

Whilst Hafod was home to both the Morfa Works and the massive Vivian Works, across the river the Eastside had four copper works (Upper Bank, Middle Bank, White Rock and the Port Tennant Works) and was the destination of two vitally important canals, the Smith's Canal whose southern terminal ended at Foxhole, and the Tennant Canal that linked the mineral wealth of Neath to Fabian's Bay, via Crymlyn Bog.

In order for the town to move to its next stage of growth, a substantial amount of land at Tirlandwr was severed off from the Eastside to form the North Dock, developed on the land that sat between the original course of the River Tawe and the New Cut. Thirty years later, Fabian's Bay began disappearing under first the Prince of Wales Dock, then the Kings Dock and finally the Queen's Dock, whilst Swansea's new patent fuel business was established and grew around them.

The Eastside was home to three of Swansea's seven mainline stations, but not before new housing was demolished to accommodate the miles of railway tracks needed to link the docks to the rest of Wales and beyond. Another fifty years passed, and it was the turn of the railway lines to be ripped out, and in their place came a dual carriageway that linked Swansea and its port to the M4, part of Britain's new motorway system. A major casualty of this was Fabian Street, the main commercial thoroughfare of the Eastside, now just a memory buried under an anonymous part of Fabian Way.

At the centre of this period of change were the people of the Eastside.

Before the industrial boom that hit the area in the mid-1800s, the Eastside was rural, but over the following forty years, Swansea was a magnet to those that weren't afraid of hard work, including coppermen, mariners, dockers, railwaymen and many other tradesmen and labourers, nearly all of whom established their families in the area. Many of the Eastsiders of today are descendants of that hardy stock, but whilst we are all proud to say we are Welsh, many Eastsiders can trace their family back to their origins in West Wales, England, Ireland, Belgium, and beyond, something directly reflected in my own family - the Stewart's from Plymouth, the Davies's from Pembrokeshire, the Crowley's from Co. Wexford, and the Wilkinson's from Leicester.

When we say we are 'from the Eastside' this is what it means, this is who we are.

***

Part One of this book is laid out in the form of a historical timeline that includes both English history (what many of us were taught in school) and Welsh history (what most of us <u>weren't</u> taught in school) that covers the period from the Iron Age to the Victorian Age and attempts to show when the areas of Kilvey, St. Thomas, Danygraig and Port Tennant are first recognized.

The Victorian Age saw the British Empire take its place at the centre of world commerce, and **Part Two** deals with the industrial development of Swansea during this period and specifically the substantial changes made to the Eastside. With this growth came the need for housing to support the people that arrived on the

Eastside from West Wales, Cornwall, Devon, the West Country, the Midlands, Ireland, Belgium, Germany and beyond, whilst at the same time the introduction and influence of the various religious denominations also made its mark on the local population.

Part Three discusses a small group of industrialists whose determination forever changed the fortunes of Swansea and simultaneously altered the shape and definition of the Eastside forever - the Grenfell family, the Tennant family, the Benson family, and the Briton Ferry Estate.

Part Four of this book follows no particular timeline but is a collection of individual chapters that cover various Eastside landmarks as well as aspects of Eastside life from the Victorian times to the end of the 21st Century that I hope will be of interest to the reader.

PART ONE - Gower, Swansea, and the Eastside.

In order to properly address the history of the Eastside of Swansea, and specifically Kilvey, St. Thomas, Danygraig and Port Tennant, it is necessary to first look at the documented history of first Gower and then Swansea.

Although it is very difficult to pinpoint with any certainty evidence of an early permanent settlement in the Gower area before the arrival of the Normans in the late 11th century, there are over sixty 'Scheduled Ancient Monument Sites' or SAMs listed in the area, with evidence of the existence of life from the Palaeolithic Age through to the Iron Age. The sites include Britain's oldest cave painting at Cat Hole, a cairn at Giants' Grave (now Parc le Breos), the Neolithic tomb known as 'Arthur's Stone', on Cefn Bryn, and probably the most famous find of them all, 'The Red Lady of Paviland' (later proven to be a male) found in Western Europe's oldest burial site, thought to be over 33,000 years old.

In 1954 an oval enclosure approximately 300 ft long by 200ft wide and believed to be an Iron Age earthwork was discovered on the northern side of Kilvey Hill. In 1968, local historian Bernard Morris, assisted by senior boys from Bishop Gore and Gowerton Grammar Schools, carried out some excavation works there and a bank was located at each side of the ditch, estimated to have been originally 3m wide and 1.5m deep with steep sides and a flat bottom. A sherd of a Samian bowl was found beneath the inner bank, and the age of the site was reassessed and placed as c125-150 [1]. There were also a small number of stone cairns, or rings of stones, found close to the top of Kilvey Hill, although the period they come from is unknown. [2]

In the 19th century, there were a number of finds linking Romans to Swansea and Gower that included a section of Roman mosaic floor found in an Oystermouth churchyard in 1860, Roman hoards (coins, pottery, etc.) found at Llythrid in 1823, east of the River Tawe at Pentrechwyth in June 1835, and in Port Tennant in January 1836. [3]. During the construction of the North Dock in 1846 a regularly formed paved ford was discovered by Colonel Grant

Francis, thought of as 'Roman workmanship', and in recent years there have been items found at Parc le Breos, Parkmill, Pengwern Farm in Ilston and on Mumbles Hill; however, there are no records to date of any Roman settlements in the area.

The Romans first landed on British soil in 55BC led by Julius Caesar, but it was not until 43AD that they set about conquering Britain under the leadership of Aulus Plautius, the first governor of the new province. Within four years Fosse Way had been constructed running from Lincoln on the east coast to Exeter in the southwest of Britain, during which time the Romans were met with resistance from numerous tribes, although some were content to work with them rather than fight against them.

The main tribes in Wales at that time were the Deceangli in the far north, the Ordovices in the northwest and upper-central region, the Cornovii in the northeast, the Silures in the central and south-eastern regions, and the Demetae in the southwest. Whilst these tribes regularly fought against each other, it was the tribes of the Ordovices and Silures who regularly battled with the Romans. They were finally defeated by 75AD, allowing the Romans to consolidate more than half of their legions on the Welsh border areas of Shrewsbury, Chester and Caerleon. The Romans probed further into Wales as far as Caernafon in the north and, operating from the regional base at Caerleon (Isca Augusta) in South Wales, they travelled west and built additional fortifications in places such as Neath (Nidum), Loughor (Leucarum), Carmarthen (Moridunum) and Llandovery (Alabum), all approximately one day's march apart on the road known as Via Julia Maritima.

By 476 AD, the Romans had left Britain and England saw the emergence of the Anglo-Saxon tribal kingdoms of Wessex in the South West, Northumbria in the North, East Anglia in the East, and the biggest tribe in Mercia, an area we know today as The Midlands. Other minor kingdoms and territories included the kingdoms of Essex, Kent and Sussex.

By the 8th century, under the orders of Mercia's Kings Aethelbald (716-767AD) and his successor Offa (757-796AD), a border between the tribes in Wales and Anglo-Saxon England was roughly constructed by the building of first Wat's Dyke and then Offa's Dyke, which between then ran from Prestatyn in the north to Chepstow in the south. The tribal 'kingdoms' of Wales at that time included Gwynedd, Powys, Ceredigion, Brycheinog, Ergyng, Gwent, Dyfed and Glywysing, Ystrad Tgwi and Gwyr.

By the 5th Century, 'British' Celts spoke a language later known as Brythonic, from which the languages of Wales, Cornwall and Breton developed. The term 'combrogi' ('countryman') was in use from which the word 'Cymru' came, later to be used as the term for the country of Wales. The Germanic Anglo-Saxon tribes had invaded Britain via its eastern coast and were known by the Celtic name 'Saeson' and (in Gaelic) 'Sasanaigh'. The Saxons called the Britons 'Wealas' from the Germanic word 'walha' or 'outsider', likely the origin of the words 'Welsh' and 'Wales', and something also reflected in the suffix of the name Cornwall. There is no definitive point in time when the region became known as either 'Wales' or 'Cymru', and it could be argued that these names actually mean the opposite of each other ('countryman' and 'outsider').

According to the 'Brut y Tywysogion' ('The Chronicle of the Princes'), the first Viking raid on Wales was recorded in 852AD [4] and likely coming from Dublin, where the Vikings, referred to as 'Black Pagans' first raided in the late 8th century before later establishing a settlement there. Rhodri ap Merfyn (820-877AD) aka Rhodri Mawr (the Great), was the ruler of Gwynedd, Powys and Seisyllwg, and according to 'the Brut', engaged in a number of battles with both Anglo-Saxon tribes and Viking marauders, including a notable victory in 856AD where the Danish king Gorm was killed. He repelled two further Viking raids in 872AD, before finally meeting his end five years later during a Saxon invasion led by the Mercia king Ceolwulf II. After Ceolwulf's death in 879AD Mercia ceded control to the self-styled 'King of the Anglo-Saxons', Alfred the Great.

The relationship between the Welsh tribes and the Vikings was a complex one. It appears that many of the Vikings that visited the coastal areas of Wales did so as traders, however as battles over kingdoms and wealth continued across England and Wales, it was not uncommon for Viking raiders to side with either the Welsh or with the Saxon tribes if it meant the defeat of a common enemy. Alfred the Great, with the help of forces from a number of Welsh tribes, battled with the Vikings across Anglo-Saxon England and defeated them in 893AD at the Battle of Buttington near Welshpool in mid-Wales. Two years later, after wintering in the Severn Valley, the Vikings carried out raids in South Wales, whilst in c900AD there were a series of Viking raids in North Wales, one of which resulted in the death of Meryn ap Rhodri.

In c909AD, Rhodri Mawr's grandson Hywel Dda (Hywel the Good) became King of Seisyllwg and ruled over large parts of Wales. He held a truce with the Anglo-Saxon kings and restricted Viking raids through much of his forty-year reign. His legacy was the codification of Welsh law, which was based on compassion and compensation rather than physical punishment or internment, and clearly recognized the rights of women who, amongst other things, could divorce their husbands after seven years for a host of reasons. After his death in 950AD Viking raids resumed, and in 987AD they seized 2000 men from Anglesey, who were sold as slaves in Ireland. During the same period, the Vikings also attacked the north and east coasts of England, as well as northern Europe. Many chose to settle in the west of France, and under the leadership of Gaange Rolf (also known as 'Rollo') the 911 Treaty of Saint-Clair-Sur-Epte was signed with King Charles III of West Francia, 'Charles the Simple', that recognized the establishment of The Duchy of Normandy, 'The Land of the North Men'.

For much of the 10th century England was ruled by various members of the House of Wessex, but when in 990AD the Danish king Sweyn Forkbeard laid waste to large areas of England, King Ethelred 'the Unready' (ill-advised' or 'of no counsel') gave Sweyn a financial payment to return to Denmark, funded via a land tax levied on citizens known as Danegeld. Nevertheless, Sweyn continued his raids in the north of England, but after Vikings made settlements there, an enraged Ethelred decided that all Danish settlers had to be forcibly expelled, and on St. Brice's Day, 13th November 1002, Sweyn's sister Gunhilde was amongst those massacred.

Sweyn returned to England a few months later at Sandwich (now in Kent), and for the next ten years rampaged across England, finally targeting London. Fearful for their lives, the English earls proclaimed Sweyn the first Viking King of England on Christmas Day 1013. His reign was short as he died five weeks later on 3rd February 1014, at which time his eldest son Harald became King of Denmark, whilst his youngest son Cnut proclaimed himself King of England. However English nobility recalled King Ethelred from his exile in Normandy to reclaim the throne, and until his death in 1016, Ethelred was at war with Cnut. On Ethelred's death, his son Edmund 'Ironside' lay claim to the throne, but instead the Witenagemot (or 'Witan', the King's Council) elected Cnut, and following the Battle of Assandun in 1016 Cnut signed a treaty with Edmund, who ceded control of all of England with the notable exception of Wessex.

The treaty stated that on the death of either one of them, the other would be King of all England. Edmund died the following year, likely assassinated, and Cnut the Great became King of England. After the death of his brother in 1019, he was also made King of Denmark. On Canut's death in 1035 his two sons Harold Harefoot and then Harthacnut succeeded him as king, their combined rule spanning twenty-six years (1016-1042). However, as neither of Canute's sons had a successor, the House of Wessex reclaimed the throne. The new king was Edward the Confessor the seventh son of Ethelred 'the Unready' and Harthacnut's half-brother, as both were sons of Emma of Normandy, who had first married Ethelred (1002-1016) and following his death had married Cnut the Great (1017-1035).

In 1055, after various battles in Morgannwg, Gwent and Dehuebarth, where he was aided by Swein Godwinson, the Earl of Wessex, Gruffudd ap Llywelyn, King of Gwynedd and Powys and from the bloodline of Rhodri, claimed sovereignty of all of Wales, something recognized by King Edward 'the Confessor' of England in exchange for his loyalty. His rule lasted until his death in 1063 when he was defeated near Snowdonia by Swein's younger brother Harold Godwinson, who had become the new Earl of Wessex after Swein was exiled from England in 1047. Legend has it that

Gruffudd's head was severed, and dispatched by Harold Godwinson to King Edward the Confessor.

Welsh historian John Davies [5] stated that Gruffudd ap Llywelyn was 'the only Welsh king ever to rule over the entire territory of Wales...Thus, from about 1057 until his death in 1063, the whole of Wales recognised the kingship of Gruffudd ap Llewelyn. For about seven brief years, Wales was one, under one ruler, a feat with neither precedent nor successor.'

Wales would never have one ruler again.

On 5th January 1066, Edward the Confessor died without an heir to his throne and after a meeting of the Witan, his brother-in-law Harold Godwinson, whose family were related by marriage to Sweyn Forkbeard, was crowned King Harold II. Two other men also held a claim to the crown, Harold Hardrada (Harold of Stern Council) the King of Norway, who was supported by Tostig Godwinson the younger brother of the new King of England, and William the Duke of Normandy, a cousin of the late King Edward also known as William the Bastard.

Harold Hardrada signalled his intentions by entering England in the north and ransacking towns and villages as he went, he defeated English forces at the Battle of Fulford on the 20th September 1066. King Harold II was in the south of England at that time, as he had expected an attack from William of Normandy, but on getting news of Harold Hardrada's actions he rallied his troops and headed north. After riding for four days and nights, he surprised the invaders at East Riding in Yorkshire and was victorious at the Battle of Stamford Bridge on 25th September where both Harold Hardrada and Tostig Godwinson were among those killed. Despite substantial losses both at Fulford and Stamford Bridge, the new king turned his army and marched south to intercept an expected invasion by William of Normandy, however, William had already landed at Pevensey Bay in Sussex on 28th September and was prepared for battle.

Sixteen days later on 14th October, King Harold II fell and died in action at Hastings, legend has it hit by an arrow through his eye.

His weakened army was defeated, and the reign of the Anglo-Saxon kings had come to an end. After fighting and winning only one battle, William became the first Norman King of England, William I, also known as William The Conqueror.

William I (c1028 - 9th September 1087): England was initially the focus of King William's attention and there were no official advances on Wales, however in 1067, he made his cousin William FitzOsbern the Earl of Hereford, Roger de Montgomery was made Earl of Shrewsbury, and Hugh d'Avranches was made Earl of Chester, thus establishing three lordships along the border between England and Wales, known as the Welsh Marches. Each had the full power of independent action should they wish to expand their lordships into Wales, whilst acting as the first line of defence against Welsh raids.

Castles were built on the 'border' between Pura Wallia, the mid to north area of Wales ruled by Welsh Princes, and Marcher Wallia, which ran across South Wales from the Severn River in the east to Pembroke in the west. Although part of a feudal system headed by the king, the Marcher lords were allowed to raise armies, battle other earldoms, set up towns and markets, and impose their own local taxes. In short, they ran their lordships as small kingdoms, and should a lord die without leaving an heir, the estate would revert to the ownership of the king. In 1077, while en route to St David's Cathedral, William made a pact with Rhys ap Tewdwr the ruler of Deheubarth, who agreed to pay forty marks a year to keep William from invading South Wales, an arrangement that lasted until William's death in 1087.

William II (c1060 - 2nd August 1100): After William I's death, his eldest son Robert Curthose took control of Normandy and as William's second son Richard had died in 1070, his third son William Rufus 'The Red' became King William II of England. William's youngest son Henry was left with a monetary inheritance.

In 1090, Iestyn ap Gwrgant Prince of Morgannwg, dispatched Einion ap Collwyn, who had previously served William in England and France, to solicit the aid of Norman soldiers in a battle with Rhys ap Tewdwr, and Einon persuaded Robert FitzHamon, Lord of Gloucester and twelve other knights to bring a large army to the aid of Iestyn. Rhys' forces were much smaller than their opposition, and he was defeated in a battle near Hirwaun. Although he survived, his army incurred heavy losses and his son Goronwy was beheaded.

Another of his men Cynan, reputedly a bastard son of Rhys, left the battle and travelled towards the 'Vale of Tywi' (Tawe), pursued by Iestyn. Cynan tried to escape through a lake called Crymlyn, a marsh between Briton Ferry and Swansea, however, he was drowned there and the location became known as 'The Pool of Cynon' or 'Conan's Pool.' [6] Rhys ap Tewdwr managed to avoid capture that day but met his death three years later in a conflict against Bernard De Newmarch at the battle of Brycheiniog.

William's main focus was on regaining land in the north of England, and in 1092 he defeated King Malcolm III of Scotland and reclaimed Cumberland and Westmoreland, and three years later dispossessed Robert de Mowbray and reclaimed Northumbria. In 1096 his elder brother Robert decided to join the Crusades and in exchange for 10,000 marks to fund his trip, handed the control of Normandy to William. In August 1100 William died in a hunting accident, shot by an arrow from one of his own men, allegedly under the instruction of William's younger brother Henry. On his brother's death, Henry rushed to London to claim the throne, taking advantage of his older brother Robert's absence.

Henry I (c1068 - 1st December 1135): Many of the Norman barons in England favoured the return of Robert, so Henry quickly set about strengthening his grip on the crown via his Charter of Liberties, making concessions and granting favours to those that supported him. Robert returned from the Crusades and invaded England in 1101, but shortly after relinquished his claims on the throne in return for Henry's territories in Normandy, along with a substantial annual annuity. In 1106 Henry invaded Normandy, capturing Robert, and imprisoned him for life, first at Devizes Castle in Wiltshire, and then Cardiff Castle, where he died in 1135.

Kilvey and St. Thomas

The first Norman Marcher to lay claim to Gwyr (Gower) c1100 was Henry De Newburgh, Earl of Warwick, also known as Henry Beaumont, who by 1106 had erected a timber-built castle at the mouth of the River Tawe that overlooked the inlet to the sea. There was likely no town or hamlet at this location at this time, but the castle became a focal point and the town was built around it, and it is likely that the borough and the original privileges of its burgesses may have been set up by Henry Beaumont. A burgess was someone from the upper ranks of townspeople who could own land, buy and sell property, had legal and administrative responsibilities in the town and who owed services and taxes to the Lord, and many if not all of Swansea's burgesses were Anglo-Saxons, encouraged to resettle in Wales by the Marcher Lords.

The Brut Y Tywysogion states:

'Harry Beaumont came to Gwyr against the sons of Caradog, son of Jestyn, and won many of their lands from them, and built the castle at Abertway, the castle of Aber Llchwr, the castle of Llanrhidian, and the castle of Pen Rhys, in the place where Rhys ap Caradog ap Caradog ap Jestyn was slain, and established himself there, and brought Saxons from Somerset, where they obtained lands; and the greatest usurpation of all was his in Gower.' [7]

De Newburgh's Gower extended eastwards from the peninsula and was bounded by the rivers Llwchr, Amman, Cathan, Twrch and the Tawe. There were two distinct divisions within the lordship specific to language used - Gower Anglicana, the English-speaking area that covered much of the peninsula, and Gower Walicana, the outlying areas that were Welsh-speaking. A separate distinction was used by the Normans to separate uplands and lowlands, supraboscus and subboscus, the smaller and separate Welsh-speaking area division (subboscus) defined the areas above and below the forest that ran between Loughor and the peninsula, where castles were built to protect the Lordship from Welsh armies who could cross at Loughor and the Burry Estuary.

In 1113, Gruffydd, son of Rhys ap Twdwr, returned from exile in Ireland with the aim of reclaiming what he believed were his territories, and between 1114 and 1116 he attacked a number of Marcher castles that included Carmarthen, Kidwelly, and Llandovery. He also attacked the garrison at Swansea Castle and burned down the outworks, however, an unsuccessful attack on Aberystwyth Castle saw him defeated and his troops disbanded.

On the death of Henry De Newburgh in 1119, his Gower lordship passed to one of his sons, also Henry, known as Henry of Warwick, and after he died without issue, the estate passed to his nephew William De Newburgh, the third Earl of Warwick, and it was he that issued the first Charter of 'Sweynesse' (Swansea) in c1158-84. [8]

The Charter addressed 'all barons, burgesses, and men, English and Welsh", and dealt with the physical boundaries of the town and its outlying pasturage, allocating to every burgess a burgage of "seven acres beyond the wood and above', an area later known as the Town Hill. It also clarified the rights of the burgesses that had been trading in the town for many years. The eastern boundary of Warwick's land is stated as 'Pulkanan' (Cynon's Pool) on Crymlyn Marsh, the eastern border of Kilvey that in pre-Norman times had stretched to the River Nedd. After the death of Henry I in 1135, Stephen of Blois the grandson of William I, came to the throne.

King Stephen (c1092 - 25th October 1154): His reign was notable in that it included 'the Anarchy', a civil war between his supporters and those of Empress Matilda daughter of Henry I, that covered both England and Normandy. The Welsh were quick to take advantage of this uncertainty, and in 1136 the army of Hywel ap Maredudd of Byrcheinog took on the troops of Roger De Beaumont near Gorseinon, where over five hundred mostly Norman soldiers were killed in battle. The location later became known as Garngoch (red cairn), possibly in reference to the blood spilt there.

Henry De Newburgh, the youngest brother of Roger De Beaumont, recaptured Swansea Castle c1138, and as 'Henry of Gower' he restored it as caput of Gower and minted coins there c1140, some of which bore the name of King Stephen and others the name of Henry in Latin 'HEDRICIDE DE NOVOB', along with the abbreviated place name 'SVENSHI, SWENSI, SVEN, and SVEN. Some of these coins were part of the Coed Y Wenallt hoard found near Cardiff in 1980. [9] Matilda's son Henry Curtmantle succeeded Stephen on his death in 1154, and Henry II become the first of the Angevin kings of England.

Henry II (5th March 1133 – 6th July 1189) In 1160, Henry appointed his Chancellor Thomas Becket as the new Archbishop of Canterbury in an effort to weaken the control of the Church in England. Unfortunately for the king, Becket took his new role seriously and quickly took the position of defender of the church. He complained that the king's taxing of the church was unwarranted and maintained that only the church could and should try members of the church who have committed secular crimes, and their disagreements finally came to a head in the Constitutions of Clarendon in 1164, a set of legislative procedures that restricted ecclesiastical privileges.

Becket fled to France where he sought the support of King Louis VII as well as that of Pope Alexander III, but in July 1170 Becket and Henry came to an agreement, and he returned to England in early December the same year. Within days of his return, he excommunicated some of Henry's followers and on 29th December four knights were dispatched to Canterbury to arrest him, however after he refused to accept his arrest, they hacked him to death in front of the altar. His murder caused consternation across the Christian countries of Europe, and on 21st February 1173, he was canonised by Pope Alexander III and venerated as 'St. Thomas the Martyr' by both Catholic and Anglican Churches.

In 1166, Waleran de Beaumont, Earl of Warwick and grandson of Roger de Beaumont, succeeded Henry de Beaumont as Lord of Gower, however, he had serious money problems and mortgaged the Lordship, and in 1189 after clearing the debt owed to Bruno of London, Henry II reclaimed Gower as his own. Following the uprising of the Welsh princes who united against Henry II in 1164-1170, Rhys ap Gruffydd (1132-1197), the grandson of Rhys ap Twdwr and known as 'Lord Rhys', emerged as the strongest ruler in Wales, and in 1171 he met with Henry II, who travelled through Wales on route to Ireland, the problem of Thomas Becket now behind him. After proclaiming his loyalty to the king, Lord Rhys was made Justiciar of South Wales, showing that he controlled the southern half of Wales.

Losing his first son William in infancy, Henry II was subject to a number of plots led by three of his four other sons, Henry 'The Young King', Richard, and Geoffrey, and after the death of 'The Young King' in 1183, his third son Richard became heir to the throne. Known as ' Lionheart' because of his military prowess, Richard was present when his father died on 6th July 1189, and some historians think he may have been responsible for his father's death.

Richard I (8th September 1157 – 6th April 1199) was Duke of Normandy, Aquitaine and Gascony in France, and became King of England on 3rd September 1189. Although born in England he lived in the Duchy of Aquitaine, and as a military man, he spent many years fighting in conflicts outside the country, and was keen to honour his father's commitment to take part in the Third Crusade, an attempt to reconquer the Holy Lands to be led by three European monarchs, namely Richard, Phillip II of France and German King Frederick I, who was also the Holy Roman Emperor.

After assembling an army to accompany him on the Crusade, King Richard appointed regents to administer the country in his absence. His brother Geoffrey had died in 1186, and his youngest brother John, unhappy with Richard's administrative arrangements, set up an alternative royal court. After John's plot to take control of the country was unsuccessful, his mother persuaded Richard to allow John to rule in his absence. John made it known that Richard had died on the Crusades and positioned himself to be heir to the throne, however, Richard returned in 1194, and John left England for Normandy.

In South Wales, with no loyalty to Richard I, Lord Rhys attacked the Marcher lords in Pembroke, Haverfordwest and Gower and captured castles at St Clears, Laugharne and Llanstephan. He built a number of castles himself, with Cardigan being the earliest 'native build' castle in Wales, and the first Eisteddfod was held there in December 1176.

In April 1197 Rhys died suddenly, recorded in the Brut in this way:

'...there was a great pestilence throughout the island of Britain ... and that tempest killed innumerable people and many of the nobility and many princes, and spared none. That year, four days before May Day, died Rhys ap Gruffydd, Prince of Deheubarth and unconquered head of all Wales.' [10]

The pestilence followed a five-year period of famine and mortality caused by scarcity, and would shortly be followed by an 'unprecedented plague of people and murrain of animals' that continued for a number of years. [11] In March 1199, Richard was wounded by a crossbow arrow whilst putting down a revolt in Southern France. The wound was infected and he died a few weeks later on 6th April 1199 having spent less than a year in England during his reign, and his brother John was recognised as his heir and proclaimed King of England.

John (24th December 1166 – 19th October 1216) John, became King in 1199, and was the youngest son of Henry II and Eleanor of Aquitaine. Known as 'John Lackland', Henry had planned to pass over extensive lands to his son as a wedding present. Fearing the expansion plans of the Marcher Lords, Llewellyn ap Iorwerth, known as Llewellyn Fawr (the Great), Prince of North Wales, swore allegiance to the new king, an agreement that guaranteed retention of his lands. His marriage to the King's illegitimate daughter Joan further strengthened his position.

The Lordship of Gower had passed from the Warwick family into the new king's ownership, and in 1203 he gifted the land to one of his most loyal military leaders William De Breos, 4th Lord of Bramber.

King John's Charter of 1203 to William De Breos granted 'all the land of Gower with all the appurtenances' and highlighted the boundaries of the Lordship, which includes the land east of the Tawe from 'Glais to the Meynhiron (or stone sepulchres, and the

Meynchiron to Crimlyn (the Crymlyn Brook) and from Crimlyn to Pulcanan (the pool in Crymlyn Bog). [12] Whilst the name 'Kilvey/Kylvai/Cilfai' is not specifically mentioned in this charter, it is clear that the land referred to is what would become known as the 'Manor of Kilvey', although the earliest mentions of Kilvey appear to be referenced in 1311 [13] and in 1314 [14].

Unfortunately for De Breos, by 1206 he and the King had fallen out over substantial unpaid debts, and the king reclaimed De Breos' land in both Sussex and Devon. The people of both Gower Anglicana and Gower Wallicana petitioned the monarch because of De Breos's oppressive treatment, and in 1207 Gower was also reclaimed by the king. King John visited Swansea in May 1210 on his way to Ireland, and issued separate charters to both groups, assuring the safety of both groups.

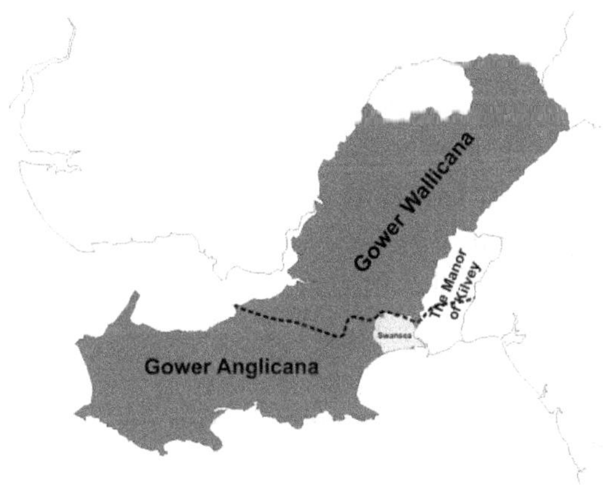

Map of Gower showing Gower Anglicana and Gower Wallicana

A few months later De Breos fled to Ireland with his wife and child, dressed as beggars. His wife Maud and son William were later captured whilst trying to travel to Scotland, and were both starved to death whilst jailed in Windsor castle. William De Breos made his way to France where he died in exile in c1211. In the same year, Llewellyn attacked the lands of the Earl of Chester, but after King John sided with the Earl, it was only the intervention of Llewellyn's wife that kept his position intact. In 1211 Llewellyn still had control of Gower, however, this was disputed by the Earls of Warwick. In 1214, King John increased the financial demands on the Marcher lords in order to fund his plans to regain lands lost in Northern France. Incensed by this, they revolted against the king, and Llewellyn Fawr sided with the lords.

The following year the king was forced to meet with the Marchers at Runnymede on June 15th where he signed the Magna Carta, a document that ensured that the king would abide by the same rule of law as his subjects. The document also confirmed that any outstanding disputes in Wales would be dealt with under Welsh law, and all Welsh prisoners were released. King John's second Swansea Charter of 1215 expanded the privileges of the town's burgesses, allowing them tax-free access into towns across England and Wales, with the exception of London. The king agreed that Giles de Breos (second son of William) could come out of exile in France and claim his family's lands, but Giles died in 1215 before he could return. A few months later King John also died and was succeeded by his nine-year-old son Henry.

Henry III (1st October 1207 - 16 November 1272) became king in October 1216, and the young monarch was placed under the regency of Sir William Marshall, Earl of Pembroke until he came of age, whilst a council of thirteen executors, already appointed by the dying King John, ensured continuity of governance. Llewellyn Fawr signed an agreement with Henry III known as The Treaty of Worcester, however, Reginald De Breos, William's third son and Llewellyn's son-in-law had also spoken with the king and laid claim to all his father's lands and titles. On learning this, Llewellyn retaliated by attacking De Breos castles at Brecon, Abergavenny and Swansea, but in c1219 John De Breos, the grandson of William 4th Lord of Bramber and nephew of Reginald, regained the lordship of Gower as dowry from his marriage to Llewellyn's daughter Margaret.

Reginald De Breos died in 1227 and was succeeded by his son William, a despised figure known to the Welsh as 'Gwilym Ddu', or 'Black William', whose daughter Isabella had married Llewellyn's son Dafydd. In 1230, Llewellyn Fawr returned home to find Gwilym Ddu in bed with his wife Joan, and after he had publicly hanged 'Black William', he placed his wife on house arrest for a year. Llewellyn's execution of William De Breos was viewed by the crowds that celebrated his death as an act of Welsh strength against their English oppressors.

By 1256 Llewellyn ap Gruffydd (aka Llewellyn the Last) the grandson of Llewellyn Fawr, was Prince of Gwynedd, and with ambitions to emulate his grandfather, he widened his sphere of influence in Pura Wallia. Henry III's focus was on unrest within the ranks of his barons, led by Simon De Montfort, and by 1258 the unrest had evolved into a civil war. De Montford defeated Henry at the Battle of Lewes and imprisoned the king and his son Edward. In 1265 Llewellyn signed the Treaty of Pipton with De Montfort, to whom Llewellyn paid 30,000 marks to ensure he would not be attacked, and in return De Montfort recognised him as 'Prince of Wales'. However, Prince Edward escaped and his troops defeated and killed De Montfort at the Battle of Evesham in the same year. Henry was released and regained the throne, and in 1267 he signed the Treaty of Montgomery with Llewellyn, who paid Henry a further 20,000 marks. When King Henry died in 1272 his son, also known as Edward Longshanks, was on a crusade and was crowned as the new king in his absence.

Edward I (17/18th June 1239 – 7th July 1307) England had been led by a royal council until Edward returned to England in 1274, and his immediate focus was on Wales. Llewellyn Fawr refused multiple requests to pay homage to the new king, and in 1277 Edward invaded Wales with the largest army assembled in Britain since 1066. Facing an embarrassing defeat, Llewellyn surrendered and was forced to sign the Treaty of Aberconwy that stripped him of all concessions allowed to him under the Treaty of Montgomery. In addition, he was made to pay a fine of 70,000 marks, swear an oath of fealty to Edward, and drop any claim of fealty from other Welsh princes, and was left with only a small area of land west of the River Conwy (Uwch Conwy).

After five years under the rule of Edward and his lords, the Welsh rebelled, initially led by Llewellyn's brother Dafydd, who captured Hawarden Castle and slaughtered its garrison. Llewellyn then led the revolt and declared war on Edward. The Archbishop of Canterbury attempted to negotiate a settlement but was rebuked, and a Welsh council issued a statement on 11th November 1282 telling the Archbishop that Edward could not be trusted, and declared that irrespective of any fealty shown by the princes the council '…would nevertheless be unwilling to do homage to a stranger whose language, customs and laws are totally unknown to them.' [15]

On 11th December 1282 Llewellyn was ambushed and killed at the Battle of Orewin Bridge, his severed head sent to Edward at Rhuddlan who sent it to London, where it was placed on the gate of the Tower of London as proof of his death, and the following year, the head of his brother Dafydd was placed next to it. The rebellion was over, and with it any hopes of independence. In 1284 the Statute of Rhuddlan brought Gwynedd under the legal and administrative system of England, and Edward built a number of new castles in Wales. The Marcher lands elsewhere in Wales were not affected, and the Welsh armies, now split up amongst the various royal armies that fought under Edward's banner, successfully nullified the threat of Welsh uprisings via the tactic of establishing and securing military and administrative centres in the lordships, that in turn attracted tradespeople from England, many of whom would become town burgesses. [16]

As a direct consequence of this, by the late thirteenth century many of South Wales' boroughs, including Swansea were, from a population perspective, more English than Welsh. Edward punished Wales by restricting social and economic opportunities as well as restricting the civil rights of Welsh people, and in 1301 he gave his son Edward the title of Prince of Wales, handing him all the royal estates in Wales. Although born in Caernarfon Castle, he is regarded as the first 'English' Prince of Wales, something designed to further challenge and dilute Welsh heritage. Edward known as 'The Hammer of the Scots' died in February 1307 at a military camp at Burgh by Sands, south of the Scottish border, and his son Edward II (aka Edward Caernarfon) became king a year later.

Edward II (25th April 1284 – 21st September 1327) inherited a kingdom that had been in conflict with the Scots, the Welsh and the Irish, and that had a difficult relationship with France, and in 1309, in an effort to ease tensions with the latter, he married

Isabella, the daughter of King Phillip IV. In the early years of his reign, he fought Robert the Bruce, losing decisively at Bannockburn in 1314. However, rather than focus on external threats as his father had, he surrounded himself with friends who acted as his advisors, and aimed his power at what he felt were internal threats to his rule, and in particular Roger Mortimer, a Marcher lord who ruled Carmarthen and south-central Wales, one of the leaders of the reforming opposition to the king.

Gilbert De Clare had led the barons in urging the king into reforms called 'the Ordinances of 1311' that heavily curtailed regal powers and gave some control back to the barons, but after De Clare died in The Battle of Bannockburn with no heir to his lordship, Edward partitioned his lands and split them between the husbands of De Clare's three sisters, Hugh Audley, Roger Damory and Hugh Despenser, who was the king's closest friend and rumoured to be his lover. Despenser had built up both land and titles in South Wales, and revelled in the independent powers in the region by virtue of his acquisitions, and had begun to rival and threaten the established Marcher lords. Not content with his share of De Clare land, he plotted against his brothers-in-law, and also coveted the Gower lordship, at that time held by William, the 2nd Baron De Breos.

William De Breos had no surviving son and heir so petitioned for his son-in-law John Mowbray to succeed him, but Despenser claimed that De Breos had sold the reversion of Gower multiple times, to the king's brother-in-law Edward Bohun, to John Mowbray, to Roger Mortimer, as well as to Despenser himself. Aware of Despenser's actions, Mowbray took control of Gower in 1320, even though De Breos was still alive (he died in 1326). Despenser persuaded the king that this was illegal and that Mowbray should be removed, and the lands forfeited to the king. Richard De Foxcote of Gloucester was tasked by the king to take possession of Gower, but shortly before reaching the River Tawe he and his small group were confronted by 'a great multitude of Welshman, unknown to him, and armed' and loyal to Mowbray, who met him at the Chapel of St Thomas the Martyr in the Manor of Kilvey and they prevented De Foxcote 'executing the mandate so that he could do nothing therein without danger of death.' [17]

Shortly afterwards, a larger armed group led by Richard de Rodney took control of the lordship on behalf of the king.

Between November 1337 and February 1340, the Chapel of St. Thomas was used on a number of occasions as the location of the signing of documents. [18] Jeruard ap Meuric and David and Philip ap Lucas gifted '1/2 a. of land, by Welsh measure, at Tyr Map Sayr in Klyvei', as well as various lands 'measured by the rod of Margam' gifted by Llewellyn ap Meuric and David and Philip ap Lucas, David ap Wachan ap David ap Eneas, and Gronow ap Cradoc Wyth to Sir Robert de Penryse, and witnessed by various individuals including Morgan Thoid, listed as 'steward and also bailiff of Kylvei'.

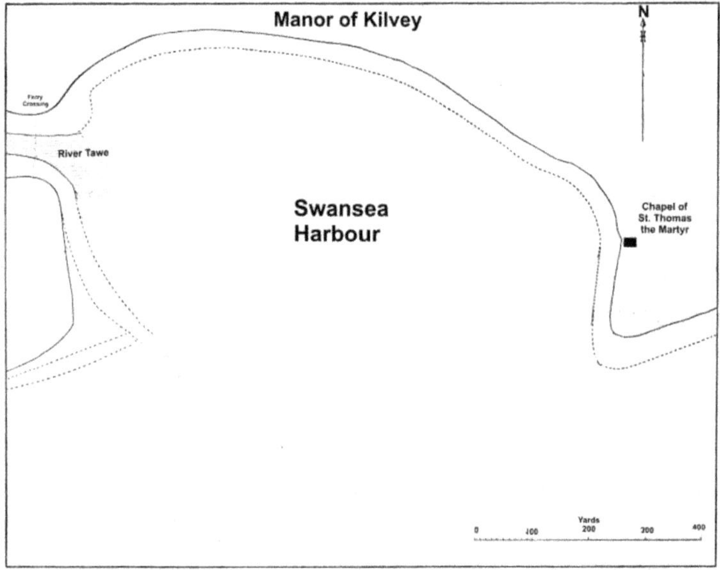

Map showing the likely location of the Chapel of St. Thomas the Martyr

Aware that Despenser was a threat to them all, the Marcher lords formed a coalition that included Roger Mortimer of Wigmore, who had returned from Ireland, and also the powerful Thomas, Earl of Lancaster, the king's cousin. Together, they requested the king have Despenser answer to the many complaints set out against him or else they would not recognise him as their king and threatened to put him in the custody of the Earl of Lancaster. Edward refused, and 'The Despenser Wars' began on May 4th 1321. Newport Castle was the Marcher Lords' first target, followed by attacks on the castles at Caerphilly, Cardiff and Swansea, and Despenser would later claim a loss of twenty-three manors.

They also attacked the English lands of Despenser's father and rampaged through sixty-seven manors in seventeen counties. Many innocent people suffered because of the attacks, and the people of Swansea, amongst others, petitioned the king for help. The Marchers requested the Despenser family be exiled, but again the king refused to act. On August 1st the barons entered London and threatened to set the city on fire 'from Charing Cross to Westminster,' and informed Edward that he would be deposed if the Despensers were not exiled. This time the king agreed, and after exiling the Despensers, he pardoned more than 400 men for crimes committed on Despenser lands. Edward however, was preparing to take on the Marcher Lords, and on December 5th issued a safe-conduct decree to Hugh Despenser; his father Hugh the Elder followed on December 25th.

The king assembled his own army, including a number of loyal English lords, to take the battle to 'the Contrariants' [19] and after forcing the Marchers back into Wales, he turned his ire on a long-term foe, the Earl of Lancaster, capturing and beheading him. Roger Mortimer was captured in 1322 but escaped to France in 1324 where he became the lover of the king's estranged wife Queen Isabella, who had travelled to France as a peace mediator in 1325 and had not returned to England. Mortimer and Isabella planned their return, and in September 1326 their forces invaded England.

The following month Hugh Despenser the Elder, who was left to defend Bristol, was captured and beheaded, his body cut up and fed to the dogs. His head was sent to Windsor and put on a pole on public display. Edward turned to his Welsh supporters for help, and he and the young Despenser fled to Wales, where Despenser was hated. The two men took a boat from Chepstow to Lundy, but weather and tides forced their boat inland to Cardiff. From there they travelled to Neath from where various royal items including the King's 'Great Seal' were dispatched to Swansea Castle. With no support found locally, Edward and Despenser decided to return to Caerphilly Castle and were captured at Llantrisant on November 16th.

Many of Edward's supporters were captured and executed, and Hugh Despenser went through a series of tortures before his mock trial on November 24th 1321, where he was cited for crimes against the state, church, crown and the king's wife. He was deemed guilty of all charges and sentenced to be hanged, drawn and quartered. At his execution, he was tied to a post that was then dragged around the streets by four horses. He was then hoisted onto the gallows where his penis and testicles were severed from his body, his heart and intestines removed, and then beheaded. His body was then quartered and the four parts were sent to Carlisle, Bristol, York and Dover for public display.

The king was not executed immediately, however his title was passed to his son Edward, who became King Edward III on January 25th 1327. Edward II, who had reverted to his old title of Edward of Caernarfon, was executed on September 27th 1327 and was buried at Gloucester later that year. Legend has it he was held down and had a red-hot poker inserted into his anus and had died from the internal injuries suffered. There is some debate as to whether this was the method used for Edward's execution, and some historians have put forward an alternative argument that he was not executed at all, but was instead taken away to live the rest of his days in an unknown location.

Edward III (13th November 1312 -21st June 1377). After a number of minor conflicts with France in 1337, Edward III signed a truce with France's ally Scotland in 1338 and also formed alliances with Portugal and Rome. The initial conflicts with France would escalate into what would later be called 'The Hundred Year War' an ongoing dispute over the right to rule France, that continued until 1453 (116 years later). In a charter to Swansea dated March 1st 1327, the king restored the forfeited lands of those who had been affected by the insurrection of the Despenser Wars and officially granted Gower to John De Mowbray's widow Alina De Breos, who in turn was succeeded by her son John De Breos III.

Edward granted a second charter to Swansea in 1336 that reconfirmed the earlier charters of Henry II and Edward II. It was during this period that the bubonic plague (later known as the Black Death) decimated the population of rural Britain. Believed to be spread by flea-infested rats, it was first recorded in June 1348 in Dorset and reached London within a few months. By the following June, it was countrywide but subsided by December that year. It is estimated that between 40%-60% of the population were infected and died, resulting in a shortage of labour across the country. A second surge of the plague occurred in 1361, which took the lives of a further 20% of the population.

In 1352 Thomas De Beaumont made a claim on the Lordship of Gower. Successful with his claim, the lordship was back in the hands of the Earls of Warwick, but within a short time, there was a new challenge, based on the fact that Prince Llewellyn had gifted Landimore and Kilvey to Morgan Gam in c1217, and that Gower came under the jurisdiction of Carmarthen. After much deliberation, the Lordship of Gower retained the lands in dispute and its fealty was clarified as direct to the crown, rather than via Carmarthen.

Much of Edward III's reign was taken up by military excursions into France, some led by his son Edward of Woodstock, The Black Prince, including at Poitiers in 1355 where he captured the French King John II. This put a huge financial strain on the kingdom that resulted in the defaulting of many debts. His military ambitions were curtailed, and by 1360 Edward had renounced his claim to the French throne. He died in September 1376 and was succeeded by his 10-year-old grandson Richard of Bordeaux, son of the late Edward of Woodstock, who had died three months earlier.

Richard II (6th January 1367 - 14th February 1400) was only ten years old when he succeeded his grandfather in September 1377 and was supported in day-to-day governance by a series of nine 'continual councils', changed annually, designed to ensure that no one man could be in a position of influence. Richard took a leading role in the quelling of the 1381 Peasants' Revolt that occurred as a direct result of the loss of a substantial number of England's population due to the Plague. Substantial gaps in the labour market allowed workers to expect higher wages that by definition had a negative effect on the wealth of the barons. The young king met with its leaders, initially ceding to many of their requests only to later rescind any agreements made. Many of the leaders of the revolt were executed, including Wat Tyler whose head was cut off and displayed on a pole on London Bridge.

After coming of age and assuming full responsibilities, Richard did away with the continual councils and enlisted members of his close circle of friends as advisors, something that caused consternation in parliament. In 1337 he gave in to some of the parliament's requests, and by 1338 many of his confidantes had either fled the country under sentence of death or else were executed. In 1396, the king committed Thomas De Beaumont to the tower for high treason, at which time he revised the ownership of the Lordship to Gower to Thomas De Mowbray, and ordered the records of the earlier pleadings be removed from the records. However, due to De Mowbray's forfeit for standing against the king, in 1398 Gower was again in Richard's hands, and the king visited Swansea the following year on route to Ireland.

Richard's relationship with his parliament was fractured at best, and after discovering he had tried to get support from the French, he was arrested and a parliamentary session was called, later known as the 'Merciless Parliament', after which many of his followers were tried for treason and executed. In 1399 Richard, now essentially a figurehead, was forced to abdicate and died in prison the following year aged 33, likely of starvation. His cousin Henry Bolingbroke, grandson of Edward III, and the son of John of Gaunt who had previously been exiled by Richard, became King Henry IV.

Henry IV (15th April 1367-20th March 1413) became king in 1399 and for much of his reign was in poor health, and it was he that had to deal with the last Welsh uprising, later known as The Welsh Revolt, led by Owain Glyndwr who had been a loyal soldier to King Richard II. Reginald de Grey, Earl of Ruthin, stole land from Owain Glyndwr who took his claim to Parliament but was unsuccessful. After further exchanges between the two men where Lord Grey called Owain a traitor, Owain assumed his hereditary title of Prince of Powys and attacked Lord Grey's lands. The attacks gained support across Wales, and by 1401 Owain was proclaimed Prince of Wales by his countrymen, his rapidly growing following likely aided after Parliament issued The Penal Laws against Wales of 1402. As talk of independence grew stronger, he captured Harlech and

Aberystwyth Castles. Henry's forces retaliated in the north, and the Cistercian monks were thrown out of Stata Florida by Henry who used the abbey as a military base.

Owain was in control of Mid and South Wales, and within three years controlled most of Wales, and was confident enough to set up a Welsh parliament at Machynlleth, from where he clarified he wanted independence, a return to the laws of Hywel Dda, and a separate Welsh church. He sought alliances with Spain and France and was part of the 'Tripartite Indenture' with his son-in-law Edward Mortimer and Thomas Percy of Northumberland, where Percy would claim the north of England and Mortimer the south and west of England, whilst Owain's Wales would extend north to the River Mersey, south to the River Severn and would include Cheshire, Shropshire and Herefordshire.

This was not to be as Percy was captured and publicly beheaded after The Battle of Shrewsbury, whilst Mortimer died at the siege of Harlech Castle. In an effort to further align with France, Owain sent what was later to be known as The Pennal Letter [20] in which he set out his plan for an independent Wales, and pledged the church would align with Pope Benedict XIII of Avignon rather than the church in Rome. He signed a formal treaty with the French who put troops in Wales, but by 1406 the French had completely withdrawn from Wales. By 1412 the revolt was over, Owain Glyndwr disappeared and was not heard of again.

King Henry's health was failing, and he was disfigured by skin disease (possibly leprosy), and from 1410 his son Henry of Monmouth was de facto king. On the King's death in 1413 he was buried at Canterbury Cathedral and his son became King Henry V.

Henry V's (16th September 1386 - 31st Aug 1422) rule was shorter than that of his father, but he is remembered for his military prowess, honed fighting against the troops of Owain Glyndwr, and culminating in his victory at Agincourt in 1415. In 1417 he introduced the use of English as the official language of government. The 1420 Treaty of Troyes recognised him as regent and heir to the French throne after marrying Catherine of Valois, daughter of King Charles VI of France, however, nine months after the birth of his son Henry, he died of dysentery in August 1422. Two months later the French monarch also passed away, and the infant King Henry VI of England also became King of France.

Henry VI (6th December 1421 - 21st May 1471) was assisted in governing by a Regency Council that handled the administration of England and English Territories in France, however by the time he took full control in 1437 there were deep divisions between the council's members, who were split into partisan lines that resulted in poor decision making in both England and in France. Henry had a number of mental breakdowns, and his wife Margaret of Anjou, niece of Charles VII, attempted to rule in his place. His cousin Richard, Duke of York, took control of parliament, an act that led to what became known as the War of the Roses, and Henry was deposed in March 1461, defeated at The Battle of Towton by Richard's son, who claimed the throne as Edward IV.

Edward IV (28th April 1422- 9th April 1483) The first decade of Edward's rule was turbulent, involving a number of encounters between his supporters and those of the deposed Henry VI, who was imprisoned by Edward in 1465. This resulted in what became known as 'The Readeption', the restoration of Henry VI to the throne in 1470. Edward was forced to flee to Flanders, but with the assistance of Flemish financial backers, he returned to England and after defeating Henry's supporters at the Battle of Barnet and the Battle of Tewkesbury, he reclaimed the throne in April 1471. Henry VI was captured and died in the Tower of London in May 1471.

In 1470 Edward gave the Lordship of Gower and Kilvey to William Herbert, 2nd Earl of Pembroke, and passed to him 'the castle and manor of Swaneseye, the lordship or land of Gower, and the lordship or land of Kylvey.' [21] The widow of John De Mowbray objected to this and put in a new claim, but to no avail, and in 1481 the lordship was fully under the control of William, Earl of Huntington, son of William Herbert, but by 1483 the lordship was taken from him and had once again reverted to the crown.

Edward became seriously ill and in March 1483 likely aware he was dying, named his brother Richard the Duke of Gloucester as the protector of his 12-year-old son Edward, The Prince of Wales.

Edward passed away on April 2nd 1483, but **Edward V** (2nd November 1470 – c. June 1483) would never be crowned king. He and his younger brother Richard of Shrewsbury Duke of York were sent to the Tower of London by their uncle Richard, who in order to claim the crown for himself, had clerics state that Edward IV's marriage was bigamous and therefore invalid, and thus his sons could have no legitimate claim to the throne. Edward and Richard were never seen again, likely murdered on the orders of the new King Richard III.

Richard III (2nd October 1452 – 22nd August 1485) had stolen the crown from his nephew and became king on 6th July 1483, but his was a short and tumultuous reign. He was immediately met with hostility from a friend and ally of Edward IV, Henry Stafford, 2nd Duke of Buckingham, who in 1483 led an unsuccessful revolt against Richard in what would later be known as the Buckingham Rebellion. In August 1485 Richard fought against Henry Tudor in a battle at Bosworth Field in Leicester, where with the help of 5000 Welsh troops Henry defeated Richard, who is remembered as the last King of England to die in battle.

Henry VII (28th January 1457 - 21st April 1509) became king on 22nd August 1485. The first Tudor King, his marriage to Elizabeth of York unified the houses of Lancaster and York, and his emblem was the Tudor Rose, a combination of both the red rose of Lancaster and the white rose of York. His marriage was important as it helped nullify future claims on the throne from either house, although it did not remove the threat completely, and he was forced to quell a few minor rebellions and executed anyone he felt was a threat to his lineage. He maintained peace throughout his reign managed by The Court of the Star Chamber, which allowed him to act quickly and decisively. Court proceedings were held in secret, the accused would often have no legal representation, and his Justices of the Peace acted as the enforcers of law and order.

William Herbert, who in 1479 had exchanged the earldom of Pembroke for the earldom of Huntingdon at the request of the king, received a pardon from Henry VII on 22nd September 1486:

'Pardon to William Herbert, knight, lord Herbert, alias William late Earl of Pembroke, and late Chamberlain in South Wales, alias late Chamberlain of Edward late prince of Wales, alias William Herbert late earl of Pembroke, son and heir, and tenant of the lands of William late earl of Pembroke, alias William earl of Huntingdon, of all fines, issues, forfeit and accounts due from him, to August 2 last'. [22]

The Lordship of Gower was back in the hands of the Herbert family but after William's death c July 1490 at only 35 years old, with no son to assume direct lineage rights the title 'Earl of Huntingdon' was not passed on, however, the Lordship of Gower was passed to his son-in-law Charles Beaufort Somerset who was made Earl of Worcester in 1514.

In October 1526 the Earl leased "all the manner mines of coal now found or that hereafter can be found and all the coals of the said mines within the said Lordship of Gower and Kilvey or the members of the same" [23] to Sir Matthew Cradock for a period of 80 years, at the agreed rent of £11 per annum. The title 'Baron Herbert' was passed on to William's grandson Henry Somerset, and in 1532 Henry, now 2nd Earl of Worcester after his father passed away in 1526, issued a new Charter to Swansea that essentially re-confirmed the 1306 De Breos charter.

In the space of two years, King Henry VII had lost both his eldest son Arthur, the Prince of Wales, and also his wife Elizabeth, and was in mourning until his own death from tuberculosis on 21st April 1509. His second son Henry, like his father known as Henry Tudor, succeeded him as King Henry VIII.

Henry VIII (28th June 1491 – 28th January 1547) was the second son of Henry VII and became heir on the sudden death of his brother Arthur, who at 15 years old had married Catherine of Aragon. Five months after the marriage both he and his wife were taken ill with 'sweating sickness' but whilst she recovered, he passed away on April 2nd 1502. After Arthur's death, Henry married Catherine, a process only sanctioned by the Catholic Church after Catherine had sworn that she and Arthur had never consummated their marriage. The ongoing tension between France and Spain in

Europe captured the interest of Henry and in October 1511 he aligned with his father-in-law Ferdinand II of Spain, and together with Venice, stood against the Papal aspirations of the French, sending over 10,000 men to take part in the 1st Invasion of France, in reality, was a series of battles at Guinegate, at Therouanne and at Tournai.

Whilst in France his brother-in-law James IV of Scotland invaded England, but the Scots were heavily defeated by the Earl of Surrey at the Battle of Flodden on 9th September 1513, and James himself was a casualty of the battle. A truce was sort between England and France, and Henry and the French King Francis I met on 7th June 1520 at the Field of Gold near Calais, but Henry favoured an alliance with Charles V of Spain, and when Charles V attacked France, Henry pulled his troops from France. England and France signed The Treaty of the More in August 1525, which involved various payments made to England as well as ensuring Henry's claim to the title King of Scotland. In return, England agreed to assist in the release of King Francis of France who was held by Charles V of Spain, whilst France agreed to retain John Stuart, Duke of Albany, who would not be allowed to return to Scotland.

As the son of Elizabeth of York, Henry was acutely aware that as he represented both Houses of Lancaster and York, a male heir would nullify claims on his crown from either side. His marriage to Catherine had produced a daughter Mary, born in 1516, but with no male heir, he approached Rome for an annulment, arguing his marriage was against 'divine law', something which had already been approved by the Church when he had asked to marry Catherine. The issue became known as 'the Kings Great Matter' and after passing a number of Acts culminating in the Act of Supremacy on 3rd November 1534, the House of Commons formally recognised Henry as 'the only head, sovereign lord, protector and defender of the Church', effectively separating the church in England from the control of the Catholic Church in Rome. His first marriage was annulled, and Henry VIII married Anne Boleyn on 25th January 1533, and he introduced the Act of Succession that ensured that his daughter Mary was illegitimate in the eyes of the law, whilst it recognised the legitimacy of the children of Henry and Anne Boleyn.

Thomas Cromwell was appointed chief minister and Henry's principal secretary in April 1534, and he ensured that all Papal payments were abolished with the monies going to the Crown instead. The church was closed down in 1536, resulting in 'The Dissolution of the Monasteries' that took four years, and resulted in the greatest redistribution of property in England since the Norman Conquest in 1066. Many of Henry's supporters took advantage of the Dissolution, and in Gower, the family of Rice (Rhys) Mansel of Penrice and Oxwich became one of the wealthiest in South Wales as a result of investing in monastic lands that including Margam Abbey and its estates.

England's break with Rome coincided with the Protestant reform in Germany, but whilst the changes in England were rooted in Henry's quest for a male heir rather than a question of faith, in Germany the fallout with Rome was led by Martin Luther, a theology professor and one-time priest who openly questioned many of the teachings and actions of the Catholic Church. Free of the shackles of the church, Henry had Anne Boleyn executed on 19th May 1536. She had not produced a male heir but did give Henry a second daughter, Elizabeth. Within two weeks of Anne's execution, he married Jane Seymour who, after giving birth to his much-wanted son and heir Prince Edward on 12th October 1537, died a few weeks later following complications after the birth.

Thomas Cromwell was tasked with devising a plan to nullify the threat to the crown by the Marcher Lords, and as a result, a plan to bring Wales under English law was devised culminating in the passing of The Act of 27 in 1536, meaning it was proclaimed in Henry's 27th year as king. The first of two 'Laws in Wales Acts' was passed with no consultation or representation from Wales, and formed a 13-county Wales that would be governed by the English parliament. The Marcher lordships separating England from Wales became the counties of Radnor, Brecknock, Montgomery and Denbigh, whilst Monmouth became an English county, however, the border established left some Welsh-speaking areas in England. The South Wales lordships of Gower, Kilvey, Glamorgan and Morgannwg were amalgamated into the new county of Glamorgan.

The governance of Wales was handled by The Court of Great Sessions which met twice a year in each of the thirteen Welsh counties, with each county appointed a Sheriff and nine Justices of the Peace. All administration in Wales was carried out in the English language and no one using the Welsh language 'shall have or enjoy any manner of office', and the English law of primogeniture was introduced and the Welsh law of 'cyfran' was abolished, which meant henceforth a man's inheritance passed to his eldest son only, rather than all sons inherited equally. Under the 1536 Act, the counties of Wales could now elect members to the English Parliament, and the first members took their seats in 1542. The second of the two 'Laws in Wales Acts' was passed in 1543, and further recognised the equality of Welsh citizens with the English, however, it appears that the cultural impact on Wales was not considered at all. These acts have since erroneously become known as the 'Acts of Union', and many historians maintain that the harmonising of laws was their primary purpose.

Thomas Cromwell tried to develop a Northern European Alliance and with this in mind had persuaded Henry to marry the German Anne of Cleves in the hope of strengthening relationships, but the marriage was annulled within six months and was likely not consummated. Henry had Cromwell arrested for treason and heresy, and he was executed on 28th July 1540. Henry married his fifth wife, 17-year-old Catherine Howard, only 19 days after the annulment of his previous marriage and on the same day as Cromwell's execution. The marriage ended with her being stripped of her title of Queen in November 1541, followed by the execution of two of her lovers in December 1541, and ended with her execution on 15th February 1542. In the same year, Henry joined with Emperor Charles V of Spain to fight against the French, only to see Scotland, now ruled by Henry's nephew James V, side with their long-term allies the French.

The Scottish king dispatched a large force of 18,000 men across the border into Cumbria and was met by an English force of around 3000 men led by Sir Thomas Wharton. The campaign ended on the day it started following a decisive defeat of the Scots at the Battle of Solway Moss on 24th November 1542. James V died of fever a few weeks later leaving behind a six-day-old daughter Mary, who would later come to be known as Mary, Queen of Scots.

Henry's sixth and final marriage was in July 1543 to Catherine Parr who as queen consort would survive him by twenty months, and who was instrumental in the passing of the Third Succession Act that restored the linage rights of Henry's daughters Mary and Elizabeth, although his son Edward was first in line to the throne. Henry VIII died on 28th January 1547 at the age of 55 and was succeeded by his 6-year-old son Edward VI, but due to his age a Regency Council actually ran the government, and it was during this period that Protestantism was established across England and Wales.

Edward VI (12th October 1537 - 6th July 1553) likely suffered from tuberculosis, and recognising that the king's illness was terminal, the Regency Council ensured succession planning was in place. Edward's will ignored the Crown Act of 1543, bypassed both of his half-sisters Mary and Elizabeth, and instead named his cousin Jane Grey as his heir. Edward reigned for only nine years, and on his death, his will was disputed. Nine days later his half-sister Mary, a Catholic, was proclaimed Queen despite a statute law to prohibit this.

Mary I (18th February 1506 - 17th November 1558) daughter of Catherine of Aragon, became England's first Queen regnant, and quickly set about reversing the Protestant reforms that had previously been put in place. She ordered the death of nearly 300 dissenters, burnt at the stake in the Marian persecutions, which earned her the name 'Bloody Mary'. She regarded her half-sister Elizabeth as a threat to her sovereignty and placed her in the Tower of London for nearly a year for her support of the Protestant faith. Mary married Prince Philip of Spain on 25th July 1554 within days of meeting him, however, when she died without an heir on 17th February 1558 at only 42 years old, her half-sister Elizabeth, daughter of Anne Boleyn, succeeded her.

Elizabeth I (7th September 1533 - 24th March 1603) became Queen of England on 17th November 1558 at the age of 25, and immediately ensured the establishment of the Protestant Church.

The Protestant Settlement of Edward VI initially became known as the Elizabethan Religious Settlement, and would later become 'The Church of England'. Whilst Elizabeth recognised Catholicism as a threat to the Crown, she nevertheless tried to manage the inclusion of many elements of the Catholic Church so as to pacify her Catholic subjects.

For a number of years, a threat to Elizabeth's crown was her cousin Mary. Granddaughter of Henry VIII's sister Margaret, and the only legitimate child of James V of Scotland, Mary, also known as 'Mary Queen of Scots', had married Francis the Dauphine of France in 1558, and was Queen Consort of France between 1559 and his death in December 1560. She returned to Scotland after the death of her mother in 1560 and assumed control of the Scottish government. In July 1565 she married Henry Stuart Lord Darnley, gaining her the support of Catholics in England, however, the marriage was not supported by her mother's half-brother James Stuart Earl of Moray. Forced to expel Moray and his supporters into England, he was pardoned and allowed back into Scotland the following year.

Mary was implicated in the death of her husband Henry and married the Earl of Boswell, who was also implicated in the murder. In 1567 she abdicated in favour of her infant son James, and the Earl of Moray was appointed regent of her son King James VI of Scotland in her absence. Unfortunately Moray's pro-Protestant position had made him many enemies, and in January 1570 he was shot and killed by James Hamilton of Bothwellhaugh, notable as being the first official assassination by a firearm. Mary fled south to England where she was imprisoned for nineteen years before being executed for treason at Fotheringhay Castle in Northamptonshire in 1587.

Although her Protestant positioning regularly angered both Ireland and France, Elizabeth I's reign is regarded by many as a 'Golden Age,' and her marine fleet reached America, Russia, the Middle East and Asia, and although cautious in military excursions, the defeat of the Spanish Armada in 1588 led by Walter Raleigh remains a point of note in English history. The last Tudor Monarch, Elizabeth died at Richmond Palace on the 24th of March 1603, and within hours of her death, the Royal Council, led by Robert Cecil, proclaimed James VI of Scotland, son of Mary Queen of Scots, as James I of England.

James I (19 June 1566 – 27 March 1625) was only one year old when made James IV of Scotland, and became James I, King of England on 24th March 1603. He married Anne of Denmark by proxy in August 1589, formally marrying her in Oslo, Norway in November later that year. They had two sons, Henry Frederick who died aged 18 of typhoid, and Charles (later Charles I), as well as a daughter Elizabeth. James proclaimed himself 'King of Great Britain and Ireland', however, the parliaments of Scotland and England remained separated, and he endured regular conflict with the English Parliament throughout his reign and survived two substantial plots to overthrow his court.

Sir Walter Raleigh was amongst those tried for conspiracy in July 1603 in what became known as 'The Main Plot' to remove James from the throne and was imprisoned in the Tower of London. Raleigh was released after 13 years, only for James to have him executed two years later in 1618. A second unsuccessful plot by English Catholics occurred on 4th and 5th November 1605 when Catholic plotters wanting freedom of worship were foiled in their attempt to blow up the Houses of Parliament. Led by Robert Catesby, their failed attempt became known as 'The Gunpowder Plot', remembered today as 'Guy Fawkes Night', named after the plotter who was discovered guarding the explosives and who, amongst others, was later hanged, drawn and quartered.

In 1623, it was intended that James's son Charles would marry Maria Anna Habsburg, the Spanish Infanta, in order to improve relations between the two countries, later known as 'The Spanish Match', at which time James had agreed to repeal the anti-Catholic legislation put in place by Parliament. This proved to be a disastrous plan as neither person would change the faith to accommodate the other, so the planned pairing never happened, and Parliament subsequently doubled down on its anti-Catholic stance, and a war with Spain was discussed.

A devoted Protestant and patron of the arts, he sponsored the writing of the King James Bible which is still in common usage today. Although an educated man, he gained the epithet 'The Wisest Fool in Christendom' for his apparent lack of application of common sense, although this has since been questioned by historians. He died on 27th March 1625 aged 58 years and was succeeded by his son Charles I.

Danygraig and Port Tennant

In the 17th Century **Charles I** (19th November 1600 - 30th January 1649) become heir to the thrones of England, Scotland and Ireland in 1612 after the death of his elder brother Henry Frederick, the Prince of Wales. A firm believer in 'the divine right of Kings' in word and deed, he clashed with both church and government throughout his reign, all of whom strongly objected to his unilateral actions. His marriage to Henrietta Maria, the youngest daughter of King Henry IV of France, upset the Reformed religious groups of England and Scotland, all of whom believed his sympathies lay with the Catholic faith, whilst his levying of unrealistic levels of taxes on the kingdom without prior consultation, greatly upset both parliament and subjects.

Charles and the Archbishop of Canterbury William Laud wanted to enforce uniformity across the religions in England, Wales, Scotland and Ireland upsetting English Puritans, Scottish Covenanters and Irish Catholics, and by 1642 matters had come to a head, resulting in a war fought between the Royalist forces of King Charles, led by his nephew Prince Rupert of the Rhine Duke of Cumberland, and Parliamentary forces led by Sir Thomas Fairfax, later known as The English Civil War, although fighting actually took place across England and Wales. The Parliamentarians also had an agreement in place with the forces of the Scottish Covenanters.

At the commencement of the English Civil War, Gower and Swansea, now part of Glamorgan, continued to have loyalty to the Crown, including local lord Henry Somerset, 5th Earl of Worcester as well as many of the town's dignitaries, such as Walter Thomas of Swansea, his son William Thomas of Danygraig and Bussy Mansel of Briton Ferry. [24] Parliamentary sympathies were also in evidence amongst some of the region's landowners as well as the local Puritan clergy, and there were likely to have been quite a few people who were neither Royalist nor Parliamentarian, who instead favoured self-preservation, irrespective of who ruled the country.

A merchant of substantial wealth, Walter Thomas was a descendent of the 11th century Welsh prince Einon ap Collwyn, and had been Swansea's Portreeve (mayor/principle magistrate) in 1615 and 1626, High Sheriff of Glamorgan in 1636, and deputy steward in 1643 and 1645. Walter's son William Thomas lived at Ty Mawr, (The Great House) in Danygraig on the east side of the River Tawe, and was married to Catherine, the sister of Bussy Mansel of Briton Ferry, and had been appointed High Sheriff of Glamorgan in 1645. In 1650 amongst his listed assets he 'owned premises in Wind St and Fisher St', 'three water gryst mills…called the Bryn Mills' and also had 'benefit of the Passage Boat there'. Bussy Mansel was the youngest and only surviving son of Arthur Mansel of Briton Ferry and Jane, daughter and heiress of William Price of Briton Ferry, and was the grandson of Sir Thomas Mansel, baronet, of Margam, who had died in 1631. [25]

From the time of the first Marcher Lord, Gower and Swansea held a strategic role in the eyes of the Crown as both a garrison town and a useful port of entry to the west of Wales and beyond. The local lord could be relied on to recruit and supply men to fight its wars, and in addition, the region was a good source of revenue, be it through the collection of taxes on the local residents, its exports including coal, or via oaths and loans from local dignitaries. By July 1643, many Puritans had left Swansea for friendlier climes, whilst others opted to join the parliamentarian forces. The more prominent amongst them had suffered the indignity of their goods being seized, after the Commissioners of Array for Glamorgan ordered the taking of the estates of all 'convicted separatists, fugitives and other disaffected persons within the several hundred of Swansea, Neath and Llangyfelach'.

This was tasked to Royalists Bussy Mansel and William Thomas who were authorised to sell any and all goods confiscated and lease out any land and tenements seized. Further to the King's call to arms, in August 1643 the Commissioners of Array instructed Walter Thomas, William Thomas and Bussy Mansel to gather 120 men from the 'Hundreds' of Swansea, Llangyfelach and Neath, arm them and then send them to Cardiff to join with troops gathered from the other South Wales hundreds, from where they would all march on to seize Gloucester from parliamentary forces.

In January 1645, Swansea was no longer under the control of Royalists. The custody of Swansea Castle had been stripped from Governor Walter Thomas, and for a few months was under the control of Richard Donnell, until on 17th November Parliament appointed Phillip Jones as his replacement as Governor of Swansea and Swansea Castle. The castle was decommissioned as a garrison in case of a resurgence of Royalist forces, something that was enforced across South Wales with the notable exception of Pembroke Castle, which was deemed vital to any military excursion into Ireland.

Referring to the original structure, Swansea Castle was later described in Cromwell's 1650 Survey of Gower as 'a decayed Buildinge called the Castle of Swanzey'. [26] On the same day it was announced that 22-year-old Bussy Mansel, now no longer a Royalist, was promoted to the position of "Commander-in-Chief of the Forces in the County of Glamorgan, subordinate to Sir Thomas Fairfax". Walter and his son William Thomas did not shift their alliances, and both men suffered the indignity of having their estates confiscated and fines levied against them. Walter was fined £400, an amount later reduced to £313, and William fined £786, a sum later reduced to £336, whilst William's estates were placed in the hands of his brother-in-law Bussy Mansel, who in 1647 was made High Sheriff of Glamorgan.

Charles I was captured by Scottish troops in Newark in May 1646 and was handed over to Parliamentarian troops in Newcastle, effectively ending the English Civil War and Royalist estates were given to parliamentarian supporters, including the estates of the Earl of Worcester, whose lands in Gloucester, Monmouthshire and Glamorgan were passed to Oliver Cromwell, the parliamentarian Lieutenant-General of Cavalry, and 2nd in Command of 'the New Model Army' led by Sir Thomas Fairfax. It was expected that the king would accept parliamentarian conditions to form a constitutional monarchy, but his refusal caused further problems between various factions across England, Wales, Scotland and

Ireland, and in December 1648, upset at the support for the king from some Royalist sympathisers, the English Parliament was dissolved and a Rump Parliament elected in its place.

Charles' refusal to make a compromise resulted in the Second Civil War, made up of uprisings and military excursions later known as The Wars of Three Kingdoms (1648-51), the Bishops Wars (1638-1640) and Cromwell's 'Conquest of Ireland', each of which saw the superior military capabilities of forces led by Fairfax and Cromwell defeating their opposition. Oliver Cromwell visited Swansea on two occasions, the first visit on 19th May 1648 on his way to Pembrokeshire to suppress an uprising led by Colonel John Poyer, who after defeating Royalist forces when the governor of Pembroke Castle, refused to hand over the castle to the Parliamentarian cause, and instead joined the Royalists. Poyer surrendered to Cromwell on July 11th 1648 and was later executed at Covent Garden, London.

The Minute Book of the Common Hall of Swansea recorded Cromwell's visit:

'At which time came into this town the truly honourable Oliver Cromwell Esquire, Lieutenant General of all the forces of this Kingdom of England under the command of the Parliament, Lord of this town, the Seignory of Gower, and the Manor of Kilvey, with the members thereof, who gave unto the poor of this town to be set out at interest for the benefit and advantage of the said poor the sum of ten pounds and the sum is referred to the Portreeve of the town for the time being.' [27]

After a failed attempt to escape, Charles I was imprisoned at Carisbrooke Castle on the Isle of Wight where after being tried and found guilty of high treason, he was sentenced to death. He was beheaded on 30th January 1649 at the Palace of Whitehall, London, the only English monarch to be executed. After his execution, the English Rump Parliament announced the establishment of 'The Commonwealth of England' however on 5th February 1649 Scotland, not consulted over Charles I fate, recognised the then-exiled Charles II as their rightful king, an act that would be a catalyst for the Third Civil War.

Catholics in Ireland were also restless and in late 1649, Cromwell and his troops were dispatched to quell the Irish dissent, and stopped at Swansea for a second time on his way to Pembroke. Whilst in Swansea he was the chief guest at dinner held by the Governor of Swansea Philip Jones, the Minute Book of Common Hall of 2nd September 1649 recording that:

'By the desire of the alderman of the town whose names are underwritten, there was provided for the Right honourable Oliver Cromwell, Lord Lieutenant of Ireland, and Lord of this town and for all his followers, a dinner in the house of William Bayly, then Portreeve. Now, to defray the charge of necessaries towards that provision, we have thought fit to take ten pounds out of the town stock. And whereas the greatness of the charge of free quarter within this town was such on their march, of horse and foot, to Ireland, that we were forced one night to entertain in the inns forty horse with some foot on the public charge of the town amounting to six pounds eight shillings, we see fit to take same out of the common stock of this town, all amounting to sixteen pounds and eight shillings.'

Oliver Cromwell was responsible for a Survey of Gower in 1650 supervised by Bussy Mansel and John Price, who was now High Sheriff of Glamorgan, and it was during the Commonwealth period that Swansea's first official market was set up in 1652, open twice-weekly near the remains of the 'new' castle. In addition, an annual programme of town fairs was held in May, July, August and October each year. The title 'Portreeve' was replaced by the new title of 'Mayor', and on 21st January 1658 Swansea had its first Member of Parliament William Foxwist, who stood as MP until parliament was dissolved on 22nd April 1659, however when parliament resumed in March 1660, he returned as the Member for St. Albans. It was also during this period that Bishop Hugh Gore established the Swansea Grammar School, apparently at the suggestion of Bussy Mansel.

On June 20th 1650 unhappy that the Scots supported Charles II, the English Rump Parliament authorised an attack on Scotland led by Oliver Cromwell, who had succeeded Thomas Fairfax as Lord General and Commander-in-Chief. The English and Scottish armies fought in various locations in both Scotland and England, and by the end of 1651, the English parliamentarians were finally victorious, at which time military rule was imposed in Scotland under General Monck.

On 25th June 1651 Bussy Mansel was added to the High Court of Justice, and in 1653 he was a member of Cromwell's 'Barebones Parliament', one of six members representing Wales. In 1654 he was Militia Commissioner for South Wales, and in the following year, he was made a Justice of the Peace for Glamorgan. After acting as a Commissioner for the Safety of the Protector, he was tasked with the command of all militia forces in South Wales, horse and foot, 'to lead them against the enemy if need be.' [28]

After his defeat at the Battle of Worcester on 3rd September 1651, Charles II went into hiding, and following a failed attempt to escape to a Royalist safe haven in Wales, made his way to Shoreham in West Sussex from where on 15th October 1851 he took a boat to France. Oliver Cromwell was made Lord Protector of England (which included Wales), Scotland and Ireland on 16th December 1653, and was responsible for two Charters of Swansea made in 1655 and 1658, the second being an addendum to the first charter. After his death on 3rd September 1658, Cromwell was given a state funeral, organised and overseen by Philip Jones of Swansea.

Oliver's son Richard Cromwell succeeded him as Lord Protector, but lacking both his father's reputation and political guile, his time in the position was short and he was removed by the army on 25th May 1659 and the Rump Parliament, led by Charles Fleetwood and John Lambert, was recalled. Fleetwood and Lambert were opposed by Governor of Scotland General George Monck who after returning to England was instrumental in the disbanding of the Rump Parliament and the setting up of the Convention Parliament, designed to be little more than a mechanism to hand back the crown to the king. There are no records in Swansea marking the death of Oliver Cromwell, but there are documents that show costs relating to the proclamation of Richard Cromwell as the new Lord Protector, who had also inherited his father's lands and titles. [29]

By October 1659, Cromwell's Swansea charters had been set aside, and the role of mayor was replaced by the new Portreeve, William Jones. On 1st May 1660, Charles II was declared the rightful King of England, backdated from the date of his late father's execution, and records show that the proclamation of the new king was celebrated in Swansea with 'bells, bonfires, and beer.' [30] The Convention Parliament was dissolved in December 1660 and was replaced by the Cavalier Parliament of Charles II, who had returned from exile and was crowned on 23rd April 1661. After the Restoration, the Lordship of Gower and Kilvey returned to the Somerset family, the Earls of Worcester, who were rewarded for their loyalty to the king.

William Thomas of Danygraig returned to Swansea after residing in Carmarthen for a number of years, and records show him listed as an Alderman of Swansea in 1662. In the same year he took a lease on Swansea Castle and ground from the Earl of Worcester; not the 'ruinous old building' mentioned in Cromwell's Survey of Gower 1650, but the 'ancient building called the new Castle', originally built in 1332 by John Mowbray. His lands were returned to him but after his death without issue, they passed to Bussy Mansel.

Charles II (29th May 1630 – 6th February 1685) Charles II's return to the throne was swiftly followed by the implementation of the Pardon, Indemnity and Oblivion Act, designed to pacify the majority of Cromwell's followers via a general pardon for all crimes carried out under the rule of the parliamentarians, with the exception of serious crimes such as rape and murder. All crown lands confiscated previously were immediately restored, however goods, lands and estates confiscated from anyone else were not covered by the Act and disenfranchised parties, including Royalists sympathisers and their families, were left to fend for themselves, either privately or via legal means.

Excluded from the Act was anyone involved in the trial and execution of Charles I. The trial of the king had involved over one hundred people including witnesses, associates, and 59 commissioners who had signed the king's death warrant, ten of whom were executed. Many were given life sentences, whilst some, fearing for their lives, went into exile. Oliver Cromwell had died in

1658, but on 30th January 1661 the 12th anniversary of Charles 1st execution, Cromwell's corpse, together with that of his son-in-law Henry Ireton and that of the trial's presiding judge John Bradshaw, was taken to Tyburn Gallows in the centre of London and given a posthumous execution. Their bodies were first hanged and then beheaded, their headless corpses dumped in an unmarked ditch, and their heads left to rot on spikes above Westminster Hall. Cromwell's head was said to have remained there for over twenty years before it was dislodged in a storm and taken by a soldier for safe-keeping and is said to have passed through the hands of various people before it was acquired by the Wilkinson family, and in 1960, nearly 300 years later after his posthumous trial, it was donated by Dr Horace Wilkinson to Sidney Sussex College at Cambridge, Cromwell's alma mater.

South Wales and Swansea in particular had become a Puritan stronghold, and a series of penal laws were introduced by parliament with the aim of persecuting both Catholics and members of the various Non-conformist groups alike. The Act of Uniformity was introduced in May 1662 that forbids anyone to hold ecclesiastical office unless they had been ordained, and within two years the Conventicle Act was passed, aimed directly at those attending religious meetings that did not use The Book of Common Prayer. In 1665 the government introduced the Five Mile Act that prohibited ministers from living within five miles of a 'corporate town' or any other location they had previously served. The word 'corporate' offered some solace to the ministers of Swansea, as it referred to a town or borough represented in parliament, but nevertheless, persecution was intense, and many Puritan leaders left for the Americas.

One such individual was John Miles, who was minister of a Baptist congregation in Ilston on the Gower peninsula, where he had replaced the royalist William Houghton in 1649. He grew the congregation quickly, and by 1660 it had over 250 members. Removed and replaced by William Houghton after the Restoration, Miles and many of his congregation left South Wales and settled in Plymouth, Massachusetts, where he established its first Baptist church at Rehoboth. In 1667 he was expelled from the area and moved south to Wannamoisett on Rhode Island, where he established a settlement called Swansey (now called Barrington), where he died in 1684.

In 1661, Charles II married the Infanta of Portugal, Catherine of Braganza, a Catholic. Her dowry included the Portuguese lands of Tangiers and Seven Islands of Bombay, a payment of 2 million Portuguese crowns (then the equivalent of £360,000), plus access to the Portuguese trading routes of Brazil and the East Indies. In 1668 the East India Company were given a lease to develop the Seven Islands of Bombay for a nominal fee of £10 in gold, but English Tangiers was abandoned in 1684. He spent much of the next twenty years in various disputes with his parliament, be it through his military excursions or his religious policies, but it was his willingness to get close to France and his openness to the practices of the Catholic faith that were particular irritants. His wife had been unable to give him an heir, which meant his brother James the Duke of York, who had become a Catholic in c1668, was heir to his throne, so to ease the government's concerns of a return to Catholic royalty, Charles agreed to the marriage of James' daughter Mary to the protestant William of Orange.

Charles continued to espouse freedom to worship, and in March 1672, issued the Royal Declaration of Indulgence, which suspended the penal laws previously enacted to punish Catholics and Non-conformists. The fear of James becoming king remained as strong as ever, and in 1679 parliament introduced the Exclusion Bill to ensure he was removed from the line of succession, however, Charles dissolved parliament and prevented it from being passed, and dissolved parliament a further three times by March 1681.

The king valued those close to him that showed loyalty, and in 1682 the Somerset family were rewarded for their support, and the Earl of Worcester was made Duke of Beaufort. [31] Charles II died on 2nd February 1685, converting to Catholicism on his deathbed, and his brother succeeded him as James II of England and Ireland, and James VII of Scotland.

James II (14th October 1633 - 16th September 1701) was crowned on 23rd April 1685, and in November of the same year, he dissolved the English Parliament. In August 1686 he dissolved the Scottish

Parliament due to their unwillingness to remove legal restrictions on practising the Catholic faith, before introducing a Declaration of Indulgence in 1687 in an effort to establish freedom of religion across the British Isles. Seen as an affront to the Church of England, it culminated in the 'Trial of Seven Bishops' for sedition, all of whom were subsequently acquitted, further damaging the king's already fractured relationship with his government.

Frustrated by his inability to get his own way in Britain, in 1686 James created The Dominion of New England which included the New England colonies of Massachusetts, New Hampshire, Plymouth, Connecticut, New Haven, and Rhode Island, and would later add New York (renamed from New Amsterdam) and New Jersey in 1688. Governed by Sir Edmund Andros, the New England Puritan communities were deeply concerned when their land titles were questioned, resulting in payments to the crown for the reconfirmation.

During the Restoration period, Bussy Mansel changed his allegiances from Parliamentarian back to Royalist again, seemingly without any loss to either his assets or reputation, and in 1660 he was elected Member of Parliament for Cardiff in the Convention Parliament. Whether this can be attributed to his acute survival instincts or his family ties, or perhaps a combination of both, is open to debate, but he was regarded by many as a 'trimmer', a term further expanded on thirty years later by George Savile, Lord Halifax in his book 'The Character of a Trimmer' as 'someone who trimmed their sails to accommodate prevailing politic winds.' [32]

In 1688, thirty years after the death of Oliver Cromwell, the Duke of Beaufort carried out a Survey of the Manor of Kilvey [33] and the document notes:

'...about six years ago Bussy Mansel Esq. one of the freeholders of the said Manor, hath erected a Windmill on Kilvey Hill within the said Manor, and hath also erected a Watermill there called New Mill.'

It also shows that he also owned coal mines in Kilvey, and had four fishing weirs 'on the Salt sands opposite St. Thomas Chapel.'

Bussy Mansel become a very wealthy and politically influential man who in 1677 became High Sheriff of Glamorgan, was MP for Glamorgan in 1679 until 1681, and again in 1689 until his death in 1699.

In June 1688, James II's second wife Mary of Modena gave birth to a male heir, James Frances Edward Stuart. This was a step too far for the parliament, and seven prominent Protestants wrote to William of Orange inviting him to take the English throne, guaranteeing him their support. In November of that year the King was deposed in the bloodless "Revolution of 1688" or "Glorious Revolution", an event that re-emphasised Parliament as the ruling power and not the Regent. The 1689 Bill of Rights further clarified this and established the right of parliament alone in the law-making process, whilst at the same time making clear the limits of a sovereign's power. The bill was given Royal Assent by James II's daughter Mary and her husband William of Orange, who was formally offered and accepted, the role of joint sovereigns. James II fled to France rather than face William and his flight was considered an abdication by parliament.

William III (14th November 1650 - 8th March 1702) **and Mary II** (30th April 1662 - 28th December 1694) jointly reigned until her death in 1694. William was not readily accepted as sovereign in Scotland, where his troops slaughtered many of the McDonald clan at Glen Coe in 1692, nor in Ireland where citizens still believed that James was the rightful king. In 1689 James II arrived in Ireland, and with French support, he declared war on England, however, William's forces successfully defended both Londonderry and Enniskillen, and in 1691 William led troops in defeating James' forces at the Battle of the Boyne, effectively ending the conflict. Whilst William dealt with the problems in Scotland and Ireland, Mary managed the government in England in her own name, content for her husband to take the lead when he returned to England.

William led the European opposition to the expansion plans of Louis XIV of France, resulting in the War of the Grand Alliance (also called the War of the League of Ansberg) where Louis' expansion plans were ended by the alliance led by Britain, the

United Provinces of the Netherlands and the Austria Habsburgs. Queen Mary died of smallpox in 1694 at the age of 32, and when James II died in exile in France in September 1701, Louis XV proclaimed his son Louis, the Dauphin of France as James' rightful heir, which caused great consternation in Protestant Britain. Seven months later William III died, and with no direct lineage, his crown was passed to his sister-in-law Ann, daughter of James II.

Queen Ann (6th February 1665- 1st August 1714) was the youngest sister of Mary II, and took the throne on 8th March 1702. She married Prince George of Denmark in 1683, and her adult life was fraught with medical issues. Pregnant 18 times between 1683 and 1700, only five pregnancies reached full term, and her one surviving son died in 1700 at the age of eleven, meaning she had no successor to her crown. A devout Anglican, she favoured the Anglican-leaning Tories in government and accepted the 1701 Act of Settlement that had previously set out parliament's role in handling the succession to the throne that ensured a Protestant regent, a system still in use today.

The Tory government was also active in the forming of the Act of Union between England and Scotland, finally given Royal approval in March 1707, where amongst other things, taxation would be uniform across Great Britain, although Scotland would retain its own laws and law courts. The following year, when asked to give royal assent to a Scottish Militia Bill that would allow the arming of a separate fighting force in Scotland, Queen Ann vetoed the proposal for fear of a future uprising, and in doing so became the last British monarch to veto a government bill. Ann died on August 1st 1714, the last of the Stuart monarchs, and as her nearest Protestant relative, the throne was passed to George Louis/Ludwig of Brunswick-Luneberg.

George I (25th May 1660 - 11th June 1727) was the first Hanoverian King of Great Britain, taking the throne on 1st August 1714, although there was a failed attempt to remove him and replace him with James Francis Edward Stuart (The Old Pretender), half-brother of Queen Anne. It was during George's reign that a 'cabinet of government' was first put in place where decisions are made by a government headed by a prime minister, led by the Whigs and Britain's first 'de facto' Prime Minister, Robert Walpole (although his actual title was First Lord of the Treasury and Chancellor of the Exchequer). Frustrated with his inability to affect domestic policy, George focused on foreign policy, resulting in an alliance with France. He died from a stroke on 11th June 1727 whilst on a visit to Hanover, and his only son George Augustus was named his successor.

George II (30th October 1683 – 25th October 1760) was born in Hanover, coming to Britain for the first time in September 1714, when he was formally pronounced Prince of Wales, and succeeded his father as king on 11th June 1727. His relationship with his father had been strained for a number of years, and on succeeding him George II was expected to replace Robert Walpole who had become one of his father's most trusted ministers. Contrary to expectations, he allowed Walpole to control both domestic and foreign affairs, and it was Walpole that guided the king away from the military excursions he otherwise favoured. George had a fractious relationship with his son Frederick, the Prince of Wales, who took a stand in opposition to his father's government, problematic enough to force the resignation of Robert Walpole in 1742.

On the 31st March 1751 Frederick, Prince of Wales died, and his son Prince George became heir to his grandfather's throne at the age of 22. The conflict known as The Seven Years War in Europe began in 1756, placed the forces of Britain, Hanover and Prussia on one side, and those of France, Austria, Saxony, Sweden and Russia on the other, however, this also overlapped a wider conflict between Britain and France over control of North America and India (1754-63). George II died on 25th October 1760 and was buried on 11th November 1760 at Westminster Abbey.

George III (4th June 1738 – 29th January 1820) (4th June 1738 – 29th January 1820) was born on 4 June 1738 in London, the eldest son of Frederick, Prince of Wales, and Princess Augusta of Saxe-Gotha, the first Hanoverian king to be born in Britain, and who spoke English as his first language and succeeded his grandfather, George II, in 1760. He was crowned King of Great Britain and Ireland on 25th October 1760, although his title changed on 1st

January 1801 after the union of the two kingdoms, from which time his title changed to the 'United Kingdom of Great Britain and Ireland'. He was devoted to his wife, Charlotte of Mecklenburg-Strelitz, and they had 15 children, 13 of whom reached adulthood. As a gift to her, he bought the Queen's House, which was later enlarged and became known as Buckingham Palace.

Britain's national debt was vast given the high cost of maintaining a military presence to deal with ongoing conflicts with France and Spain in an area as vast as the crown had claimed in America, together with the loans given to the East India Company, who were responsible for administrating India on the Crown's behalf, and by 1770 there was an annual requirement of £4 million to service the debt. The king was not directly responsible for the loss of the colonies, but did oppose any bid for independence, and supported Parliament's position when the declaration of American independence was made on 4 July 1776. The war ended with the surrender of British forces in 1782.

The loss of the American colonies put a strain on the king who, as a family man, was already distraught at the behaviour of his sons and the secret marriages of his brothers. The Royal Marriages Act of 1772 was passed at George's insistence, stating that under the Act, the sovereign must give consent to the marriage of any lineal descendant of George II. He had serious bouts of illness in 1788-89 and again in 1801, although by 1789 after a bill authorised his son to act as Prince Regent on his behalf, he had a 'full recovery' and the Bill was not passed. After a number of mental relapses in relation to other illnesses, George was deemed mentally unfit to rule in 1810, and in May 1811 he accepted the need for the Regency Act, and his son George, the Prince of Wales, became Prince Regent.

His second son Frederick Augustus the Duke of York founded The Royal Military College at Sandhurst but is better remembered today as "The Grand Old Duke of York" of the nursery rhyme, which relates to the Flanders Campaign of 1793-4, and more specifically Britain and Austria's ignominious defeat by the French at Tourcoing in Flanders in May 1794. In his final years, George III had become frail and blind and died at Windsor Castle on 29th

January 1820. After a reign of almost 60 years, his son George succeeded him as George IV.

George IV (12th August 1762 – 26th June 1830) became king on 29th January 1820, although he had become Regent in 1811 as a result of the illness of his father. Estranged from his father for many years, George IV's extravagant lifestyle earned him the title "The First Gentleman of England". Secretly (and illegally) he married a Catholic, Maria FitzHerbert in 1795, only for the marriage to be annulled by his father under the Marriages Act. In an agreement to clear his mounting debts, he married Princess Caroline of Brunswick in 1795 but tried to divorce her after his accession in 1820, but Caroline died in 1821 before any divorce could be arranged. After the death of his father, he resumed royal visits, first to Ireland and Hanover in 1821, and then in 1822 he visited Scotland, the first monarch to do so since Charles II's Scottish Coronation in 1651.

In 1829 his ministers persuaded him to agree to the Roman Catholic Relief Act that reduced and removed many of the restrictions on Roman Catholics previously introduced by the Act of Uniformity, the Test Acts, and the various remaining Penal Laws. On the 26th June 1830 aged 67, George IV died at Windsor Castle where he had spent his final years in seclusion. His only daughter Princess Charlotte had died giving birth to a stillborn child in 1817, so the throne passed to George's youngest brother William, Duke of Clarence, who became heir presumptive at the age of 61, when his brother Frederick, Duke of York, died in January 1827.

It was during George IV's reign that George Tennant's ambitious plans to link the Neath Canal to Fabian's Bay finally bore fruit. His canal opened in 1824 [35] and the area we know today as Port Tennant was created.

William IV (21st August 1765 – 20th June 1837) reigned from 26th June 1830 until his death on 20th June 1837. As the third son of the monarch, he was not thought to be in line for an inheritance to the throne and joined the Royal Navy at the age of thirteen. By the age of 20 he was the captain of the HMS Pegasus, and became a rear admiral in 1789. In the same year, he was made Duke of Clarence, and ended his active Royal Navy career a year later, after which he spent much of his time in the House of Lords. An advocate of the slave trade, something he had seen first-hand whilst serving in the Caribbean, he was considered the nemesis of leading abolitionist William Wilberforce who, in his first Parliamentary speech, he referred to by name when stating "the proponents of the abolition are either fanatics or hypocrites and in one of those classes I rank Mr Wilberforce" [36].

Wilberforce and the Abolitionists were successful in their endeavours, and after the Emancipation Act of 1833, slavery was finally abolished in the British Empire on 1 August 1834. Whilst children under the age of six were freed immediately, under the terms of the Act, all other former slaves continued to work without pay for their former owners as 'apprentices' until they were finally released in 1838. Plantation owners in the British Caribbean received nearly £20 million in government compensation for the loss of over 700,000 slaves. Many of the plantation owners were leading British politicians and businessmen that had never set foot in the Caribbean, whilst the former slaves received no monetary reparation, monetary or otherwise.

Between 1791 and 1811 he lived with his mistress, the actress Dorothy Bland (better known by her stage name 'Mrs Jordan') and their children under the family name of 'FitzClarence', however in 1818, William married Princess Adelaide of Saxe-Meiningen, who gave him two daughters, the first surviving only hours and the second only a few months. A major part of William's seven-year reign was the discussion and subsequent action relating to the Reform Crisis. This involved proposals to reform the electoral system of Great Britain that allocated local ministers to parliament that had been more or less unchanged since the 15th Century. The system showed substantial imbalance, favouring areas known as 'rotten' or 'pocket' boroughs owned by aristocrats or landed gentry, who would get more MP's allocated to their areas than large towns, some of which had no representation at all. In August 1830 the Duke of Wellington's Tory government lost the general election to Earl Grey's Whig Party who pledged parliamentary reform.

After three successive Reform Bills were rejected, the first in the Commons and the remaining two by the House of Lords, the Reform Act of 1832 (also known as The Great Reform Act) was passed. The Act did away with rotten boroughs, clearing up the injustices felt by the large towns and cities, and for the first time in British history the vote was given to any man that paid a yearly rental of £10 or more. The Act specifically defined a voter as a 'male person', thus women were excluded from the process completely. William IV died on 20 June 1837, and although he had at least ten illegitimate children, the throne passed to his niece Princess Victoria, the only child of George III's fourth son Prince Edward, the Duke of Kent, who had come of age only a month earlier.

Queen Victoria (24th May 1819 – 22nd January 1901) was the only daughter of Edward, Duke of Kent, the fourth son of George III, and was born at Kensington Palace, London. After William IV's death on 20th June 1837, Victoria became queen at the age of 18, and her coronation was held on 28th June at Westminster Abbey. On February 10th 1840, Queen Victoria married her first cousin Prince Albert of Saxe-Coburg and Gotha, who became HRH Prince Albert. He was not given the official title Prince Consort of Great Britain and Ireland until 1857.

An educated man who had attended the University of Bonn in Germany, as the queen's husband he had no real power of his own, but quickly became her most trusted adviser on both domestic and international affairs. Together with Prime Minister Lord Melbourne, Albert advised how to best use her influence as sovereign to sway opinion in what had now become a constitutional monarchy.

The queen and her husband understood the need to be seen as 'working royals', and thanks to the development of the country's growing railway network travelled around the country. Victoria took her first train journey in 1842, the first sovereign to travel by train and they expanded their civic duties to include attending the opening ceremonies of things such as colleges, museums, and industrial facilities, all of which were reported on in the growing newspaper trade. The queen's move to a neutral position amongst Britain's political parties is also attributed to Albert's advice, and after the original parliament building had been demolished by fire in 1834, she attended the first State Opening of Parliament at the Palace of Westminster on 3rd February 1852, a tradition that has been followed by every British monarch since.

Victoria came to the throne at a time of change and development previously unseen by British monarchs. What was once a rural country centred around agriculture, was fast becoming an industrial powerhouse built around its growing towns and cities. Considered a champion of social injustice, Albert openly encouraged Victoria's interest in the social welfare issues of the country. He was the driving force behind the Great Exhibition of 1851, a World's Fair event run over five months that celebrated British culture as well as the scientific and technology-driven advancements that drove Britain's growing industrial outputs. Industrial innovations such as the invention of the steam engine had revolutionised Britain's mining and marine industries whilst also developing a new railway industry. Successes with the development of rail meant the growth of Britain's civil engineering knowledge as bridges, tunnels and viaducts were built. Industrial towns grew quickly, but with the factories came significant and long-lasting social costs to the working class as child labour, poverty, disease and pollution became the norm.

There was substantial Irish immigration into both Britain and the USA during this period, much of it as the direct result of the eviction from their homes during and following a potato blight that had caused mass starvation and death in Ireland. Drawn by the availability of work, many people arrived in South Wales and settled in and around Swansea, at this time establishing itself as the copper smelting capital of the world.

Following the Public Health Act of 1848, Swansea held a public enquiry into the conditions of the town's sewage, drainage, water supply, and sanitary conditions. Swansea had suffered a serious outbreak of cholera in 1832 and was in the midst of a second outbreak, and whilst the centre of town itself was a case of immediate concern, much of the work involved the outlying townships that had been built up either side of the River Tawe to support the town's massive copper industry, including Tre Vivian

(Hafod) on the west side of the river and Foxhole and Pentrechwyth on the east side. The subsequent report led to the setting up of the Swansea Local Board of Health in 1850, and in the following year, Swansea's first sewer was built.

Between the 5th October 1852 and 30th March 1856, Britain was involved in the Crimean War, the first war to be covered by regular correspondents. The public, fuelled by newspaper reports, had shown a great interest in the campaign as many men had served their country never to return home. The conflict resulted in a victory for the allied forces of the UK, France, the Ottoman Empire and the Kingdom of Sardinia, but whilst many reports revelled in the successes, William Howard Russell, a reporter for "The Times" newspaper, vividly described the previously unreported realities of war, including the poor decision making of officers and the chronic shortage of equipment, as well as the fact that whilst nearly 3500 men had been lost in battle, over 20,000 men had died because of typhoid and cholera.

Britain's military successes were celebrated across the Empire, and streets in towns and cities across the country still bear the names of battles fought and won, and Swansea was no exception. In the St. Thomas area, Alma Street (now the southern half of Miers Street), Balaclava Street, Inkerman Street and Sebastopol Street were built and named after Crimean battles, whilst intersecting all four of these streets is Delhi Street, named after an uprising in the Indian Rebellion of 1857-58. Cawnpore Street, named after the Indian uprising at Cawnpore in 1857, ran parallel to Delhi Street, between Alma Street and Balaclava Street, but by 1871 that name had gone as the street had become part of Fabian Street.

Prince Albert was on hand to guide the queen through a dispute with the United States in 1861 when, in what became known as the Trent Affair, Albert's political savvy is credited with the delaying, reviewing, and revising of despatches that contained potentially threatening ultimatums that could have resulted in war. It was during the Trent Affair that Albert fell ill and was diagnosed with typhoid, and on December 14th 1861 he died, leaving behind his wife and nine children, most of whom had married into other Royal families of Europe, as well as 42 grandchildren. As a couple, Victoria and Albert were often seen in public, attending but after her husband's death, her seclusion was the subject of much criticism.

Devoted to her husband, Victoria sank into depression and was rarely seen in public over the next 12 years, during which time a strong republican sentiment had surfaced in the UK, encouraged by the founding of the Third French Republic in 1770 after the collapse of the French Empire. Whilst in mourning she did not neglect her duties and met with ministers and visitors as normal. She gradually resumed her public duties between 1871 and 1880, and her popularity increased as the British Empire grew, and on the 2nd January, 1877 Victoria became Empress of India, some twenty years after the Indian Rebellion.

After her self-imposed seclusion, the government sensed an excellent opportunity to quell the growing republican sentiment in the country via the fiftieth anniversary of Victoria's reign, and in 1887 the Golden Jubilee celebrations were announced. The queen herself did not improve public sentiment when after being told of the cost of the planned celebrations by then Prime Minister William Gladstone she was alleged to have replied "The people must pay". Large public events were scheduled across the Empire from 21st June to coincide with the first day of the 51st year as queen, and on 20th June a feast was held at Buckingham Palace attended by 50 foreign kings and princes, nearly all of whom were related to her by blood or marriage, as well as the governing heads of colonies and dominions from across the British Empire.

On June 21st, she travelled by coach in a lavish procession to a thanksgiving service at Westminster Abbey, accompanied by a mounted bodyguard of seventeen uniformed European princes, and a troop of Indian cavalry and that night beacons and bonfires were lit across Britain. Statues were erected in many locations and parks were opened to celebrate the event, one such park being Victoria Park in Swansea, which officially opened on Jubilee Day. Whilst some republican thoughts remained, the Golden Jubilee celebrations had the desired effect that the government had hoped for; both Queen Victoria's popularity and support of the Empire were as high as they had ever been.

In 1897 the country celebrated the Queen's Diamond Jubilee, and whilst not as grand as the Golden Jubilee, the prime ministers of the self-governed dominions of the Empire were invited to London, and Empire-wide events were planned for 22nd June. Public events were held in town squares and local parks across Britain, street parties were held and beacons were lit around the coast, including the 'Jubilee Beacons' lit at Mumbles and on Kilvey Hill. [37] Whilst Britain's influence across the world was now at its strongest, there were significant pressures put on the government by the country's own growing working population, but as had happened after the 1877 Jubilee, the public's involvement in celebrations served to further strengthen the bond between Queen, Country, and Empire.

At the turn of the 20th century, Britain was involved in the Boer War in South Africa, where British troops fought against the self-governing Afrikaner (Boer) colonies of the Orange Free State and The South African Republic (the Transvaal). The Queen would not live to see the victory, as on 22nd January 1901, after weeks of ill health, she died at Osborne House on the Isle of Wight, her son and heir Edward and her grandson Emperor Wilhelm II of Germany, at her deathbed.

Queen Victoria reigned for 64 years and led Britain through a time of significant economic progress, an age of industrial expansion that made Britain the first global industrial power that produced much of the world's coal, iron and steel, as well as its textiles. She left behind an Empire of over 400 million subjects that covered a quarter of the globe on which it was said "the sun never set", a phrase supposedly first used in connection with the Habsburg Empire of King Charles V in the 16th century.

It was during Victorian times that the Eastside of Swansea developed from a mostly rural area wrapped around a small bay, into an integral part of an industrial Swansea that was to play a key role in the growth of the British Empire.

Bibliography

[1] Cadw, "Scheduled Monuments - Full Report: Earthwork on Kilvey Hill," 1968. [Online].

[2] Colfien, "Colfien - Kilvey Cairn V," [Online]. Available: https://coflein.gov.uk/en/site/305622/.

[3] W. Morgan, An Antiquarian Survey of East Gower, Glamorganshire, Swansea, 1899, pp. 68-70, 71-72.

[4] T. (. Jones, Brut y Tywysogyon or Chronicle of the Princes (trans.), Cardiff: Board of Celtic Studies History and Law Series 11, 1952.

[5] J. Davies, A History of Wales, Penguin, 1990, pp. 100-101.

[6] W. Morgan, An Antiquarian Survey of East Gower, Glamorganshire, 1899, p. 66.

[7] A. (. Owen, Brut y Twyysgion - The Chronicle of the Princes, vol. Gwentian Chronicle of Caradoc of LLancarvan, Cambrian Archaeological Society, 1863, p. 89.

[8] W. Thomas, The History of Swansea, From Rover Settlement to the Restoration, Gomer Press, 1990, p. 7.

[9] G. Boon, 'Welsh Hoards 1979-1981' p.37, National Museums and Galleries of Wales , 1986.

[10] T. Jones, Brut y Tywysogion, or Chronicle of Princes: Peniarth MS 20 Version, University of Wales Press, 1941, p. 138.

[11] M. Charles Creighton M.A, A History of Epidemics, Cambridge University Press , 1891, p. 17.

[12] W. Jones, History of Swansea and the Lordship of Gower, vol. 1, Royal Institute of South Wales, 1920, pp. 192-193.

[13] H. W. O. Richard Morgan, Dictionary of the Place-Names of Wales, Gomer, 2007, p. 207.

[14] E. T. Pugh, Glamorgan County History, vol. 3 'The Middle Ages', Cardiff, 1971, p. 215.

[15] I. Bremner, "BBC History: Wales: English Conquest of Wales c.1200 - 1415," 2011. [Online]. https://www.bbc.co.uk/history/british/middle_ages/wales_conquest_01.shtml.

[16] W. Robinson, "Swansea," in *Boroughs of Medieval Wales*, University of Wales Press, pp. 263-286.

[17] e. H. C. M. Lyte, Calendar of Patent Rolls 1317-21, London, 1898, pp. 547-548.

[18] "Roll containing copies of 9 charters," in *Penrice and Margam Estate Records* , Vols. GB 0210 PENRICE - 296 p 176-177, The National Library of Wales.

[19] B. Wells-Furby, "The Contrariant Uprising of 1321–2: A New Perspective," *Bristol and Gloucestershire Archaeological Society,* no. 130, pp. 183-197, 2012.

[20] T. N. L. o. Wales, "Pennal Letter," 2000. [Online]. Available: https://www.library.wales/discover/digital-gallery/manuscripts/the-middle-ages/pennal-letter. [Accessed 18 July 2022].

[21] W. Jones, History of Swansea, vol. Two, Royal Institute of South Wales, 1992, p. 63.

[22] G. Britain, Calendar of the Patent Rolls - Henry VII A.D. 1485-94, vol. 1, London: Hereford Times Limited, 1914, p. Membrane 9 (19) p141.

[23] W. Jones, History of Swansea, vol. 2, Swansea: Royal Institute of South Wales, 1992, pp. 76-77.

[24] W. Thomas, The History of Swansea: From Rover Settlement to the Restoration, Gomer Press, 1990, pp. 190-191.

[25] W. Thomas, The History of Swansea: From Rover Settlement to the Restoration, Gomer Press, 1990, pp. 190-191.

[26] "Leisure--Swansea Castle-Life after the Lords of Gower," [Online]. Available: https://archive.swansea.gov.uk/afterlordsofgower.

[27] J. Lewis, The Swansea Guide: Compiled from the Most Authentic Sources., 1851, p. 14.

[28] The Parliamentary History of the Principality of Wales 1541-1895, Edwin Davies and Bell, Coinuty Times Offices, 1895, p. 99.

[29] W. Thomas, The History of Swansea: From Rover Settlement to the Restoration, Gomer Press, 1990, p. 239.

[30] W. Thomas, The History of Swansea: From Rover Settlement to the Restoration, Gomer Press, 1990, pp. 238-239.

[31] W. Jones, History of Swansea, vol. Two, Royal Institute of South Wales, 1992, pp. 86-87.

[32] G. S. M. o. 1.-1. Halifax, The character of a trimmer his opinion of I. The laws and government, II. Protestant religion, III. The papists, IV. Foreign affairs, 1848.

[33] O. o. o. t. D. o. Beaufort, "'Thirteenth' and 'Fifteenth' Articles," *Survey of the Manor of Kilvey,* pp. 363, 365, 1688.

[34] W. Jones, History of the Port of Swansea, Royal Institute of South Wales, 1992, p. 152.

[35] R. Fulford, Hanover to Windsor, Fontana Press, 1972, p. 121.

[36] T. Cambrian, "Jubilee Beacons," *The Cambrian,* p. 5, 25th June 1887.

[37] P. A. M. E. Records, Roll containing copies of 9 charters - Margam 296/2-6, The National Library of Wales, pp. 176-177.

PART TWO - The Development of the Eastside in the Victorian Age

Trade and Transport

When the Romans finally departed Britain's shores in 464 AD, they left behind a countrywide network of roads that, with a few additions, by the middle of the 16th century were known as 'The King's Highways'. Following a 1555 Act, the upkeep of these roads was placed in the hands of towns or civil parishes across the country, with work carried out deemed 'statute labour' where parishioners worked under supervision for four days a year repairing and maintaining their local highways. A 1563 Act extended this period to six days, and the statute labour system formed the basis of road maintenance plans for a further three hundred years. In addition the 1692 Highway Law was passed that taxed people at a rate of 2.5% of their income to assist with road building and maintenance costs.

In the early 17th century the commercial use of Britain's roads was limited at best, and was based on the concept of a horse-drawn cart pulling a maximum load of three tons per run over poorly prepared road surfaces that were often unusable for use because of inclement weather; in essence, a system suited only for short local trips, as horses had to be regularly rested, fed and watered. The inland manmade waterways of Britain were restricted to moving agricultural produce for the landed gentry in Southern England, and therefore the most reliable form of commercial transport at that time was coastal shipping.

The 1700s saw further changes to road financing methods, and Turnpike Trusts became commonplace. Turnpike Trusts introduced the payment of tolls that were charged for the use of a road, although the system was still supplemented by statute labour as most of Britain's roads were not turnpiked. By 1760 much of South Wales came under a single turnpike trust, and in 1827 a Parliamentary bill amendment to the Glamorgan Turnpike Act of 1823 allowed for the making of a road across Crymlyn Burrows from Briton Ferry to Swansea, as well as the building of bridges at the mouth of the River Nedd and of the River Tawe. Whilst the first road bridge to cross the New Cut at Swansea was built in 1843, over a hundred years passed before the first road bridge crossed the River Nedd, and when in 1955 it was built at Briton Ferry the road across Crymlyn Burrows to Swansea would soon follow.

By 1830 there were nearly 8000 tollgates across England and Wales, but there was open resentment from local communities, many of whom were unemployed and lived in poverty, who were asked to pay to use old roads. This resulted in the wilful damage of toll gates and milestones, and magistrates were given the power to punish those that were found guilty. In Wales, a series of violent protests between 1839 and 1843 and later known as the 'Rebecca Riots' acted as the catalyst for the abolition of turnpike trusts in the six counties of South Wales, although the last toll road in all of Wales closed in 1895 at Llanfairpwll in North Wales. A few turnpikes remained in England, but a combination of difficulty in collecting tolls, the heavy cost of road repairs, and the competition from both the canals and the up-and-coming railway networks meant that the remaining toll gates companies were forced to close, and the 1888 Local Governments Act passed the responsibility for road maintenance to Borough and County Councils.

In 1843 the first road bridge to cross the New Cut at Swansea was a hand-winched 'swivel-bridge' that could be operated from either side of the river and built to accommodate riders, horse-drawn carts and pedestrians. Around eight years later a 'double-bascule' railway bridge of wooden construction was built adjacent to the road bridge linking Warlich's Patent Fuel Works on the east bank of the river to the ship-loading facilities on the North Dock. [1] Both bridges were replaced in 1867, when on October 18th that year a combined road and rail drawbridge was opened. The railway bridge was replaced again in 1897 when a new swing bridge was opened. Designed by Swansea Harbour Trust engineer A.O. Shenk and built at a cost of £27,000, it incorporated a high-pressure hot water system that would ensure the bridge mechanism was operational throughout the winter months. [2]

A number of other bridges were also constructed around the North Dock. A swing bridge known as 'The Pottery Bridge' was built in 1847 in an area near the top of The Strand near the site of the old Cambrian Pottery Works and crossing to the north-west corner of the North Dock, while in 1851 a manually operated drawbridge was installed at the entrance to the North Dock. It was replaced in 1868 by a hydraulically operated bridge and replaced again in 1903 when a new hydraulic bridge was installed. In 1852 the Swansea Vale Railway erected a railway bridge from the east bank of the New Cut to the top end of The Float which in 1871 was upgraded to a hydraulically operated drawbridge, whilst in 1863 new high-level drawbridges were installed that spanned both the New Cut and the entrance to the North Dock, both of which were upgraded with hydraulic operating machinery ten years later.

As a result of the opening of various crossings, the Swansea Ferry, for centuries the only way to cross at the mouth of the River Tawe, officially closed in September 1850. [3]

Canal Systems

Whilst turnpike trusts were slowly improving roads, by the 18th-century industrialists in the north of England began developing canal systems that allowed for the movement of huge amounts of coal, minerals, and textiles quickly and efficiently across the country, and over much longer distances than the roads. The canals were so successful that their owners amassed considerable wealth, and because of increases in trade, helped establish the northern industrial towns of Leeds, Manchester and Liverpool. In 1769 the Duke of Bridgewater engaged engineer James Brindley to construct the Bridgewater Canal, from Worsley in Salford to Manchester at a cost of £25,000, a huge amount of money at that time. Its success was instant given that previously transportation of coal by road cost more than it did to actually mine it.

Canal transportation costs dropped the total cost of producing and transporting coal by 50%, drastically increasing demand as coal quickly became the fuel of choice, and by the end of the century over forty Canal Acts had been passed. The Bridgewater Canal remained lucrative and was later extended from Manchester to

Runcorn and from Worsley to Leigh, but the vast majority of canals that followed were poor investments as there were not enough raw materials or manufactured goods locally available to sustain them.

Adam Smith, the author of 'The Wealth of Nations,' noted in 1776 that 'Navigable cuts and canals are of great and general utility, whilst at the same time they require a greater expense than suits the fortunes of private people.' [4] In Swansea six such canals were developed, namely:

- The Clyndu Canal: privately built in Morriston by John Lockwood in c1747 and later extended in 1979 to run from the Forrest Copper Works to Landore, and incorporated into the Swansea Canal.

- The Smith Canal: built by mine owner John Smith in c1784, it ran from Gwernllwynchwych near Llansamlet to Foxhole.

- The Glan Y Wern Canal: built in c1790 to move coal from Glan Y Wern colliery across Crymlyn Bog to 'Trowman's Hole'. It ceased operations but was added to The Tennant Canal in 1810

- The Swansea Canal: Constructed by The Swansea Canal Company following an Act of Parliament in 1794, it was fully operational by October 1798. It ran over 16 miles between The Old Brewery Wharf near the Strand and Hen-Noyadd in Abercrave.

- The Penclawdd Canal: constructed in 1814, it ran from Waunarlydd to the Penclawdd Canal Dock on the Llwchwr River, but was disused by 1818.

- The Tennant Canal: Privately funded by George Tennant, it connected the River Tawe to the Neath Canal at Red Jacket Pill on the western side of the River Neath. Completed in 1818, it was linked to Aberdulais in May 1824.

A major stumbling block to the further development of Britain's canal systems in the 19th century was that the widening of existing canals or the building of new and bigger canals was impractical from both a time and cost perspective, and this was quickly exploited by railway company owners who could offer larger networks with load carrying capacities than the canal's owners could never hope to achieve. The railway companies were also shrewd enough to buy some of the canal companies, which allowed them to develop railway networks alongside key trade routes without an outcry, and then allow the canal route to simply 'wither on the vine' as it outlived its commercial usefulness.

Shipping

Until the 19th century, Britain's commercial trade relied heavily on sail-powered shipping that was responsible for the movement of coal, grain, timber and metal wares around Britain's coast and was instrumental in the prosperity of the producing areas, as well as playing a key role in the establishment and subsequent growth of the country's coastal towns and cities. In the case of Swansea, much of its coastal shipping business dealt with the exporting of coal to Somerset, Devon, Cornwall, London, the Channel Islands, France and Ireland. Routes rarely changed, but the safe passage of a vessel was dependent on the knowledge of experienced mariners that navigated with charts and instruments, and who understood bathymetry, tidal patterns, waves, weather and coastal visibility. Lighthouses were also a key component for ensuring a vessel's safety, and prior to the development of ports, coasters often utilised beaches as landing points.

A combination of the marine steam engine, the replacement of wood with iron (and later steel) for making hulls and the demand for coal as a fuel, drove the development of both Britain's coastal and international merchant fleets. Whilst the former could now operate to schedules not previously practical for sailing ships, the latter expanded global trade routes in line with the country's colonial aspirations, making Britain the world's first industrialised power. However, by the middle of the 19th Century, coastal shipping was under direct attack from Britain's new railway companies who had also taken advantage of steam power.

Commercial needs drove advances in naval engineering technology, and Britain's merchant fleet demanded bigger and faster vessels to drive sales growth. Whilst timber ships continued to be made in the southeast of England, iron shipbuilding facilities moved closer to the sources of the iron needed to build them as well as the coal that they transported, which included the ports of Glasgow, Liverpool, Newcastle and Durham. Whilst iron ships could not compete with clippers for speed when it came to transporting cargo over long distances, clippers were not large vessels and so were limited in the volume of cargo they could carry, and such was the demand for iron-hulled vessels that Glasgow's Clyde shipyard alone built 178 ships in 1860.

The 'three-or-more' mast vessels built to bring copper ore to Swansea were known as 'copper barques' many of which were 'Swansea-fitted', a system of internal trunking that helped the vessel maintain its centre of gravity whilst keeping the cargo away from the sides of the vessel's hold. The captains who manned these vessels earned the name 'Cape Horner' as they skilfully navigated the often-treacherous waters around the Cape Horn on the southern tip of South Africa to and from Chile with relatively few losses, the barque often laden with coal on the return trip.

The final phase for wind-powered merchant vessels was the development of 'iron barque' tall ships that combined huge iron or steel hulls with a four or five-mast sail set up. Run by a small crew and capable of carrying large cargoes without the need for either coal or bunkering, these 'windjammers' were the vessel of choice for bringing products like tea and wool from India, China and Australia to Britain, and would also take on the task of transporting copper ore to Swansea from countries as far afield as Chile and Cuba.

A major advance in marine steam engine technology meant ships moved away from using single-expansion engines to the new 'compound engines' that utilised superheated steam. Iron ships could now operate using only 60% of the fuel previously needed, and after the opening of the Suez Canal in 1869 had dramatically shortened the route to and from Asia, steamships soon dominated these routes. By 1875 over two thousand ships were fitted with compound steam engines, including nearly all transatlantic vessels. By the end of the 19th century, specialist vessels such as oil tankers and grain-carriers were being built, as were long-haul 'tramp steamers', merchant vessels operating outside the confines of regular routes and able to collect and carry general cargo at short notice to any destination on the instruction of their owners. From a commercial perspective, the 'Age of Sail' would soon be over.

In the 18th Century the need to develop Swansea's harbour was openly supported by many local businessmen, however Gabriel Powell the Steward of the Duke of Beaufort and known to many as "The King of Swansea", vehemently opposed change of any kind, and it was only after his death in 1789 that real improvements could be made. After the 1791 Harbour Act was passed, the Swansea Harbour Trust was formed to 'repair, enlarge and preserve the Harbour of Swansea' and after completing this work in 1794 they built the Mumbles Lighthouse as well as adding two breakwaters at the harbour entrance. Swansea's dock developments soon followed, and in 1845 the 'New Cut' was officially completed, the barque 'Charles Clark' the first vessel to sail through it on the 14th March [5]; alas the vessel was 'totally lost' off Mistaken Point, Newfoundland eight years later.

The land between the New Cut and the 'old' river formed an area initially called 'The Town Float', and later known as the North Dock. The North Dock officially opened for business on 1st January 1852, [6] and seven years later on 23rd September 1859, the South Dock opened on the Burrows area of the seafront. [7] This was followed by the East Dock, renamed the Prince of Wales Dock in honour of the Prince of Wales who together with his wife Princess Alexandra, opened the dock on 18th October 1881, followed by the opening of a dock extension on 11th March 1898 that encompassed much of what was once Fabian's Bay and Port Tennant. [8]

THE CHAIRMAN (MR GRIFFITH THOMAS, MAYOR OF SWANSEA)
AND THE TRUSTEES OF SWANSEA HARBOUR
request the honour of the presence of
The Hon. Odo Vivian & the Hon. Misses Vivian (3)
at SWANSEA on WEDNESDAY the 20th day of JULY, 1904,
on the occasion of the CUTTING of the FIRST SOD of the NEW DOCK by
HIS MAJESTY KING EDWARD VII
and at a LUNCHEON after the Ceremony.

HARBOUR OFFICES,
JULY, 1904.

TALFOURD STRICK,
CLERK TO THE SWANSEA HARBOUR TRUSTEES
SWANSEA.

Invitation to the Cutting of the First Sod of the new King's Dock 20th July 1904 (author's collection)

The port continued to grow, and on 22nd November 1909, The King's Dock was opened by King Edward VII and Queen Alexandra, followed by the opening of the Queen's Dock on 19th July 1920 by Queen Mary and King George V, a waterway that had already been operational but unnamed for over ten years. [9] By the end of the 19th century, Swansea also had nine dry docks, and an additional three were built in 1918, 1924 and 1959 respectively.

Railways

The 1700s saw the introduction of 'wagonways' at mines and quarries, consisting of a wagon that ran on a pair of wooden tracks that made it possible for a horse to pull up to 13 tons of coal, or stone per run, and by the middle of the century, the introduction of iron rails improved the weight capability of horse-drawn wagonways threefold. In 1804, the British Parliament approved the laying of railway lines to utilise horse-drawn wagons to transport limestone, iron ore and coal between Castle Hill in Oystermouth to Brewery Bank near the Swansea Canal, and in 1806 the Oystermouth Railway (later known as The Mumbles Railway) was operational. In February of the following year, the company was given the approval to transport passengers, and the world's first regular railway passenger service began on March 25th 1807, operating from 'The Mount', the world's first recorded railway station.

Seven years later at Killingworth Colliery in Durham, rather than use a stationary steam engine to wind a rope around a drum to haul wagons up an incline, George Stephenson attached his steam engine to a wagon that travelled at 6mph on iron rails spaced 4 feet 8 inches (1.42 m) apart, thus building the world's first steam locomotive 'The Blucher', and built a further eighteen steam locomotives there over the following five years. In 1825 George and his son Robert developed a railway line between Stockton and Darlington using the same rail width distances as Killingworth. Connecting the coal mines at Shildon in County Durham to Darlington, it used steam engines to haul its coal wagons. A new service was also started there using a horse-drawn railway coach called 'Experiment' that picked up passengers along the way, as there were no stations. In 1833, 'Locomotion No 1.' was connected up to 'Experiment' plus twenty-one new coal wagons that carried 'between 450-600'; it was the world's first steam-powered passenger service. In 1829, the Liverpool-Manchester railway line was close to completion. No decision had been made between stationary steam engines or steam locomotives to pull the trains, and trials took place at Rainhill in October 1829, where it was decided that George Stephenson's locomotive "Rocket' was successful. The line opened on 15th September 1830 carrying passengers and goods, as is regarded as the world's first public intercity railway.

Railway technology developed rapidly and networks spread across Britain, however the British government offered no guidelines as to where, when or how railways should run, or where they should link up. In 1844 the Railway Regulation Act legally obligated railway companies, for fear of closure of routes, to offer cheap passenger tickets on at least one service a day on each of their routes. For the first time, the working class could travel around the country at a price they could afford; this service became known as 'the Parliamentary Train' or the 'Ghost Train', as it often ran in the early hours of the morning.

In 1833 Isambard Kingdom Brunel became the chief engineer of the Great Western Railway (GWR) line that linked London to Bristol. An accomplished and pioneering railway engineer, he also designed and oversaw the construction of new bridges and tunnels along his railway routes. The GWR line was built on tracks 7 feet 3 inches apart, and ran so smoothly that GWR was referred to as 'God's Wonderful Railway.' It was so successful that it was later extended to connect Plymouth and Cornwall to the south of Bristol and further west to Cardiff, and after Brunel's completion of the Landore Viaduct, a structure nearly 587 yards (536 metres) long, with thirty-seven arches spanning the River Tawe, the line ended at Swansea's first inter-town/city railway station at High St, which opened in 1850.

Etching of Landore Viaduct (author's collection)

By 1846 over 90% of Britain's railway lines had been laid using George Stephenson's rail positioning, and the government passed the Gauge Act that stipulated that all railways lines had to be spaced to Stephenson's measurement of 4 feet 8.5 inches, a 'standard gauge' width that would ensure trains built could run on all tracks across the country. This included the routes that had previously utilised Brunel's gauge. Such was Swansea's growth, that by 1895 it had a further six main railway stations, owned and operated by five different companies. In addition to High St Station, the Rutland St.

station was the town's terminus to the Mumbles Railway, Victoria and Swansea Bay Stations were owned by London & North Western Railways, while on the Eastside of the Tawe, St. Thomas Station was owned by The Midland Railway (originally owned by the Swansea Vale Railway), the East Dock Station (adjacent to the junction of Fabian St and Port Tennant Rd) was owned and operated by Great Western Railway, and Riverside Station was owned by the Rhondda & Swansea Bay Railway (renamed as 'Swansea Docks' in 1924, and again in 1926 as 'Swansea Riverside').

As with the canal networks, the growth of Britain's railways was driven by commercial necessity, but unlike building canals, new railway lines could be laid quickly and lines extended as and when required. They could transport much larger quantities of goods than ever before, and most importantly ran on a reliable time schedule that enabled companies across Britain to get their goods to ports faster and on time, from where they could be exported to other countries. The success of the railways meant Britain's coastal shipping routes suffered badly, while long-distance road transport networks, already severely weakened by both canals and the coastal shipping routes, went into a serious decline that would not improve until the 1950s.

The railway industry operated on tight schedules that brought the concept of 'standard time' into focus, rather than relying on the methods of local time previously used. The synchronisation of clocks within a geographical region was of particular relevance when used in large countries where long-distance railway routes passed through places that differed by several hours in local time. A need for a method of a unified timekeeping system was introduced, and time zones were created when in October 1884 at The International Meridian Conference held in Washington DC, it was agreed that the prime meridian for longitude and timekeeping would be the one that passed through the Greenwich Observatory in London, coining the term Greenwich Mean Time (GMT).

Railways became the catalyst for the improvement of many existing services such as the post office which could now handle multiple deliveries a day, whilst ushering in many new ones like the telegram service that used poles and wires that were often installed alongside the railway lines. As new industries developed, the railway network was key to the movement of people that were looking for employment all over the country.

The population of towns and cities rapidly increased in size and Swansea, fast becoming the copper-smelting centre of the world, drew immigrants from Ireland, West Wales, Devon, Cornwall, and further afield, and in addition to copperworkers, the rural east side of the River Tawe was being transformed by the influx of workers employed on the docks, patent fuel works and tin-spelters, as well as with the railway companies themselves.

The Eastside Tramway

A few years after the passing of the Tramway Act in 1870, Swansea Improvements & Tramways (SITC) introduced horse-drawn passenger trams to Morriston, St. Helens and Cwmbwrla. In 1900 SITC changed to electric traction, and added a fourth route than ran between Alexandra Road and Swansea Docks. By 1905 there were ten passenger tramline routes that linked various outlying areas to Swansea, the majority of which were owned by Swansea Corporation, but operated by SITC, which was now owned by the British Electric Traction Company (BET).

In February 1891, a poorly attended meeting was held at St. Thomas School to discuss a proposal for the construction of a tram line between Swansea and Port Tennant, as well as an extension of the Rhondda and Swansea Bay Railway into Swansea. Discussions covered the potential boom in work and the likely substantial building activity close to Crymlyn Burrows given that previously such facilities had been built near the sea. Evidence was cited of similar activity near the Dowlais Works at Cardiff that resulted in the construction of buildings such as railway accommodation, and a report of the meeting in The Cambrian [10] stated that Crymlyn Burrows 'would be seized upon by capitalists and others.' Councillor Walter Lewis, the meeting's chairman, promoted the fact that it would be of great benefit to local people, as well as assuring those in attendance that it would likely 'save on the rates too', after which there was applause from the crowd.

Mr Steven Yockney, Engineer for the Rhondda and Swansea Bay Railway Company, SITC, and also for the Mumbles Railway and Pier Company, stated that assuming approval from Parliament, the proposed tram line would run 'for a mile and a quarter and would be laid under the most stringent restrictions forced on them by The Board of Trade.' He assured everyone that the narrow roads on the Eastside 'would not hinder the construction of the proposed line', and that he would ensure that a clause in the proposal that allowed for the conveyancing of minerals would be expunged, and thus its use would be as a passenger service only. After further discussion on the merits of the extension of the Rhondda and Swansea Bay Railway that would allow inhabitants of the Rhondda 'to flock into Swansea' both the railway extension and the new Swansea to Port Tennant tram line were supported by the East Ward.

In May 1904, thirteen years later, Calder & Company ran the first electricity cable for the tramline across the Tawe [11] and by September that year, a robust debate had begun around a SITC proposal to Swansea Council that indicated the use of wooden blocks as pavements adjacent to the Port Tennant tramline. [12] They were to be fitted between the Red House public house and the bottom of Lewis St, before the rest of the route was completed, with the line stopping at the terminus at the end of Port Tennant Rd. However, the case for the use of granite blocks as an alternative was put forward by concerned members of the East Ward Ratepayers Association, a group formed only weeks before when similar requests were being ignored.

The tram line running through Walter Road in the town had been paved with wooden blocks at the insistence of local residents, but the cost of maintenance had come into question based on blocks fitted previously adjacent to Cardiff tramlines. Union Street and other areas in the town had granite blocks fitted that doubled the life span of their wooden counterparts. Local Councillor J.H. Lee called the use of wooden blocks 'simply a craze' and put forward a resolution that granite blocks be used instead, and was advised by Councillor David Davies to add the line 'subject to the approval of SITC' to his resolution to ease the matter. Lee agreed, and the proposal to use granite blocks was passed unanimously.

In March 1905, the trolley wires and other necessary electrically equipment were successfully brought across the North Dock and New Cut bridges, [13] and on 4th August 1905, the Eastside tram service went through a test run to ensure everything was in working order [14]. The single-decker Port Tennant tram was tested under the personal supervision of Mr C.A. Prussman, Chief of Swansea Corporations Electrical Department and Mr Alexander of the overhead Department who, together with their men, had been working through the night on overhead equipment on the bridges, after which Mr Prussman 'personally propelled a car over (sic) both the New Cut and North Dock Bridges', and later the same day a formal Board of Inspection trip took place, this time with Mayor Alderman William Henry Spring in attendance.

On Saturday 19th August 'Route No. 8' was finally opened, and the first Port Tennant tram left the Eastside tramline terminus at the junction of Ysgol Street and Port Tennant Road, from what The Cambrian newspaper called 'The Vale of Neath' terminus, on its way to St. Helens, and, reporting on the tram's inaugural trip in its 25th of August edition [15] noted the need for only single-decker tramcars on the route due to the low height of the railway bridges on the Fabian St and Quay Parade, as well as at the bottom of Wind Street:

'Port Tennant Trams Running. Wind-street was livelier than ever on Saturday morning. The clang of tramcar gongs was everywhere, for were not the Port Tennant cars running for the first time and their "music" commingled with that of the Brynmill, Docks and St. Helen's sections. Four single-deckers were put on in the morning and were extensively patronised from an early hour. There being a run on single-deckers, overhead cars were in use on the Cwmbwrla section. But in spite of all the Port Tennant brake jogged cheerily along from the "Vale of Neath" to the Market, and what's more, carried passengers!'

In the weeks after the official opening of the Port Tennant line, the Swansea Corporation received a letter of complaint from Lord Jersey's agent. The Earl had given permission to end the line closer to the Vale of Neath public house and had provided a 40 ft long section of roadway for that purpose, and he was bemused as to why it ended at Ysgol Street. Whilst emphasising the Earl fully supported the project, the letter further stated it that he expected the line to be extended, as 'it was entirely with the view that the tramway being carried to Wern Terrace that we gave it our support'. However, after further discussion on the matter, it was agreed not to further extend the line. [16]

Tram on Port Tennant Rd - postcard (author's collection)

The Eastside trams ran for over thirty years until 28th June of 1937, when Swansea finally closed down its tram network and changed over to a more comfortable bus service provided by South Wales Transport. On 29th June, as a fundraiser for Swansea General & Eye Hospital, the last Swansea tram, manned by motorman George Evans, conductor Tom Rees, and inspector Arthur Evans, travelled from Wind Street to St Helen's depot with the Mayor, Alderman Richard Henry onboard. [17]

The Mumbles Railway, the world's first passenger railway in 1806 and powered by electricity since 1928, was sold to South Wales Transport in 1958, and after the South Wales Transport Act 1959, made its final trip on January 5th 1960, and was replaced by a bus service.

***

Housing on the Eastside

The earliest development of urban housing on the Eastside was directly in line with the introduction of the opening of copper works on the eastern banks of the Tawe in the late 1700s, when cottage-type housing was constructed at Foxhole by Freeman & Company for their White Rock Works staff. Further north at Pentrechwyth, Grenfell & Sons also built worker's housing on land leased from the Briton Ferry Estate. The second area of housing development came after the construction of the Tennant Canal in 1824, where worker's housing was built close to Fabian's Bay and the East Pier, again on Briton Ferry Estate-owned land.

The area of St. Thomas saw urban development in the mid-1800s as a direct result of the opening of the North Dock in 1852, after which several streets were constructed nearby. In contrast to the aforementioned areas, Danygraig remained mostly rural until the construction of housing adjacent to the new Swansea Cemetery, which opened in 1858. Although Kilvey is mentioned on the local census documents from 1841 it is in relation to properties on and around Kilvey Hill, as the residential area we now know as Kilvey is not listed as such until after the establishment of the parish in 1881.

Whilst the Briton Ferry Estate owned the vast majority of land on the Eastside, Henry Sharpe Pocklington owned a substantial area of land known as 'Tyrlandwr' that lay on the east bank of the River Tawe, in the centre of which was Pocklington's Farm. A tithe map of 1837-38 shows that Pocklington had sold much of this land to Starling Benson who, after various legal challenges, subsequently sold the land to Swansea Harbour Trust. In 1845 SHT excavated a New Cut straight through Pocklington's Farm that ran between the natural course of the river near Cambrian Pottery to Swansea Bay, and in the process created 'The Town Float', later known as the North Dock, on the island of land between the New Cut and the original course of the river.

The Duke of Beaufort owned a small piece of land south of Tyrlandwr and facing the sea where the Red Lion Ferry House stood, and this was also purchased by the Swansea Harbour Trust.

Payment for the land was made by the moving of earth displaced by the New Cut ('the spoils') to the shoreline of Fabian's Bay, which was also owned by The Duke of Beaufort. Pocklington also owned land immediately to the right of the farm, and this was sold to Mr Elias Jenkins, who subsequently built housing there between Morris Lane and Windmill Terrace, and on Pentreguinea Rd up as far as Canaan Chapel. The tithe map also shows a small parcel of land stretching east of Morris Lane owned by Francis Pinkney Esq, and a more substantial parcel of land that was once owned by the Mackworth family of Neath, that had passed into the ownership of Capel Hanbury Leigh Esq, Lord Lieutenant of Monmouthshire, who had married Sir Robert Mackworth's widow.

In November 1825, shortly after completion of his canal, George Tennant received a letter from a group of businessmen who wanted to build worker's housing near Port Tennant, and a follow-up letter [18] was sent after hearing that George Tennant was intending to develop housing himself:

'Sir….the various mining concerns, foundries, manufacturers, and works of different descriptions which are now carrying on between Swansea and Cwm Neath, and which present a prospect of considerable increase, have already introduced so great an influx of mechanics into the neighbourhood as to render it almost impossible for them in many places to provide a decent and comfortable dwelling, it is considered therefore that cottages erected in suitable places for the accommodation of such artisans and mechanics will ensure a fair if not ample remuneration of the person embarking their capital in such an undertaking, and they propose to carry it into effect by shares of £50 each, which will be rather more than the estimated value of one cottage.'

The plan proposed was for the construction of twenty cottages, however, the shareholders never materialised and the plan was scrapped. George Tennant secured leases on land at Salt House Point at the East Pier and once the site of St Thomas Chapel, the ruins of which had long since disappeared under the sand. The area was part of the harbour improvements undertaken in the previous thirty years, and by 1830 several companies had set up operations on the East Pier Docks, and the Burrows Inn was built in c1838, close to the Tennant Canal and Port Tennant.

Whilst UK census documents are available from 1841 [19] it is very difficult to accurately compare the data in a given location from one time period to the next, as whilst both district areas and reference number may change over that time, borders of the areas monitored may also change. For example, the Foxhole area was originally listed as part of a Llansamlet district census document that includes census data that falls outside the physical boundaries covered by this book, and this has offered some challenges as the property and population counts needed are split into two different census documents.

To further confuse matters information collected also differs from census to census. thus when reviewing and evaluating the available data I have tried to adhere to the same geographical footprint throughout, thus the total numbers used in this section to collate 'Properties, People, Male and Female' may not directly align with the totals given in the relevant district census documents. The census district document for a given area is compiled by a Census Enumerator and normally begins with a brief description of the route taken to collect data from households, and highlights the physical boundaries of that particular document. Given that the documents are handwritten, the clarity of the notes can sometimes be difficult to decipher. With the above in mind, and given the scope and intent of this book, my findings in this chapter should be considered a representation of the actual census documents and their data, rather than a full analysis of the census data collected.

In the case of the **1841 census**, the geographical area covered in this book fall under 'Lower Llansamlet' and 'Swansea' and lists a general name of a given area and where possible specific addresses, counting occupied and unoccupied properties. The number of male and female occupants is noted, but it does not record the birthplace of the occupants. The census of the area we are concerned with is covered by three separate documents, one as part of Llansamlet Lower Enumeration District 7 (and listed as part of the Neath Register), whilst the second and third census documents are

Swansea Enumeration District 26 and Swansea Enumeration District 27.

Llansamlet Lower Enumeration District 7 (part of the Neath Register), covered 'All the part which lies east of the river from Pentre Guinea to White Rock and from thence to Tyr Gwl to Pentre Guinea', and listed a total of 112 properties, with 548 people living in them. There were 68 properties listed as 'Foxhole', whilst four rows of terraced housing had been given their own name - Pleasant Row, Freeman's Row, Martin's Row and Bachelor's Row, with a total of 23 cottages between them.

The remaining properties were those listed as 'Kilvey Hill' (15 cottages), 3 cottages at Tyr Gwl, one property at Ty Gwl (possibly the main house), Kilvey House, the home of copper merchant Elias Jenkins and his family, and Kilvey Infants School. Given that many of these properties had been built by Freeman & Co. it is not a surprise to see that of the 548 people living in these properties, over 240 of the 267 men listed their occupation as 'Copperman' or a copper industry-related job.

Swansea Enumeration District 26 covered the 'Hamlet of St. Thomas in a line from Tre Gwl Gate to the river including Pentre Guinea, Meagers Buildings, and all the houses to the chain on the one hand, and on the north side of Morris's lane on the other as far as the house in the occupation of Major Thompson', and indicated that there were 66 properties inhabited by a total of 413 people, and included five public houses; the Ship & Anchor, the Globe Inn, the Mason Arms, the Cooperman's Arms, and the Red Lion. There was much more of a variety of employment by the people living in this area, and whilst Pentreguinea (21 houses) had a large contingent of copperworkers, on and around Kilvey Terrace (14 houses) there were 15 labourers and 33 'excavators', as well as masons, carpenters, mariners, a joiner, a tailor, a surveyor and a wheelwright.

The Meager Building had 9 occupied rooms, whilst Underhill Cottage, Hillfield Lodge (South), Hillfield Cottage, Bay View House, and Hillfield Lodge (North) all housed single families. George Harris, a lawyer, lived at Kilvey Cottage, and George Burrow the contractor lived on Ty Landwr, as did one other family.

Henry Bath's Copper Yard is also included in the census, listed as having two occupied houses.

Swansea Enumeration District 27 covered 'Part of the Hamlet of St. Thomas commencing on the one hand with the Red House and keeping on the South East side of Morris's lane to and including Major Thompson's, Maesteg, Danygraig as far as Danygraig gardener's house and including all houses at the East Pier', in total 46 properties inhabited by 270 people. In contrast to the two other areas above, the vast majority of male workers living in this area are labourers. There are only a handful of copper industry workers listed, and there are similar amounts of masons, colliers, and gardeners also listed.

There is also a higher percentage of women in employment than in the other two documents, with over 10% of the women listed as 'FS', or 'female servant', six of whom work at Maesteg (House) together with two male servants (MS). The enumerator's description mentions 'houses at the East Pier', but they are not specifically highlighted on the census and are included in the 15 Port Tennant houses.

The groups that are specified are Danygraig Cottage (3 houses), Danygraig (2), Burrows Row (6 houses), Fabian's Bay Cottages (5 houses), Ferryside (1 house), and Kilvey Cottages (8 houses). The 'Major Thompson' mentioned in the enumerator's notes was Major William Thompson, aged 65, who lives in the sixth of eight Kilvey Cottages. Two of the properties listed are of substantial size - Danygraig House, home of Colonel Nathaniel Cameron, and 'Maesteg' home of Riversdale Grenfell, his family and their eight servants. There are four public houses mentioned in this area, the Burrows Inn, the Union Arms, the Ship & Castle, and the Red House.

To summarise the 1841 census findings, of the 1251 people living on the Eastside at that time, nearly 1000 lived in housing that was nearly all built by their employers, and located in a compact area on and below Kilvey Hill that was bounded by Foxhole, Pentre Guinea and Morris Lane, three names that would continue to define the census boundaries over the following years. The remaining 46 properties in 'The Hamlet of St. Thomas' were spread across rural Danygraig or close to the East Pier and Tennant Canal.

The excavation of the New Cut commenced in 1840 and over the next ten-year period new company-built housing sprang up on the Eastside. In 1849 George Clark, the manager of the Dowlais Ironworks who was employed by the General Board of Health to review the conditions in the Lower Swansea Valley, mentioned one other village outside his remit, that of Port Tennant:

'…below Pentre-guinea, upon the seashore, a short distance for the east pier, and about the mouth of the Tennant canal…(where) there are several new and well-built houses, all within the borough. None of the owners on this side of the river has taken advantage of the copious springs above them (on Kilvey Hill) to secure a proper supply of water, neither has any advantage been taken on the position so excellently suited for drainage.'

The New Cut was completed in 1845, [20] and work continued to complete the locks of 'The Town Float' (aka The North Dock), and the **1851 census** boundaries were redefined from those used in the 1841 census and were covered by Llansamlet Lower Enumeration Districts 4, part of Llansamlet Lower Enumeration District 7, (still listed as part of the Neath Register), and a third census document, Swansea Enumeration District 21.

There is very little clarity given in notes for the Llansamlet Lower Enumeration District 4 area and after excluding the areas covered outside our area of interest, there are only 26 properties in the lower hamlet remaining, almost exclusively inhabited by 'coppermen' and their families, although no specific addresses are given other than 'Foxhole'. There is a similar issue with the Llansamlet Lower Enumeration District 7 document, as a large section of the census completed is outside the geographical remit of this book.

As with District 4, there is no breakdown of addresses at all, but the document can be broken down into three localities - Sarne and Kilvey (17 properties, 99 people), Ty Gwl to Foxhole (11 properties, 59 people), and Foxhole (125 properties, 659 people). In line with the previous census, the vast majority of male workers living in this area list 'Copperman' as their job, and the likelihood is that most properties Foxhole properties are owned by Freeman & Co. The main house at Tyr Gwl is now the home of Edward Brown, who is listed as 'manager of copperworks'.

Swansea Enumeration District 21 covers 'The whole of the Hamlet of St. Thomas in the Parish of Swansea including Pentreguinea, Patent Fuel, Ferryside, Kilvey, Port Tennant and Fabians Bay, in the same Hamlet. This district is within the Borough of Swansea', and once again, there is no breakdown of addresses at all. Instead, the document is broken down into the six areas mentioned in the enumerator's description, Pentreguinea (27 properties, 131 people), Patent Fuel (55 properties, 273 people), Ferryside (23 properties, 118 people), Kilvey (23 properties, 115 people), Port Tennant (53 properties, 262 people), and Fabian's Bay (30 properties (151 people,).

Properties recorded as in 'Kilvey/Danygraig' are the home of William Thomas (Farm Bailiff for the Grenfell family) and his family, and the home of Thomas Miles, coal merchant and farmer of 150 acres, whilst Kilvey/Maesteg is recorded as the home of Pascoe St. Leger Grenfell and his family. Note that in this census 'Kilvey' should be understood as 'Kilvey Hill'.

In line with the 1841 census, there are similar amounts of copper industry workers, masons and colliers living in the area, and there are now more mariners and blacksmiths living locally. Other occupations now include a lock keeper, a thatcher, a blacksmith and a shoemaker, as well as coal heavers, fuel workers, excavators, bargemen, and general farm workers. By far the biggest sector of workers listed in this area in 1851 is that of 'labourers', many of whom would have likely moved to the area to work on the New Cut and the Town Float.

Many of those people migrating to the area are listed as being born in Carmarthen, Devon, Cornwall, the West Country, the South of England, and Ireland. Male and female servants are also in evidence, although now listed by actual job titles, such as washerwoman, house-servant, and dressmaker, with the biggest single listed employer being Pascoe St. Leger Grenfell at Maesteg (House), with four male staff members and six female staff members.

It is difficult to summarise the 1851 findings in the same way as 1841 due to the changes in geographical boundaries between the two censuses, however, the accommodation has increased from 224 properties in 1841 to 394 properties in 1851, mostly in the Port Tennant and Fabian's Bay areas, whilst population numbers have raised from 1251 people in 1841 to 2004 people in 1851. Danygraig remains for the most part rural. In January 1852 the North Dock was officially opened, and The North Dock Basin was constructed between 1859 and 1860.

In June 1852 Charles Lambert opened the Port Tennant Copper Works, and in the leases and agreements between Charles Lambert and the Tennant family for land for the building of the copperworks, additional properties are also mentioned - 'Griffiths cottages, a house called 'Ty Mawr' on or near the docks, as well as the 'Union Public House' and also 'cottage and premises formerly occupied by 'Roger Thomas'. Lambert's Copper Works was built at Salt House Point. Following the opening of 'Lambert's', in c1856 an Arsenic Works was built nearby by Nicholas Jennings, and given that the arsenic was extracted from copper ore, Jennings' Works was also known as 'Danygraig Copper Works', or 'Danygraig Works'. Jennings relocated his business to Llansamlet only a year later, but the Danygraig Works continued smelting copper and arsenic under different ownership for nearly thirty years, operating until its closure in 1912.

The **1861 census** documents [21] were far more descriptive than in previous years and offer a better view of the development of the area we know today. Again there are three census documents, but now only the area at and around Foxhole is included in the Llansamlet Lower (District 3) census, whilst the remainder of our area of concern is covered by the Swansea census in Districts 29 and 30 respectively.

The Llansamlet Lower Enumeration District 3 covers: 'All the remaining part of the Parish of Llansamlet Lower comprising all the houses and cottages on the north side of Ty Gwl, Foxhole,

Freeman's Row up to Kilvey Hill, Gelli Grafog, Bwgwrn, back west side of the Middle Bank incline machine, White Rock back to the bounded side of the River Tawe, lower bank of Foxhole back to Tyr Gwl.'

Foxhole remains the most prominent address with 68 properties, including the Ship Inn, the Fox Inn, and the Lamb & Flag public houses (all listed as on Lamb & Flag Row), the Foxhole Music Hall, and an area listed as Foxhole Bank. Tyr Gwl House is mentioned again this time with cottages and a lodge, whilst 'Kilvey Row' is now the most substantial block of cottages with 24 properties. New addresses listed include Canaan Cottages, Bryn Aeron, Lamb Row, Pleasant Row, Prospect Row, Graig Cottage, Jericho Foxhole, Martin Row, Freeman Row, and Jenkins Row.

Swansea Lower Enumeration District 29 covers 'All that part of the Hamlet of St. Thomas in the parish of Swansea commencing from Richardson's Wharf alongside the Float to the Meager's Gate, thence along the road leading to Morris Lane as far as Maesteg House, thence along the road to the Cuba Hotel including houses at the back, including both sides of the road thence to Pentreguinea to the Fuel gate along the left side of the road, thence from the White Lion to the railway office including the houses at the back, thence from the Red House to Gillian Terrace as far as the corner of Alma St, Alma St, Delhi St. Thence from the Miers Arms to Inkerman St and all these workhouses and lands within the said boundary.'

The previous Swansea censuses offered only a generalised description of this area but property built around The Town Float (now known as the North Dock) and a new area of construction to the east of Morris's Lane are clarified in this census. There are 33 properties listed near the North Dock made up of the following un-named buildings/addresses: Yard (2), Offices (2), Cottage (22), Courts (3), private houses (3), plus one public house, the Cuba Hotel. There are a number of 'beer houses' or 'cwrw bach' listed in this document, where alcohol was sold directly from private houses rather than via a licensed establishment, while some houses listed are described as lodging houses. Pentreguinea (27 properties) includes the Coppermans Arms, near the junction with Kilvey Terrace (9 properties).

East Pier Road is now included, with 14 properties built there, whilst Fuel Road (34 properties) and Fuelgate Road (17 properties) likely relate to the new Patent Fuel business that had opened nearby. To the east of Morris Lane (20 properties) is Benson Street (18 properties) likely named after the family of Starling Benson. Alma Street (39 properties) and Inkerman Street (22 properties), were both named after Crimean War battles, whilst Delhi Street (15 properties) was named after an Indian military siege. Miers Terrace (8 properties) is directly above Alma St, and is built on land previously owned by the Mackworth family of Neath, and likely named after Sir Robert Humphrey Mackworth's wife Mary Ann (Molly) Miers. After Sir Robert Humphrey Mackworth died in 1794 his estates passed to his wife, and her second husband, Capel Hanbury Leigh, Lord Lieutenant of Monmouthshire named the new streets after the Crimean and Indian conflicts.

Swansea Lower Enumeration District 30 follows directly '...commencing from Mr Walkers' House near Inkerman St, thence from Fabian's Bay Inn to Grenfell Lodge, thence to Port Tennant Inn, near Lamberts Cottages including agents house, thence from Burrows Inn to Jennings Works, thence to Crymlyn Bridge, from John Thomas House to Danygraig Terrace, thence to Roger Thomas House and all other works and houses within the said boundary.'

The first part of the District 30 enumerators' directions is a continuation of the new St. Thomas street layout that began in the District 29 census document. The first address mentioned is that of 'Cawnpore Street' a row of ten houses that include a public house called the Coquimbo Inn. The street was named after the Siege of Cawnpore, a massacre in the Indian Rebellion of 1857, positioned between the bottom of Alma St and the lower section of Inkerman Street (the upper section is in the District 29 census). The children of the proprietor were born in Coquimbo, Cuba, and this is likely the reason for the name of the public house. The lower section of Inkerman Street is shown to have five uninhabited houses at the time of the census, and from the lower end of the street, the census records the Fabian Inn, the first of 12 houses that make up Fabian's Row. The next property listed to the east is Grenfell Lodge, at the gate of the drive to Maesteg House at the junction with Port Tennant Road. Moving further east are the Neath Abbey Coal Works run by a coal shipper named Thomas Thomas who lived there with his wife and daughter, followed by the Port Tennant Inn, kept by Ebenezer Jones. Although Nicholas Jennings had left the area nine years earlier, nevertheless 'Jennings Arsenic Works' is mentioned in the document as a reference point.

Workers accommodation for both the Port Tennant Copper Works and the Danygraig Works had been constructed, and 'Lambert's Row' was the collective name of 40 properties that included one unnamed public house and two small uninhabited houses, all of which stood within the confines of Port Tennant Copper Works, whilst nearby three cottages were listed as 'Jennings Houses'.

Fabian's Bay showing Port Tennant Copper Works 1873 (with thanks to Chris Todd)

Burrows Row now has 11 properties including the Burrows Inn. Morgan's Row is mentioned, as are 12 houses owned by Roger Thomas at Mile End, which is also used as a reference point. Properties on the opposite side of the road (Crymlyn Bridge is mentioned as a reference point) were John Thomas's Mile End Row, which included the Mile End inn, the Mermaid Inn, and Maltsters Row. To the west of the Mermaid Inn was the original Danygraig Terrace, a group of 15 houses, with a nearby Welsh Independent Chapel. An 1840 lease between Margaret Tennant, widow of George Tennant, and the Trustees of the Welsh Calvinistic Methodist Society for a 'chapel or meeting house at Port Tennant, in the parish of Llansamlet', was later sold to the Trustees in 1851 and is likely the same chapel. Included in a cluster of buildings on the opposite side of the road was the Island House Grocers Shop, which also housed a Day School. Above this group of houses was Danygraig Lodge (the gatehouse of Danygraig House) as well as Danygraig House (Ty Mawr) itself, noted as being 'in a poor state.' Nearby is Danygraig 'Old' Farm, previously the home of Roger Thomas, but now occupied by a copper worker, his family and lodger. The recently build Cemetery House is also listed, as are the non-residential Dissenters Chapel and the Church of England Chapel. Also listed are Danygraig Gardens, occupied by a coal trimmer and his family, and Danygraig Farm, now the home of the Grenfell's farm bailiff George Goss, together with his wife, six children, a house servant, a dairymaid, three labourers and two carters, all living on the farm. Port Tennant Road had become the main artery on the Eastside at this time with 22 properties that begin with Sidney Cottages, two houses occupied by a coal trimmer and a copper smelter, the Union Inn kept by Canal Agent and Victualler David Williams, Lewis Cottages, Francis Terrace, and a row of 10 properties that included a Police Station, a grocer's shop, and Port Tennant Post Office, kept by bootmaker and shopkeeper Thomas Howell.

In 1863, in order to develop industrial land at Crymlyn Burrows close to the Tennant Canal, Briton Ferry Estates surveyed a section of the land to ascertain high and low water levels and following this, in 1866 Shackleford, Ford & Co. opened a Zinc Spelter Works in the area that made galvanised coating for metal sheeting and buckets, as well as opening a wagon repair works; the company also built workers accommodation in Port Tennant. Unfortunately, the spelter works were damaged by fire the following year and uninsured, the company went bankrupt and had to auction off its assets.

A.F. Rolfe 'View of Swansea, dated 1840 - City & County of Swansea: Glynn Vivian Art Gallery Collection

Etching 'View of Swansea' 1862 (author's collection)

The spelter works were taken over by The Swansea Zinc Company but within two years it too was bankrupt, and the business was bought by Messrs. J. Richardson & Company who, trading as The Crown Zinc Company, bought in Belgian workers to operate the spelter plant. In 1865 the wagon repair works were under the name of The Bristol and South Wales Railway Wagon Company, however by the late 1870s, the works were owned by The Swansea Wagon Company. In 1868, Neath Brewer Evan Evans, owner of The Vale of Neath Brewery, was given a leasehold by Briton Ferry Estate to build 'five houses with gardens' on land adjacent to Tennant Canal that was previously occupied by Swansea Zinc Company, and given that his grandson was Evan Evans Bevan, it is likely that 'Bevan's Row' now bears his name.

The **1871 census** documents [22] covering the area of interest is split between Lower Llansamlet District 5 and the Swansea Districts 33,34, and 35 census documents, but whilst there are very few changes made between the 1861 and 1871 Lower Llansamlet census document, the growth of population, specifically in the St. Thomas area meant that an additional document was required in the Swansea 1871 census. The Llansamlet Lower Enumeration District 5 census document now includes the Smith's Arms as in Foxhole, and whilst the total number of houses listed as 'Foxhole' has reduced, additional addresses have been added such as Tiger Road, Thomas Terrace, Matthew Row, Hopkin Row, Owens Row, and 'Wind Mill St'. Some addresses shown in the 1861 census are no longer listed, whilst 'Kilvey Row' is now shown as 'Kilvey Road', and a Boy's School has opened in addition to the Infants School. The Rifleman's Arms is listed on Freeman's Row, whilst Conibear Row and 'Kilvey Old Windmill' are listed for the first time as properties on Kilvey Hill.

Swansea Enumeration District 33 covers 'All that part of the Hamlet of St Thomas in the parish of Swansea, commencing from Richardson's Wharf alongside the Float to Meager's yard, thence along the road leading to the Cuba Hotel including the houses at the back, thence along the road leading to Morris's Lane, Mackworth Road, Alma St as far as Maesteg House including both sides of the road, thence to Pentreguinea, to the Fuel Gate, along the left-hand side of the road, thence from the White Lion to the

Railway Office, including the houses at the back of Benson St to the Red House. Enumerator's note: The name of Alma St has been changed to Miers St.; Mr Dangerfield took this Street by mistake. I have therefore taken Inkerman St in my district. The name of Benson St has been changed to Pinkney St (Enumerator G.A. Potter)'.

Some of the properties between the North Dock and St. Thomas previously included in 1861 (District 29) are still included in this document but are reduced in number, although 'New Cut' is a new addition. This document reflects the further shaping of the St. Thomas residential area to the east of Morris Lane as whilst some street names are amended/changed, new streets were built and populated in line with industrial growth. Many of the male residents in this specific area worked either for a company based on the North Dock or else for one of a number of railway companies that had set up business in the area.

As per the enumerator notes, Inkerman St (now with 80 properties) is included in this census but should have been listed in the District 34 document instead. For the first time, the Grenfell home is listed as 'Maesteg House' and is now listed in St. Thomas, having previously been listed as 'Maesteg' and included as part of Danygraig. Bryn Sifi (1 property), Mackworth Villas, Mackworth Terrace and the Foxhole Police Station are mentioned for the first time. The counting of 36 properties on Pentreguinea (Road) likely indicates a boundary between Lower Llansamlet and Swansea districts. The White Lion Public House is now listed, as is 'St. Thomas Street' which runs from the Red House and Bridge Inn public houses to the bottom of Morris Lane. The Benson Inn is on St. Thomas Street, and Hebron Place and Ivy Bush Court are now listed, whilst Benson Street has been renamed Pinkney Street.

Swansea Enumeration District 34 covers 'All that part of the Hamlet of St Thomas in the parish of Swansea, commencing at Gillian Terrace thence to Miers Terrace and Street and Fabians Terrace (now called Fabian Street), Inkerman St, Balaclava St, Sebastopol St and Delhi St on both sides. Enumerator Note: 'Miers St" taken in this district in error. Inkerman St was taken by Mr Potter in lieu of the same.'

Of the four 1871 census documents covering the area, the District 34 census shows the biggest change in property numbers and population. New streets are added, some existing streets are either renamed or else enveloped by other streets, and a number of public houses have been established. One major change in Fabian Terrace to Fabian Street, previously a small terrace of 12 houses at the south end of Inkerman Street, and now a row of 31 properties that run from Gillian Terrace at the rear of the Red House public house to the south end of Sebastopol Street.

Cawnpore Street, previously running between the south end of Alma Street and Inkerman Street, is no more and is now part of Fabian Street. Fabian Street now has eight public houses in the row - the Farmers Arms, the Ship & Castle, the Miers Arms, the Chile Arms, the Fabian Inn, the Hamlet Inn, the Railway Inn, and the Station Inn, whilst the Windsor Arms is now listed on Delhi Street, which has been extended to cross the new Balaclava Street (51 properties) to Sebastopol Street (only 2 properties). Alma Street and Miers Terrace are now combined as one street, renamed as Miers Street (63 properties).

Swansea Enumeration District 35 covers 'All that part of the Hamlet of St Thomas in the parish of Swansea, commencing at Danygraig Farm thence to the cemetery and Shackleford's Buildings thence to Mile End Robert (sic) Thomas and Mrs Davies cottages, Danygraig Terrace thence from Burrows Inn to Jennings works, thence to Crymlyn Bridge to John Thomas house to Cemetery Row, Francis Row, Lodge Terrace thence to Lambert Cottages, back to Port Tennant Road to the Grenfells lodge and all other of the houses and lands within the... ' It is also marked as 'Port Tennant Village'.

This document aligns with about 75% of the geographic area covered by District 30 in 1861, and whilst not as descriptive as the 1861 census, many addresses remain the same, however, a new worker's housing development called Shackleford Row is now included, constructed by Shackleford & Ford, who had opened a zinc works nearby. Lodge Terrace and Cemetery Row/Road, now runs from the end of Port Tennant Road, northwards to the gate of Swansea (Danygraig) Cemetery. Lambert's Cottages, Burrows Row and Danygraig Terrace remain, whilst Mile End Row, Maltsters Row, Canal Cottages and Sea Beach Cottages are also listed, as are Danygraig House and Danygraig Farm and cottages. Port Tennant Road remains the main artery, ending at Port Tennant Road Lodge, which was previously listed as Grenfell Lodge. Quaker's Bank appears to be the new name for what was previously the location of Neath Abbey Coal Works.

The **1881 census** documents [23] covering the area of concern are split between Lower Llansamlet District 6 and the Swansea Districts 39, 40, 41, 42a and 42b census documents. The 1881 documents are not as descriptive as the previous census, but the document is significant in that it formally recognises Kilvey as a residential area for the first time. The growth of population in the St. Thomas area, rather than a major increase in properties built, has meant that in the Swansea 1881 census an additional census document was required, split into parts 42a and 42b.

Lower Llansamlet Enumeration District 6 (247 properties, 1294 people, Male 665 Female 629) covers 'Part of the Parish of Llansamlet Lower within the Municipal Parliamentary Borough of Swansea, and the Ecclesiastical District of All Saints Church Kilvey' Comprising ….. all of the houses and cottages which is lying South and East of the Road leading from Knapcoch to Tyr Gwll Terrace and Kilvey Hill Including 4 houses of Mr Owens at White Rock, South and east of Foxhole Rd including Freemans Row, Martins Row and all the houses and cottages at Kilvey Hill and all the houses and cottages which is lying North and East of Bigwrn which is bounded North and East of St. Thomas.'

Swansea Enumeration District 39 (105 properties, 570 people, Male 258 Female 252) recognises Kilvey as a residential area for the first time and notes a few new landmarks in its description, the document covering the 'Hamlet of St. Thomas, Borough of Swansea. Eastward from Ecclesiastical Dist. Kilvey. All that part of the Hamlet of St. Thomas comprising the whole of the Eastside of the North Dock basin North end returning along the side of the river to the New Cut Bridge as far as Thomas St, thence along the west side of Thomas St and the West Side of Morris Lane as far as and including Bryn Sifi House and thus to and including Pentre

Guinea. Within the boundaries are situated the whole of Workhouse Dwelling House, Dry Docks, and buildings of every description. Situate on the East side of the North Dock Richardson Street - Cuba Hotel, Coffee Tavern and Public House adjoining Midland Railway Station, Kilvey Terrace, Bryn Tawe, Warlichs Fuel Works, Fuel Inn, White Lion, Coppermans's Inn and Pentre Guinea and all houses and buildings within the above-named boundaries.'

Swansea Enumeration District 40 (210 properties, 1350 people, M 720 F 630) covers 'All that part of the Hamlet of St. Thomas comprising Eastside of Thomas Street and Morris Lane as far as but not including Bryn Sifi House, thence to and including Maesteg House returning to and including Mackworth Terrace thence along Inkerman Street (including the west side only) as far as Fabian Street, and along Fabian Street to the starting point at Red House Inn. Within these boundaries include Pinkney Street, Miers Street, Delhi Street from Inkerman Street to its western end and all courts leading from the streets named in the above boundaries and [ends]

Swansea Enumeration District 41 (198 properties, 1271 people, Male 678 Female 593) covers 'That part of the Hamlet of St. Thomas comprising the east side of Inkerman Street from Fabian Street to Mackworth Terrace thence to St. Thomas Church returning by Fabian Street to the starting point. These boundaries include Balaclava Street and Sebastopol Street'.

Swansea Enumeration District 42a (201 properties, 1313 people, Male 693 Female 620) and 42b (39 properties, 271 people, Male 147 Female 124) covers both sections and deals with 'All that part of the Hamlet of St. Thomas comprising from Vale of Neath New Station as far as the Railway Bridge at the Crown Spelter Works, there are the Western and Eastern Boundaries, the Northern Boundaries include Danygraig Farm, Danygraig Drift Colliery, Shackleford Row, Hoo St. The Southern boundaries include Vale of Neath Arms, and all cottages around Bevans Row, Arsenic Works, Port Tennant Works, Lambert Rows, East Dock and within the boundaries given are Maesteg Lodge, Danygraig Terrace, Mermaid Row, Burrows Row and all houses and works and buildings adjoining the places named.'

The description of the census boundaries is far more specific in the 1881 documents given that much of the general layout of landlord-built-and-owned residential property on the Eastside was nearly completed, with the exception of part of Danygraig which still remained rural. A number of families from Devon, Somerset, Gloucester and The Midlands are now established in the Port Tennant area, as well as those originating from Belgium, Scotland, Ireland, France, Chile and Malta, but in contrast to St. Thomas that had seen an influx of 'navigators' or 'excavators' arrive to work on the new Prince of Wales Dock, the Port Tennant workforce had few such workers, nor were there many railway workers living in the area, the main employers locally being Lambert's, the Spelter Works, the Arsenic Works and the Wagon Works.

By the time of the **1891 census** [24] whilst some streets and roads were only partially built, much of what we know today as the Eastside had been completed and the employment demography in the area was reasonably settled, based on the companies and industries that were already established adjacent to the various residential areas of Kilvey/Foxhole, St. Thomas and Port Tennant/Danygraig.

Lower Llansamlet Enumeration District 8/9 (284 properties, 1381 people, M 695 F 686) covers 'All the Remaining parts of the Parish of Llansamlet from within the Swansea County Borough and the ecclesiastical district of all Saints Church Kilvey. Comprising all the houses and cottages North and east of the road leading to Cwmdonos Brook to Knapcoch and Foxhole Road to No. 22 Windmill Terrace and on the North and East of the Bigwrn which is bounded North and East of St. Thomas. Follow the Borough boundary back to Cwmdonos Brook. Including Gwindy, Grenfell Town, Pentrechwyth, Knapcoch, Foxhole, Windmill Terrace, Kilvey Road, Owens Row, Tyr Gwll Farm, Kilvey Hill, Bachelors Hall…and Pentre Graig. The whole in the Parliamentary Division of Swansea.'

Swansea Enumeration District 39 (200 properties, 1049 people, M 501 F 548) covers 'All that part of the Hamlet of St. Thomas comprising the whole of the East side of the North Dock - from the Lock Bridge to the extreme end of the North Dock Basin

(North End) returning along the side of the river to the New Cut Bridge as far as Thomas St - and to the side of Morris Lane - as far as - and including Bryn Sifi House - and the West side of Morris Lane and including all houses in Windmill Terrace from and including No. 23 upwards and Pentreguinea Row. Within the boundaries situate the whole of the Workhouses Dwelling Houses, Dry Docks and buildings of every description situate on the East side of the North Dock Richardson Street - Cuba Hotel, Coffee Tavern and Public House adjoining Midland Railway Station, Kilvey Terrace, Benthall Place and Terrace and all new houses within the boundaries named - Bryn Tawe, Fuel Inn, White Lion Inn, Copperman's Arms, Pentreguinea - and all tenements within the above-named boundaries.'

Swansea Enumeration District 40 (208 properties, 1259 people, M 613 F 646) covers 'All that part of the Hamlet of St. Thomas East side of Thomas St and Morris Lane, as far as but not including Bryn Sifi House, thence to include Maesteg House. Returning to and including Mackworth Terrace thence along Inkerman St (including the west side only) as far as Fabian St and along Fabian St to the starting point at the Red House Inn. Within the boundaries are included Pinkney Street - Miers Street - Delhi St - From Inkerman Street to its Western end and all courts leading from the streets named in the above boundaries and Maesteg House.'

Swansea Enumeration District 41a (202 properties 1120 people, M 536 F 584) covers 'All that part of the Hamlet of St. Thomas comprising the east side of Inkerman Street from Fabians Street to Mackworth Terrace. Hence to St. Thomas Church returning by Fabians Street to the starting point - the boundaries include Delhi Street - from Inkerman Street - to St. Thomas Church, Balaclava Street, and Sebastopol Street.'

Swansea Enumeration District 41b (386 properties, 2391 people, M 1230 F 1161) - no description available

Swansea Enumeration District 42 (56 properties, 323 people, M 164 F 161) - no description available

Post-1900

The vast majority of houses on the Eastside were constructed between the 1840s and the 1920s on land owned by Freeman & Co., Elias Jenkins, Thomas Capel-Leigh, or the Briton Ferry Estate, and were either built by the landowners themselves or by private landlords who leased the land, built housing on it and, then leased the housing to others. A high number of these houses were regarded as workers' cottages, and whilst many have names directly linked to the various landowners, a small number of streets have Welsh names. Over time, the names of some streets were changed, houses that originally had names were given numbers, and as streets were extended, they were often renumbered.

Council housing on the Eastside appeared in the late 1920s, constructed on the eastern end of Danygraig Road, as well as in St. Thomas, where the street names are linked to the Grenfell family.

The Grenfells built little if any housing on the Eastside, but after their business went bankrupt and their various leases expired, their family home Maesteg House, together with its substantial grounds, reverted back to the landowners, Briton Ferry Estate. When Swansea Corporation purchased Maesteg House and its grounds to construct new council housing in the 1920s, the Grenfell family names were added following the suggestion and support of local councillors, and shortly afterwards a new private housing estate built above Windmill Terrace also took the Grenfell name.

Briton Ferry Estate had begun selling leaseholds prior to WW1, and after claims were made to the War Damage Commission in order to repair housing stock after the damage incurred to housing during World War II, further divestment of its properties followed. By the early 1950s, it had begun selling the leaseholds of its Eastside properties to housing companies such as Gwalia Land & Property Ltd, the City & Provincial Housing Association, and the Principality Property Company, as well as to smaller landlords and individuals, whilst retaining some properties that were managed by its own company, Estateways Builders.

The Influence of the Church

At the time of writing, there are only four functioning religious establishments currently on the Eastside, St. Thomas Church, Fabian's Bay Church, St. Illtyd's Church and the Ebenezer Gospel Hall (or six if both the Norwegian Church and the Waterfront Community Church on the SAI development on the docks are included), so it is easy to overlook the importance of the various Non-conformist church groups of the 1800s and 1900s who were heavily involved in the shaping of the area we know today.

'Non-conformists' are so-named as they do not conform to the governance and usages of the Anglican Church, and to best understand their importance, it is necessary to first examine the shaping of industrial Swansea at the beginning of the 1800s when the two main parishes in Swansea were both Anglican - the parishes of Swansea (St. Mary's) and Llangyfelach.

In the early 1800s the Parish of Swansea, part of the diocese of St. David, was one of the largest in England and Wales. it covered an area of nearly 7000 acres that included St. John Parish Church on High St, which itself covered areas we know today as Manselton and Hafod. It ran northwards from the sea to the Lliw Valley and the Burlais Brook, stretched west to the Blackpill stream, and crossed the Tawe to include the Hamlet of St Thomas, which covered an area below Kilvey Hill that ran eastward to the Crymlyn Bog. The rest of the manor of Kilvey fell under the auspices of the church at Llansamlet. Llansamlet covered an area of over 6000 acres and ran north to Glais, but until 1841 it was regarded as a parish within Llangyfelach. Nearly 27000 acres in size excluding Llansamlet, [25], Llangyfelach parish ran northwards from the east side of the Tawe at Foxhole, to the east side of the Lliw Valley, from St. John parish in the south, and northwards to include Bettws.

Despite the obvious size of the combined area of Swansea and Llangyfelach parishes, outside of supporting its main churches, the Anglican Church establishment offered little in the way of developing new places of worship from its own coffers, and many existing churches were still in a state of disrepair following the

Reformation of the mid-1600s when church assets were sequestered to the government. The Restoration of King Charles II had restored some semblance of order and security to the Anglican Church, but his coming to the throne upset the many Puritans across England and Wales who had flourished under the Parliamentarian Commonwealth, nevertheless, the various Dissenter/Non-conformist groups remained and prospered using private houses as places of worship.

The 1672 Declaration of Indulgence and The Toleration Act of 1689 went some way to ease the situation as public meeting places could be established, and in Swansea, various groups took advantage of this including Baptists, Quakers, Presbyterians, Independents, Methodists, Unitarians and Congregationalists, many of whom opened meeting places in the centre of town in or close to Castle Street and High Street, whilst English and Welsh Methodists built chapels on Goat Street and near Green Hill (Crug Glas). St. Mary's Church held services in English only, whilst both English and Welsh were used at St John's. Many of the existing Non-conformist groups in the town held services in Welsh or were bilingual, but as the town's population rapidly increased, services in the many new churches and chapels were held only in English, in line with worshippers' needs.

The arrival in the 1700s and early 1800s of Industrialists such as Robert Morris, John Lockwood, John Henry Vivian, John Freeman and Pascoe Grenfell, as well as the involvement of local industrialists like John Smith in Llansamlet, was instrumental in extending the footprint of the Anglican faith in Swansea. Through directly funding repairs of old Anglican churches as well as the building of new churches, their substantial investments also often included the building of worker accommodation close to their works, and they were all keen advocates of religion-based education, carried out using English, rather than Welsh, as the main language. Given the rapid growth in population in Swansea throughout the 1800s, it comes as no surprise that the various Non-conformist groups were also extremely active at this time, and the opening of new Non-conformist churches and chapels far exceeded that of the Anglican churches in the area during the same period.

Most new Non-conformist chapels held services in English only, and nearly all that opened also held Sunday Schools. Given that many of their workers were Non-conformist, the Anglican industrialists often supported Non-conformist groups too, as did local businessmen like steel and tinplate works owners E R Daniel, John Jones Jenkins, and Richard Hughes.

In the early part of the 1800s, population growth was in the main via immigrants from rural West Wales, but by the middle of the century, the immigration came from a far wider area, from Cornwall and the West Country, Ireland and even from mainland Europe, as the town changed into an industrial hotbed that offered an opportunity to many. Immigrants looked for chapels of the same denomination they had previously worshipped at, and if they were not available, then there was an opportunity to start a new group.

The various denominations looked to develop their own congregations, and the following list [26] shows the breakdown of churches and chapel buildings built in the first half of the 1800s:

Independents	22
Baptists	17
Calvinistic Methodists	12
Wesleyan Methodists	11
Primitive Methodists	4
Anglicans	5

To further endorse the growth of the Non-conformist churches and chapels compared to those of the Anglican faith, the 1851 Religious Census showed that whilst Anglican churches in Swansea had 2717 worshippers, Methodists groups had 4600 worshippers, whilst 'Older Dissenters' had over 7000 worshippers, and the census also noted that many of the Non-conformist places of worship also had Sunday Schools.

English was the language of choice in most cases, and by 1907 there were 44 English-language churches in Swansea compared to only 19 Welsh-language churches, many of which were 'Iron Churches', also known as 'Tin Tabernacles'. Iron churches sprang up in towns up and down Britain, and were seen as a tool of growth for the Non-conformists, so much so that The Oxford English Dictionary definition mentions the Non-conformists directly when referring to 'tin tabernacles' - 'applied disparagingly to buildings (esp. Non-conformist churches) made partly of corrugated iron.' [27]

The Tin Tabernacle was the idea of London Dock Company architect and engineer Henry Robinson Palmer, who felt that corrugated iron buildings were suitable for chapels, churches, and mission halls, hospitals, schools and offices. Originally made in 1820 from corrugated iron although later made from steel, the 'iron church' became a big favourite across all religious denominations as its lightweight and portability meant it could be easily transported and could be assembled quickly by a semi-skilled workforce. They were sold 'flat-pack' by companies such as William Cooper Ltd. of Old Kent Road, London. and The London Iron Church and Chapel Company, often by mail order catalogue, to customers as far and wide as Africa, Asia and America. In 1837 French engineer Stanislaus Sorel patented galvanising, and when the corrugated iron sheets were hot-dipped with a zinc coating, this gave them a high level of corrosion resistance that extended the life of the building itself. Fabricated buildings originally designed as temporary structures were now light, strong, and corrosion resistant, so when a permanent structure (such as a stone-built church) was built, the iron church was often simply dismantled and relocated to a different location, where it was reassembled.

Whilst originally sited in Newport in 1900, Swansea's most recognisable iron church is the Sjomanns Kirken, the Norwegian Seaman's Church that from 1910 stood between the entrance of the docks and the mouth of the Tawe until its relocation to the SA1 Development in 2004. The Anglicans also made good use of the iron church, and the current St. Thomas Church on the Eastside replaced an early iron church that had originally been erected in Cheltenham. After the current stone structure was completed, it was dismantled and then reassembled to become St. Stephen's on

Danygraig Road. [28] When it too was replaced by a stone building, the iron church became the church hall.

The first church or chapel recorded on the Eastside of the Tawe was that of **St. Thomas the Martyr**, named after Thomas Becket, canonised after his murder at Canterbury Cathedral in 1170. Likely built in the 12th century close to a location that would later be known as Salt House Point, at that time of its construction it would have stood in the Forest of Kilvey. In 1188, Giraldus Cambrensis and Archbishop Baldwin of Canterbury travelled through Wales preaching of the crusade accompanied by Rhys ap Gruffydd, it is likely that they passed through the Forest of Kilvey before crossing the Tawe to Swansea on their way to the Gower Peninsula, however, given that Thomas Becket was murdered in 1170, it is doubtful that the building was built at that time. Both the forest and the chapel were said to have been washed away in the floods of January 1607.

Over 200 hundred years later George Tennant bought the same land, which by this time included the remains of an old salt house, in order to construct a port at the end of his canal. [29] Tennant leased much of the land to Charles Lambert who in 1851 began construction of his Copper Works. [30] In the early 1900s, there was a hurricane in the channel that lasted some days, and after the storm subsided, local residents went out on the sands to check on the damage to their boats and found that the storm had so disrupted the shoreline that coffins had appeared from the sands and the remains of the chapel walls could be seen. [31]

In c1807 Freeman & Company owners of the White Rock Copper Works, together with Pascoe Grenfell & Sons, opened the Copperworks School for workers' children, and in 1841, under a similar arrangement, Pascoe Grenfell & Sons owners of the Middle Bank and Upper Bank Works built a new Anglican Church on ground donated by Freeman & Company, its construction supervised by Riversdale Grenfell. Known as **All Saints Church Foxhole**, it opened in 1845 as a Chapel of Ease to Llansamlet Church, and became an ecclesiastical parish in May 1881, the Benefice of Swansea St. Thomas and Kilvey, and was restored in 1883 at a cost of £960, an able to seat 500 people. Prior to the opening of All Saints, Anglican parishioners would worship at either Llangyfelach or Llansamlet Churches.

Morris Lane School opened in 1863 as an infant's school thanks to the efforts of Mary Benthall, the granddaughter of Elias Jenkins of Kilvey House, who enlisted the support of E.B. Squires Vicar of Swansea in securing a lease on the land. When the lease on the building expired in 1945, the Benthall family donated it to the St. Thomas parish with the request that it became a parish hall. [32]

The current **St. Thomas Church**, designed by Thomas Nicholson of Hereford, was built between 1886 and 1890 and replaced the iron church that stood close to the spot of the new construction. Dedicated to St. Thomas the Apostle, the new parish was created in 1888. Whilst various Grenfell family members were contributors to the church, the money used to build the church chancel and spire extensions came from the Llewellyn family of Baglan, Mrs Madelina Llewellyn being the eldest daughter of Pascoe St. Leger Grenfell. Whilst not as high profile locally as her sister Mary, she was a generous benefactor of various good causes in both Swansea and Neath, including substantial donations to Swansea Hospital. General Sir Francis Wallace Grenfell laid the foundation stone.

The Grenfell family contributions were made in remembrance of Pascoe St. Leger Grenfell who had died in 1879, however, it appears that the church was at least paid for in part by public prescription, as in the years preceding his death there was some concern locally as to how money regularly collected from parishioners for the building of a stone church was instead used buy and erect an iron church. Mary Grenfell was said to be involved in the purchase of the Iron Church from Cheltenham, and a flurry of letters was printed in the Cambrian in April and May 1878 [33] [34] [35] highlighted the restlessness of the community over this issue. The Reverend W. Evans, the curate in charge, was identified by name in the letters as the man who, over a two-year period, 'came to our doors to solicit subscriptions towards the erection of a new church' and who had gathered support from hundreds of parishioners who had 'gladly promised our mites towards this good and necessary object', and who were 'looking forward with much delight in anticipation of having in the course of a year or two a handsome new church'. However after the plans of the proposed new church had been viewed by parishioners, an iron church had been purchased instead.

This caused much upset, as on physical examination some parishioners felt that the wooden parts were rotten and the iron pieces were worn, and there were major concerns as to how much more needed to be spent on it, as well as how long it would last; 'It will cost at least £700 before it is fit for use. Would it not be much wiser to give that sum towards building a permanent church, than to spend it on what must soon be sold as old iron and firewood'. A small number of responses in defence of the purchase followed with some letters quoting the scriptures to support their point, as well as a letter from Rev. W. Evans who protested his innocence in the matter, and clarified that he had 'no part nor lot in the Iron Church, and therefore, I decline expressing my opinion as to my approval or disapproval of it'.

The final correspondence on the subject appeared in the Cambrian on May 4th when 'A Church Goer. St. Thomas' commented that 'more than 90 per cent of the inhabitants of St. Thomas and Port Tennant are against the Iron Church and condemn it' as prior to the plans, designs, and specifications of the Stone Church becoming public knowledge, 'nobody had ever heard of an Iron Church" and there was serious doubt cast over a decision that meant "spending £700 upon an old worn-out concern which cannot last but two or three years.' The new stone church was finally completed nearly ten years later, and contrary to the concerns that it was 'not worth the trouble and expense of taking it down and putting it up again', the iron church was dismantled and rebuilt near the junction of Grafog Street and Danygraig Road and became St. Stephen's Church.

St. Stephen's Church began life as an iron church but a new sandstone-built building was constructed adjacent to it between 1905 and 1907, designed by E.M. Bruce Vaughan. [36] The iron church remained and became the church mission hall.

The presence of Non-conformist worship on the Eastside was first noted from c1837 when the Trinity Calvinists had a school in Port

Tennant [37] possibly **Port Tennant Chapel**, although archived Tennant family documents show a lease signed in 1840 with Welsh Methodists, further endorsed via a new 99-year lease with Margaret Tennant in 1851 [38]. Situated on Burrows Row near the Burrow Inn opposite the original Danygraig Terrace, it is listed as demolished in 1882 to accommodate the route of the Rhondda and Swansea Bay Railway. A new church was built in its place on Ysgol St, known as **Danygraig Congregational Chapel,** officially opening in 1863. Modified in 1883, a Sunday School began in 1897 and a manse was added in the same year. It was further modified in 1913 and sat 600 worshippers. [39]

The Independent Canaan Church, its origins in the Ebenezer Chapel in Mynddbach, was established in March 1840 in the Foxhole area on land leased from Lord Jersey. Built at a cost of £706 and 6 shillings, it held its first service a few months later. The names 'Hafan Chapel' and 'Kilvey Chapel' were touted amongst others before the name 'Canaan Church' was agreed on [40]. Services were initially held in Welsh, although the Church reverted to English in the early 1900s [41]. Local roads to the new church were in a poor state of repair, and the footpath from Foxhole Road to the Church was 'strewn every Sunday with sand, giving it the appearance of a path of gold' [42]. The children of Canaan used the Copperworks School until 1883 when Canaan built its own school adjacent to the church. One of Canaan's main benefactors was Elias Jenkins, local landowner and the manager of White Rock Copper Works, who lived in nearby Kilvey House on Ty Gwl, and who together with his daughters, was active in many of the church's activities. Kilvey House was a mansion and estate that once overlooked Windmill Terrace, that many years later would be demolished to make room for a new private housing estate.

Mid to late 19th Century maps show a church/chapel at the junction of Foxhole Road and Kilvey Road that is listed as the **Tabernacle English Baptist Church,** founded in 1829 (according to a Religious Census of 1851).

The Hebron Church was established in St. Thomas in 1840 and is listed by the Welsh Church Commission as an English Baptist Church, but elsewhere it is listed as a branch of the Calvinistic

Methodist Church at Salem, Capel Y Cwm. [43], and shared the building for a short time with the Forward Movement c1895.

Forward Movement Church - The Forward Movement of the Calvinistic Methodist Church in Wales was founded in Cardiff in 1891 by the Rev John Pugh, and soon after set up in Swansea. On the Eastside of Swansea, after previously first utilising the old Hebron Church building on Delhi St., the Forward Movement Church on Port Tennant Road was established around 1895 under Frank Jackson, and was initially in an iron church. The Eastside area was described at that time as 'one of the blackest spots under the sun', [44] and from Port Tennant Road the church developed its activities in the docks areas. By the end of the century, there was also a Forward Movement Sunday School running successfully in 'this dark and neglected spot', and in late 1930, the Forward Movement Burrows Hall was set up on Wern Terrace. The iron church on Port Tennant Road was later replaced by a stone building but this was damaged during the Blitz and services were relocated to the Burrows Hall. A new church building was erected in c1950 on Port Tennant Road on the site of the old church, however the Burrows Hall unfortunately burnt down in the 1980s and was not replaced.

Fabian's Bay Congregational Church, is of English Independent denomination, with links to the Canaan Chapel in Foxhole. Its congregation had been active in the area for a number of years, initially meeting in the house of William Owen in Miers Street before with the help of the Canaan Church, opening a schoolroom in Balaclava Street in 1862 [45]. After outgrowing the schoolhouse, the Canaan Church again stepped in to help with assistance from the Ebenezer Chapel in Castle Street, and after the foundation stone was laid by O. Wills, Esq on October 13th 1871, the current stone-build Fabian's Bay Church was erected in 1872, and later modified in 1904. It seats 500 worshippers.

St. Illtyd's Church - Initially a mission house, St Illtyd's School was built to serve the need of the Catholic community of the Eastside. A bazaar raised nearly £460 before the foundation stone could be laid by Bishop Hedley in November 1883, witnessed by a large group of children from St. David's School in Swansea, and the school was opened by the Bishop in June the following year [46]. Many of the first children to attend St. Illtyd's School were from Irish and Belgian families whose fathers worked in the local smelting works and other local industries.

My grandfather Tom Crowley outside St. Illtyd's Church. Originally from County Wexford in Ireland, he worked on its construction (Author's collection)

The first mass was held in the school in February 1885, and services remained there until 1913 when a small church and residence were built at a cost of nearly £800. In 1915, Father Arthur Dawson got an agreement to construct a larger building, and by the early 1920s, the current church and presbytery were built at a cost of £6000, officially opening in February 1927. The school building is no longer used, and a new school in Bonymaen has taken its place, however, St. Illtyd's Church remains the centre of Catholic worship on the Eastside.

Mount Tabor was established in c1895 on Delhi Street and run by Reverend N. Coppin; it was likely a Bible Christian group at that time [47]. The Bible Christians merged with other Non-conformist groups to form the United Methodists, as well as in 1910, Mount Tabor was listed as a United Methodist Church, run by the Reverend Simeon Lewis Warne (Supt.), Reverend Thomas Langdon Rogers, and Reverend J. T. P. Oliver. It seated 300 worshippers. They merged with other groups such as the Wesleyans and Primitive Methodists, and in 1932 formed what became the Methodist Church. A few years later "Potter's Electrical Repair Works' utilised the old church building as a fitting shop.

English Baptist worship on the Eastside was evident at 'The Adams Sunday School' held at No. 3 Sebastopol Street, the home of Thomas and Mary Adams, who set up and organised a school for children who did not go to church. They were so successful that they expanded into a nearby reading room, however, due to local council needs, the reading room was made unavailable to them and they reverted back to using their house. In 1881 **St. Thomas Baptist Chapel**, an iron church with a brick-built Baptistry, was built at a cost of £350 at Ffynon Hyssop (The Well of Hyysop) on Farm Lane (now Kinley Street), and was the first Baptist chapel in the area. For reasons that are still not clear, on 25th September 1882, under the instruction of Reverend Thomas Williams, the church was dismantled and transported to Gorse Lane, now King Edward Road, where a week later it became an Anglican Church [48] although there was an English Baptist Church listed at the same location in 1895.

The local congregation was determined to remain intact and under the guidance of Thomas Adams, were able to get permission to use both the Cemetery Chapel and the decaying Danygraig House as places of worship. The following year Lord Jersey released a piece of land opposite the gates of the cemetery in order that a new church could be built, and on 31st October 1883, in a meeting at Danygraig House [49] it was agreed that the new church would be named **Mount Calvary Baptist Church**, a name proposed by Mary Adams. It officially opened in 1885 and seated 300 worshippers, and was further extended in 1905. The original building was designed by architect William Beddoe Rees of Cardiff.

Ebenezer Gospel Hall is a Brethren place of worship built near the junction of Wern Fawr Rd and Ysgol St, and is still active today.

Sjomanns Kirken/Norwegian Church. Originally located in Newport c1900, the iron church and seaman's mission building was dismantled and rebuilt in c1910 at Swansea's main docks entrance, where it remained as a recognised landmark and the oldest working Seaman's Mission Church in Britain until 1998, when the lease on the church was not renewed and it closed. It was later dismantled and restored, and relocated on the docks as part of the SA1 development where it reopened again in 2004.

The high number of Non-conformist churches far outweighed the Anglicans when it came to providing schooling for the working class, indeed in many cases, a Sunday school was organised before there was a church built. The Non-conformist 'cradle to the grave' overview meant that the day-to-day life of their congregations revolved around a church that as well as setting up and running savings clubs, reading rooms, woman's groups, and cultural and recreational activities, also included the funding and supporting of new 'sister' churches in other parts of town.

Given that many Non-conformist communities were made up of families whose menfolk also worked together, it was inevitable that political groups were formed or strengthened via the camaraderie of those involved in both, and the hierarchy of the church and political groups were often one and the same people, something that continued into the 20th century with the growth of the Labour movement in particular, who took advantage of this situation after electoral reforms gave the working class an easier route to local government. A practical example of this was David Williams, a Sunday school teacher and choirmaster at St. Thomas Church, as well as secretary of the Temperance League and secretary of the Boilermakers' Union, and who became the first Labour Member of Parliament for Swansea East from 1922 until 1940.

The son of a copper worker, David "Dai' Williams was born in Pentreguinea Street, St. Thomas on 8th August 1865. He left Kilvey Copperworks School at the age of eleven to work part-time with a local stone mason, before going into domestic service at Maesteg House as a pageboy. Local legend has it that he was dismissed for organising a strike of household staff in 1879 (although there are no documented records of this), and he then got a job at Middle

Bank Copper Works, where his father and brother worked. At the age of sixteen, he became the spokesman for boy employees during a wages dispute at Middle Bank, which resulted in his dismissal, along with his father and his brother, leaving William's family destitute [50]. Undeterred he became a trainee boilermaker, spending the next decades working in local shipyards. A devout churchgoer, he was a Sunday School teacher at St. Thomas Church where he was also a long-time choir member. He was also a member of the church of Wales after the Disestablishment and was also branch secretary of the Temperance League [51].

In 1898 he became Swansea's first official Labour councillor, and in 1911 was the first Labour chairman of a council committee, the Plans and Sanitary (Health) Committee, a position he held for thirty-five years. He became Swansea's first Labour Mayor in 1912, Swansea's first Labour Justice of the Peace in 1914, and the first Eastside Labour MP man to be honoured with Freedom of the Borough in 1924. He died in January 1940, and his funeral service was held at All Saints Kilvey, followed by interment in Danygraig Cemetery. David Williams Terrace in Port Tennant was named in his honour.

By the end of the 19th century the working class made up 79% of the British population, and the role of the various Non-conformist churches in working-class society was far more evident than that of the Anglican church. Whilst Mary Grenfell and her ilk were committed to supporting the local working-class community in a 'hands-on' manner, institutionally speaking the Anglican Church was more aligned with the better-off wealthy upper-middle-class industrialists, senior local politicians, senior professionals, the middle-middle class of local bank managers and store owners, and the lower-middle class of shopkeepers, teachers etc., who between them made up 19% of Britain's population.

An Anglican church such as All Saints in Foxhole was likely only able to attract a working-class congregation because the church was built by the Grenfell family on land provided by Freeman & Co. who had also built much of the local housing, and the church's congregation was made up mainly of company workers. By contrast, in the older Anglican churches of Swansea the working class were placed in unsatisfactory areas of the church in which to pray, or else often could not get a seat at all. Clear and distinct social barriers such as speech and attire made it difficult to grow the congregations of existing Anglican churches, where the revenue-generating system of pew renting [51] was in place, allowing well-to-do individuals or families to rent the pews, and in the case of St. Mary's Church, Swansea, in 1851 one individual alone owned 120 of the 953 sittings in the church, whilst many of the churches parishioners were regarded as 'applicants for sittings in vain'. Little wonder then that this practice was described as a 'potent cause of defection to the Non-conformists.' [52]

The working class was also sub-divided into social levels, those of the upper working class (skilled workers), middle-working class (unskilled workers), and lower-working class (those people living in abject poverty) which in the case of Swansea's Eastside meant 99% of the local population, but whilst there were some middle-class benefactors that supported Non-conformist growth, in sharp contrast to the Anglicans, the very existence of the Non-conformist faiths meant that in most cases the churches, chapels and halls were built and frequented by the working class themselves, and thus were proactive to their congregations changing wants and needs [53]. Nevertheless, even with an active Anglican, Non-conformist and (by the end of the 1800s) Catholic presence on the Eastside, it was likely that a considerable amount of the working-class population did not attend any church at all.

By 1875 a number of different schools were visible in Swansea, including 'British' schools, 'Board' schools, and Catholic schools. A British school, sometimes called a Lancastrian school that ran on Joseph Lancaster's system for the education of the poor, was a Non-conformist set-up that used older children to teach younger children (the monitor system), whilst Board schools were the first state-run schools set up after the 1870 Schools Act. Catholic schools were self-funded and thus received no assistance from the local government.

The list of Swansea schools at that time included three on the Eastside - Kilvey Copperworks School (Foxhole) run on Anglican Church guidelines, St. Thomas National Infants School (an

Anglican Church school opened on Morris Lane in 1863 prior to the School Act) and the British School in Port Tennant, which likely started in a church building on the original Danygraig Terrace and then later in a church building on Ysgol St.

Danygraig Board School opened in 1875 and was extended in 1885, St. Illtyd's Catholic School opened in June 1884, and in 1898 the St. Thomas Board School opened, which took in the pupils of the Copper Works School.

***

Danygraig Estate

In the 10th century, Danygraig was a very small part of the cantref of Eginoc, an area of arable land on the lower slopes of Kilvey Hill, with only a handful of people living and working there at that time. After Normans settled in Gower in c1100, it became part of the Manor of Kilvey, at which time it is believed The Forest of Kilvey stood on the combined area of what we know today as Kilvey, St. Thomas, Danygraig and Port Tennant.

In the 18th century, the area was still a rural one, although the forest had disappeared, possibly due to a massive wave that struck the shore in January 1607 that devastated the counties of Somerset, Devon, Glamorganshire and Monmouthshire, flooding towns and villages close to the shoreline, and killing upwards of 2,000 people. Maps, leases, censuses, etc. from the 19thth century show the names of Danygraig Fawr, Danygraig Ganol, Danygraig Fach and Danygraig House occur ** which suggests the land was likely split up by landowners and then leased to multiple people that lived and worked on the land.

** In many official archived documents of this period and earlier, Welsh words were often spelt phonetically or with alternative 'English' letters e.g. 'V' used instead of 'F', as there is no 'V' in the Welsh alphabet.

On 13th September 1626 'a mansion called Danygraig' (also known as 'Ty Mawr'), 'a cottage called 'Gellygrove', as well as other local lands that included 'Tir y Gwl' were bequeathed to Catherine

Thomas the wife of Walter Thomas, by her father Hopkin David Edwards Esq of Swansea, as per his will of 13th September 1626 [54]. Walter, who was Portreeve of Swansea a year earlier, and was the steward for the Earl of Worcester, became known as Walter Thomas of Swansea and Danygraig. It is not clear if he ever lived at Ty Mawr, however his fourth son William did.

William Thomas of Danygraig was married to Katherine, the sister of Bussy Mansel of Briton Ferry. Like his father, he was a staunch Royalist, and from 1643-44 he held the position of High Sheriff of Glamorgan. The Cromwellian survey of 1850 shows that 'William Thomas Esq' was also the freeholder of 'Tir Neast Vrase' and also of 'Tir William ap Evan Penry'. William Thomas was 'of Danygraig' and appeared to live at the house and had servants there.[43] According to Patricia Moore's 'Three Seventeenth-Century Travellers in Glamorgan', John Taylor, the self-styled "Water Poet" visited Walter Thomas 'the richest man in Swansea' in 1652, before he called on his son William 'in his house, Danygraig, across the Tawe.' [55]

As Royalist control wavered across the country, Bussey Mansel changed his position from Royalist to that of Parliamentarian, however, Walter and his son William Thomas remained loyal to the Crown, and both men suffered the indignity of having their estates confiscated and fines levied against them. Walter was fined £400, an amount later reduced to £313, and William was fined £786, a sum later reduced to £336 [56] and William's estates were placed in the hands of his brother-in-law Bussy. Records show William Thomas listed as an Alderman of Swansea in 1662, and in the same year, he took a lease on 'Swansea Castle and ground' from the Earl of Worcester, not the 'ruinous old building' mentioned in Oliver Cromwell's 1650 Survey of Gower, but 'an ancient decaying building called the new Castle' originally built in 1332 as a palace by Bishop Gower, [57] although some historians say it was actually built by John Mowbray. William Thomas was later pardoned and his estates returned to him, and on his death without issue, they passed to his brother-in-law Bussy Mansel.

A survey by the Duke of Beaufort in 1686 [58] shows that Bussy Mansel Esq is a freeholder of 'Tir Gwillim ap Lewis' alias

'Danygraig Fach' (occupied by Daniel Vaughan), and is also a freeholder of ' Tir Neast Vrase' . Some of the land at Danygraig in 1686 was held by William ap William, who had been preceded by William David ap David and Lyson Jenkin. The same document states that the ruins of the Chapel of St. Thomas near Salt House Point were in 'the late Borough of Bettus' [59].

In Gabriel Powell's 1764 Survey of The Lordship of Gower carried out nearly one hundred years later, the area was still referred to as 'the Borough of Bettws (that is by St. Thomas's Chapel)' [60]. Powell's survey shows the Hon. George Venables Vernon Esq (then head of the Briton Ferry Estate) as freeholder of 'Tyr Gwillim ap Evan called Danygraig Fach' occupier Roger Jones, and is also freeholder of 'Tyr Neast Vrase' alias 'Dan Y Graig Genol, also occupied by Roger Jones, whilst land previously leased to John William ap William was now in the hands of David Williams who had 'Lands at Dan y Graig'.

Between c1806 and 1826 Danygraig House is listed as the home of Thomas Lockwood [61] who came to Swansea as a partner in the copper smelting and coal mining business of Lockwood, Morris & Co., set up by Richard Lockwood, John Morris Snr. and Edward Gibbon in Morriston and who was Sheriff of Glamorgan in 1810. Originally from London, in 1806 the Lockwood family were 'of Danygraig Farm' and were 'cutting willow and ash; there, in 1807 they had 'a good wheat harvest', in 1819 whilst on a walking tour, Captain Jenkin Jones called it 'a very pretty seat' [62], and in 1823 the Lockwood's ' kept cattle.'

In 1827-28 Danygraig House was advertised as a 'Beautiful Marine Residence' 'to be sold or let by Private Treaty' and was 'the residence of a Gentleman'. Briton Ferry Estate papers show that in 1828, Colonel Nathaniel Cameron bought the lease on Danygraig from Thomas Lockwood [63]. A plan of 'Danygraig Estate (c1818), part of an 1887 collection of documents describes the land as a large gentleman's house and farm, in line with the advertisement for sale or rent in August 1827 [64].

The plan shows Danygraig House (close 1001) also known as 'Ty Mawr', and east of it is Dan-Y-Graig Fawr Farm (close 1005), described respectively as 'House and Lawns', and 'Farmhouse with Barns, offices etc.'(close 1004), situated approx. at the top of where Hoo Street and Crymlyn Street now stand.

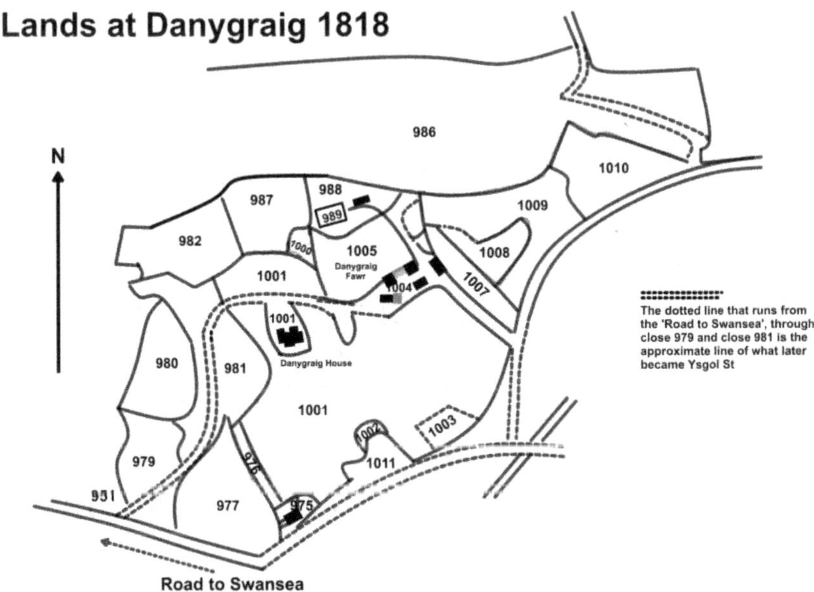

The parcels of land (closes) contained are described based on usage. Around the house is a meadow (close 1001) and a kitchen garden (close 989), and above the house turnips are grown (close 987), and there are parcels of pasture(close 987 and close 988). Above the house 'on the Graig' is woodland(close 986). There is also an area described as 'underwood' (close 981)and four 'plantations' (closes 1000, 1002, 1003 and 1010) as well as some stands of alder (close 1006). Crops to the east and west of the house include wheat, oats, barley and seeds (closes 1005, 1007 and 1009).

Briton Ferry Estate papers of 1830 show that the house at Danygraig Fawr was the home of Nathaniel Cameron, and a new lease 'for three lives' was taken out by Colonel Cameron on 1st January 1839, who was still shown as a resident at the time of the 1841 census, when there was a grant of the annuity (yearly tenancy or lease) by Nathaniel Cameron and others to Thomas Grove Esq [65]. The papers also show that a lease was signed in March 1830 on land at Danygraig Fach and Danygraig Ganol to the Grenfell family in January 1835 [66].

References to Danygraig House in 1848 include one by Samuel Lewis, who wrote: 'The seat Tan-y-Graig (sic) is pleasantly situated within its limits…', [67] and in the diary of Charles Morgan, 'Cross the ferry to get a picnic tea…tried Colonel Cameron's Lodge, no one at home. Howell the gardener comes…and invites us, as we are all gentlefolk, to Danygraig, the empty residence of the Colonel's miserably arranged house sadly out of repair and barricaded. Really prettily situayed, tis thought of for a lunatic asylum. The garden is very fertile and full of rhubarb, fruit and weeds, hot houses full of nettles.' [68]

In 1851 and 1852, the Trustees of the Committee of Visitors for the United Asylum of Cardigan, Carmarthen, Pembrokeshire and Glamorgan visited the Danygraig Estate and agreed to purchase a substantial part of it for the purpose of establishing the United Counties Lunatic Asylum.

***

The United Counties Asylum

The passing of the 1774 Madhouse Act, the 1800 Criminal Lunatics Act and the 1808 County Asylums Act showed awareness of mental health issues across the UK, and after the 1828 County Asylums Act was introduced empowering local magistrates to ensure the correct administration of admissions, discharges and deaths, and to send the annual records to the Home Office; the onus to carry out the tasks was quickly passed on to local counties. Counties could borrow money to build new facilities, subject to repayment of the loan over a 14 years period, and thus by the 1830s, the question of building new pauper asylums in South and West Wales had been a subject of discussion for some time. Pauper asylums had traditionally been privately run affairs or else supported by charitable, often church-run, institutions.

The growth in population in the urban areas meant a more coordinated approach was needed, however, the Poor Law Unions (formed after The Poor Law Amendment Act 1834) went some way to exacerbating the treatment of patients given the limited understanding of mental health issues at that time, they were often placed in the main 'population' of Union workhouses for prolonged periods, although the 1834 Amendment Act stimulated they could be held in a workhouse for 'no more than a fortnight' and that the institution required a residential medical officer, whose role included the justification of the restraint of a patient.

By the mid-1840s, the choice in front of the United Counties of Cardigan, Carmarthen, Pembrokeshire and Glamorgan was threefold; use existing private asylums based on assurances that they could handle increased numbers, utilise and adapt existing buildings, or build new asylums. The passing of both The Lunacy Act and the County Asylums Act in 1845, introduced in tandem with the aim of developing a public network of county asylums put further pressure on the United Counties to resolve the matter, and a committee for the United Counties Lunatic Asylum was formed with the aim of building a lunatic asylum for 300 inmates.

A number of locations across the four counties had been considered and dismissed for various reasons, however, in April 1847 an agreement was reached to build a new facility on the site of a farm near Loughor which was subsequently approved by the Secretary of State. Alas within a few months the decision was reversed as it was felt it was worth more as an industrial site, so the search continued, and by early 1848 the focus was on Danygraig, east of the River Tawe.

The land in question was owned by the Briton Ferry Estate and had a current partial-leaseholder at Danygraig House, Colonel Nathaniel Cameron, who had been Swansea's first Mayor from November 1835 when the Municipal Reform Bill came into operation, and for the year of 1836, although he had not lived on the site for some time. United Counties were informed of the current lease situation on part of the land, and after a number of surveys and site visits were carried out in August 1849 the Committee reported [69] that they were happy to go forward with '…the purchase from Lord Jersey of the fee of so much of the before-mentioned lands, and also of such other pieces (including the land on which the cottages and enclosures mentioned in the Surveyor's report of the 2nd

August 1849 have been or are intended to be erected or made) as specified by the Clerk of this Committee in a letter addressed to Lord Jersey's solicitors on the 8th January 1849, and as said solicitors, by letters dated 15th January 1849, and 26th March 1849, agreed on behalf of his lordship to sell to this committee' and 'for the surrender to his Lordship of the remainder of the ground to be purchased of Col. Cameron as aforesaid'.

A number of conditions were attached to the purchase that related to immediate possession, including the land currently leased by Colonel Cameron, an agreement not to carry 'coals or ore' over the land to be purchased, and that no buildings or machinery be built on the land, as well an agreement to ensure a supply of water from springs or other sources. The Committee was aware of the potential for development of the lands surrounding the Asylum plot and noted that 'since the time when the solicitors acting on the behalf of his lordship agreed by the letters before mentioned to sell to the committee the lands specified in the letter to the Clerk to the Visitors of 8th January 1849, certain houses have been commenced to be built on part of such lands under some agreement for a lease or leases granted as it is said by Lord Jersey's agent, and other portions of such lands have been marked out as gardens or other enclosures' and that 'the erection of such houses and enclosures are highly objectionable, and detract from the value of the property agreed as aforesaid to be conveyed to them.'

Aware that in the event of the various leases of adjoining land being either lapsed or foreclosed on by Lord Jersey, the contract included a condition that 'no part of the lands so to be surrendered to Lord Jersey shall be set apart for or used as a cemetery.' The land agreed upon was 106 acres of land at Danygraig which included both Danygraig House and Danygraig Fawr Farm, at a total cost of £10,250, which included the outstanding lease that remained on Nathaniel Cameron's lease at a cost of £5,250. It would, however, take nearly two years before the purchase was approved by the Secretary of State in April 1851.

Speaking at the Cardiganshire Quarter Sessions, the clerk of the Peace advised that the conveyancing of the land had not been completed, and was held up due to claims made against Colonel

Cameron, who 'had registered debts against him to the sum of £20,000', however it was hoped that things would be resolved within two weeks. This particular impasse was finally sorted out when the Jersey Estate bought back what remained of Nathaniel Cameron's lease for £5,250, and the contract was finally drawn up and signed by Lord Jersey. With the above agreement in place with United Counties, BFE nevertheless continued to lease land for both residential and industrial purposes on nearby land, including a number of leases to Thomas Miles of Danygraig Colliery to quarry stone nearby, noting that the asylum construction company may be a customer and rates should be kept at 'a fair market price'. [70]

Alas, things did not progress smoothly, and although a government loan had been approved, the mortgage document had still not been signed off by the United Counties, and on 5th April 1852, a meeting was held by the 'Committee of Magistrates for the purpose of erecting the Lunatic Asylum' confirmed the delay in procedures and that a further adjournment had been agreed, but also reconfirmed that Danygraig had been purchased from the Earl of Jersey and his leases, for the purpose of building a new asylum.

The United Counties Committee was facing a serious problem as when agreeing to purchase Danygraig they had ignored government rules that dictated that locations selected for new asylum facilities should 'not be near to any nuisances such as steam engines, noisy trades, offensive manufactories, etc'. Committee clerk, Thomas Dalton acknowledged the rules were understood but said that the committee was swayed by 'the known healthy locality', and cited a supporting surveyor's report that praised the sheltered aspect of Danygraig House and its outstanding views. Furthermore, the area's close proximity to the new rail links meant that there would also be good access to the four counties, and the collective benefits of this location aligned perfectly with the objectives of the committee.

It was at this point that Charles Tennant, son of the late George Tennant, got publicly involved in the process, writing to the local press to highlight the unsuitability of Danygraig for such a facility. In reality, the eastern winds blowing from the copper works around the banks of the Tawe had turned the slopes of Kilvey Hill into a barren wasteland, so from the perspective of the general health and wellbeing of the patients, he may have had a valid point, but Tennant's motives were for his own benefit.

The relationship between the Tennant family and the Briton Ferry Estate was a complicated one. A lawyer by profession, George Tennant had represented the Fifth Earl of Jersey, George Child-Villiers, the grandfather of the current earl, during which time he frequently visited South Wales. Realising the potential in the area, he wanted to develop his own interests and settled in Cadoxton, and opened the Tennant Canal in 1824. However, there is correspondence in the Tennant Estate Papers dating from 1812 that indicate the Earl's wife's distrust of George Tennant. Lady Jersey owned Child's Banks, and in a letter to Lancelot Dent, a wealthy British merchant who would go on to be a founder member of the Hong Kong Shanghai Bank (HSBC), she accuses George Tennant 'of acting to further his own interests' whilst represented the earl. [71] This distrust did not stop Childs Bank from continuing to extend loans to him, but the bank insisted on strict compliance with regard to the full and on-time payment of interest on all of his outstanding loans, which in turn had a knock-on effect of crippling the cash flow of all of his ongoing projects, as well as delaying payments of debts to his other lenders.

When George Tennant died on 27th February 1832, his second son Charles, and Charles' younger brother William took control of their father's businesses in South Wales. Most of their father's assets were tied to land leased from the earl including the Tennant Canal, and nearly all were financed via loans from Childs Bank. At the time of George Tennant's death, he had personal assets worth £10,000 [72] and in his will, dated 30th August 1831, after providing his two unmarried daughters with modest annuities, he left all his property to his wife, and to his second son Charles he 'devised all property vested in him by mortgage or trust'. However, his estate owed over £60,000 (over £7 million in 2022), and after William passed away only eighteen months after his father in October 1833, it was left to Charles to handle his father's business affairs in South Wales, and in order to reduce outgoings and maintain interest payments, many of the leases held by the Tennant family were released or exchanged.

The Tennant Canal had operated since May 1824, but the increase in railway development in the area had a serious negative effect on the canal's profitability, and in 1846 the Tennant family made an unsuccessful attempt to sue the Vale of Neath Railway for the loss of projected income streams. That said, the Tennant family had retained a lease on some land on Fabian's Bay, close to where the canal joined the bay at Tennant's port, and Charles Tennant leased this land to Charles Lambert, who was building a copper works at 'Port Tennant', something that Lord Jersey had objected to.

The motive behind Charles Tennant's cries of protest was not for the health and wellbeing of those that would live at the asylum, but rather it was directly linked to the protection of his agreement with Charles Lambert. Nevertheless, his complaints in the local press had the desired effect, and in June 1852 the United Counties Committee sent a Mr Grainger, a medical inspector employed by the Board of Health, to inspect the location. Tasked with evaluating not only the copper smoke pollution but also whether 'any noxious miasmata' that emanated from the Crymlyn Bog would likely prove detrimental to the health of the inpatients of the proposed asylum.

During his inspection visit, it was noted that Lambert's Copperworks had now become operational and that copper smoke was in evidence. After completing his visit, Mr Grainger's extensive report [73] which included interviews with a number of local residents as well as Charles Tennant's chief engineer William Kirkhouse, concluded that the site was not suitable for purpose 'on sanitary principles', and within days of the inspection, a press report of 7th August said that 'after minute investigation' the Secretary of State has decided that 'Danygraig is evidently unsuited for the erection of a public Lunatic Asylum'. On 30th October 1852, a press notification by the Visitors (Committee Members) of the United Counties' Lunatic Asylum [74] officially confirmed the abandonment of the plan to purchase land at Danygraig.

The suggestion of Mr Dalton the Committee clerk to cancel the agreement with both sides bearing their own costs was swiftly declined by the legal representatives of the Earl of Jersey as well as those of Colonel Cameron, who expected payment of £1000 to cover expenses and loss brought about by the delay. With the real probability of legal action to follow, the Home Secretary was consulted, after which all costs were met by the Committee and the agreement was cancelled, with Lord Jersey subsequently paid £1094 10s 9d.

***

Burial in Swansea

As the pace of the Industrial Revolution increased after the beginning of the 19th century, so did the explosion of growth in the urban population, especially in the industrial areas where people were drawn to the employment opportunities developing around them. With this came a magnification of the problems of adequate community health and sanitation, as well as the requirement for additional burial grounds. There were ten graveyards in Swansea, all associated with churches and chapels, all limited in size, and by the early 1830s, nearly all were full, including the burial ground of Swansea's main church St. Mary's, and the burial ground at St John's Church in High Street was being used to assist. Given that water supplies were from local springs and wells, the overflowing of sewerage, as well as drainage from graveyards, was a considerable health problem.

By the mid-1840s the squalid and unsanitary conditions faced by Londoners due to overflowing burial grounds were being studied by two sanitary reformers, Edwin Chadwick, who was secretary of the Poor Law Commission, and Dr George Alfred Walker. Their work caught the eye of the UK government, and a Select Committee was formed to review the findings of both men. Dr Walker reasoned that gases given off by human putrefaction could be deadly to anybody who inhaled them (the pythogenic theory), and that legislative action was urgently required as burial was a key part of the wider issue of urban sanitation; '…the filth and corruption of the urban burial yards generated poison and disease'. [75] The British government finally began to enact changes to the status quo after the 1848 Cholera epidemic further compounded the burial problem, and amended the Nuisances Removal and Diseases Prevention Act in 1849.

Earlier the same year a Swansea church had refused to bury a Nonconformist in its churchyard, and in so doing raised an issue that directly affected a large number of local residents that prompted a call for a public meeting on the subject of establishing a cemetery to accommodate all faiths. An invitation-only meeting had been held in the last week of April 1849, where some attendees questioned why the new cemetery should be a 'general one' rather than have a number of separate sections within the new cemetery designated to the various faiths. Nevertheless, on 3rd May the proposed public meeting was held at the Swansea Town Hall to discuss the establishment of a General Cemetery 'without distinction of religious opinion'. Such was the importance of the meeting that nearly all religious denominations had representatives in attendance. [76]

The majority of those attending the open meeting agreed that 'a general cemetery' was the way forward, including both Pascoe St. Leger Grenfell and the Vicar of Swansea The Rev. E. B. Squire, and it was left to a Baptist Minister Reverend D. Evans to explain that 'no exclusion had been intended' during the previous meeting. He assured everyone present that anyone could be buried in a Nonconformist cemetery 'with that view no part of the ground was to be allowed to be set apart by consecration', at which point one gentleman wryly observed: 'That would exclude Churchmen, Jews, and Catholics.' Unperturbed by the ensuing laughter, Mr Evans confirmed that in addition, members of the clergy might also be buried there.

These comments were not enough to satisfy the Chairman of the meeting (M. Moggeridge Esq) who felt that Rev. Evans' comments 'was sufficient proof that the Non-conformist cemetery was not open to Churchmen.', a view endorsed by a Catholic priest present, The Rev. C. Kavanagh, who said that he too was of the opinion that the Non-conformist position was one of exclusivity rather than one of inclusivity being accepted by everyone else, or else if it was open to all 'it was only to those who would submit to exclusive regulations about consecration'. The following editorial in "The Principality', [77] was published on 11th May and supported the gist of the public meeting of the 3rd May:

‘**The Non-conformist Cemetery at Swansea** - The recent refusal to bury a Dissenter at Swansea has, as our readers are aware, created a good deal of excitement in that town. The consequence has been that two cemeteries have been proposed—one to be open to all, and another that will exclude all who —and they are a large and influential class —attach a value to consecrated earth. This latter is the cemetery the Non-conformists propose to support. That they have a perfect right thus to act we readily admit, but we more than question the propriety of such a step. Why not build a cemetery which may admit the Churchman as well as the Dissenter? Death is our common lot, where then the impropriety of a common grave? Let a part be consecrated for the Churchman. The Dissenter should be as ready to respect his conscience as he is to require that the Churchman should respect his own.

In most cemeteries, the plan we recommend has been found to work well, and so it would at Swansea would the Dissenter bear with his weak brother, who on this point may not be so enlightened as himself. There is something very ungraceful at the very least in virtually inscribing on our burial grounds --"No Churchman buried here!” in making them the arena of religious controversy - in mingling with the solemn feelings that should prevail there the bitter rivalries of which life is too often and too necessarily the scene. It is no reply that consecration is nothing but a popish relic to the Churchman it is more than that—and for men who ask that conscience should be respected that is enough. It surely becomes the advocates of toleration to avoid anything that savours in the least of intolerance. We cannot blame Churchmen for refusing to inter Dissenters if we pursue a similar course of conduct of ourselves. A spirit of liberality is now abroad; let us not show that that spirit of which we so proudly boast—which we so fondly nursed - is departing from our midst.’

That year the government passed the Public Health Act, the first piece of legislation that attempted to deal with issues of public health across the country. The act meant that towns with a death rate of 23 per 1000 were obligated to set up a Local Board of Health, or alternatively if 10% of the town’s population petitioned for the setting up of a Board. It was compulsory for municipal corporations, but advisory in other towns, and following the Act,

Swansea Corporation held a public enquiry to determine the current state of the town's water supplies, drainage, sewerage and sanitary conditions.

Led by Mr George Thomas Clark, Superintendent Inspector of the General Board of Health, his subsequent report [78] laid bare the dire state of Swansea's infras tructure. Clark pointed out that the town's burial grounds were full, and made clear that the intolerable living and unsanitary conditions that many of Swansea's residents had to deal with on a daily basis would inevitably lead to more deaths. The lack of the most basic services coupled with the crowded living quarters built around narrow streets and courts in some areas of the town meant that illness was inevitable.

The slum areas in the centre of the town he said, had 'dirty, ill-drained streets, and close habitation of the people', and an 'entire absence of water rendering cleanliness, comfort and (good) health 'unattainable'. Clark noted that housing in the north of the town (meaning the Greenhill area) was surrounded by open ditches, was without drainage or a water supply, and had yards filled with garbage, and in some over-crowded houses, people lived in the same rooms together with pigs and sometimes donkeys. Contaminated water was used to drink and bathe in, and the risk of epidemic and contagious diseases such as typhoid and diarrhoea was ever-present.

An outbreak of cholera occurred in the 1830s and again in the Greenhill area in 1849 when an epidemic took the lives of more than 150 people. The toxic smoke from Swansea's growing copper industry belched into the air daily and caused, or at the very least intensified, a range of bronchial conditions and diseases such as consumption and fever, whilst at the same time harming animals in the area and rendering the once-healthy environment of Kilvey Hill to a barren wasteland. However, in 1854, a report to the Board of Health from Swansea doctor Thomas Williams [79] asserted the exact opposite; he argued that the smoke's antiseptic qualities actually kept diseases at bay:

'The direct chemical and pathological effects of the copper smoke upon the human body must be carefully separated from those indirect consequences, which flow from its destructive and corrosive operation upon the surface vegetation of land. In this way, beyond doubt, unless the entire tendency of modern science be utterly false, a thousand causes of disease are rendered inoperative. If it were possible to maintain a permanent infusion of copper smoke in the atmosphere of a given locality, the author records his deliberate belief that the population of such locality would be permanently exempt from those epidemic diseases, whose causative germs, whatever they may be in essence, whose causative germs, whatever they may be in essence, travel and multiply from place to place in the atmosphere.'

George Clark's scathing report resulted in a further public enquiry leading to the setting up of the Swansea Local Board of Health in 1850. Under the conditions of the Act, the local Board of Health was responsible for employing a dedicated Health Board staff that included an Officer of Health (who was required to be a qualified medical doctor) plus supporting administrative staff including a clerk, a treasurer, a surveyor, and it was 'compulsory' to appoint an 'Inspector of Nuisances'. In practice, this role was that of the sanitary inspector to investigate complaints and act against public health 'nuisances' such as refuse, sewage, smoke dust, smells, industrial emissions, polluted water, noise etc.

Dr W.H. Michael was appointed as Swansea's first Medical Officer and was paid £150 per annum, however, due to objections from ratepayers, he resigned after only one year, and the role was not filled again until 1865 when Dr Ebenezer Davies was appointed. For all intents and purposes, the local Board of Health was the Swansea Corporation, however, it was legally distinct from it. The local Board of Health had full responsibility for the town's sewers, its street cleaning, its public 'necessities' (lavatories) including providing them if they were not available, as well as for the paving of public streets. Previously the Corporation's paving commissioners were responsible for keeping certain streets in the town clean mostly by contracted pauper labour. It could also supply water if there was no private supplier available, and in 1852 the Swansea Local Board of Health purchased the Swansea Waterworks Company. The Board was allowed to set up houses for the reception of the dead prior to internment, and could apply to the

General Board to close existing burial grounds if deemed necessary, and also allocate and purchase land for new burial grounds. In addition to the above, the local Board could also regulate and if necessary close down slaughterhouses, as well as set up new facilities that met the required standards.

Up until this time the Anglican Church had controlled the whole process of handling 'death' via local parish churchyards. The Church controlled services and burials and retained the fees that they themselves deemed were required for burial. However, as per George Clark's report, the town's burial grounds were full, and a solution was needed urgently in the shape of a town burial ground. In 1852 the government passed the Metropolitan Burial Act, followed by a series of Acts and Amendments over the following years that, when consolidated in 1857, became known as The Burial Acts, which acted as the backbone of the national system for public cemeteries. The requirement for a town burial ground was not exclusive to Swansea, and new cemeteries opened nationwide, managed by Burial Boards (introduced in 1854).

It was now the Burial Boards, and not the Anglican Church, that was responsible for the interment of the dead, often fixing expenses at the Poor Rate, a local tax levied by a parish to finance the relief or support of the poor. Cemeteries were laid out with consecrated ground for Anglican use, and un-consecrated ground for the use of Non-conformists, and the Burial Boards dealt with the sale of grave plots where necessary and in 1856 the Swansea Burial Board was set up. In short, the new system established the cemetery as the successor to the parish churchyard. Given the increase in Dissenter churches across the UK, the new cemeteries welcomed all denominations and church services. This greatly weakened the Anglican Church, as not only did it loosen its grip on the public's interpretation of death and its perception of how it should be handled, it had a major and lasting effect on how the Anglican Church would henceforth be funded.

The New Swansea Cemetery

In 1847 the Joint Counties Asylum Committee travelled to the Eastside of Swansea with the aim of building a lunatic asylum to serve Cardigan, Pembrokeshire and Glamorgan and negotiated to buy 106 acres of land at Danygraig, including Danygraig House and Danygraig Fawr Farm, however, the deal fell through, and when Lord Jersey was approached by the Burial Board who wanted to utilise a large section of the land for the new Swansea Cemetery, an agreement was made.

The cemetery grounds opened in late 1856 and were laid out in 1857, at a cost of £7,000, whilst a further £3,232 was spent on building two chapels and a house for the keeper. In 1881 another £3,000 was spent enlarging the plot to 16 acres, and with the addition of a small extension paid for by the Burial Board to what was formerly a private road to Danygraig House, a new public road was constructed leading to the cemetery gates known as Cemetery Road, the name changing some years later to Ysgol Street.

The first burial to take place at Danygraig Cemetery [80] on 20th October 1856, was that of Father Charles Kavanagh.

Father Charles Kavanagh came to Swansea in c1838, at which time the only meeting place for the Catholic community was a rundown old chapel on Nelson Terrace in the centre of the town, but by 1847 he had built the Church of St David and an associated school in the Rutland Street area in 1851. St. David's was later enlarged, and a new presbytery was constructed in 1864. As the majority of his parishioners lived in the Greenhill area above High St known as 'Little Ireland', it became essential to build a school and a church there. St. Patrick's School was built in Greenhill in c1852 and took the place of a Sunday School that Father Kavanagh held on the corner of Brook St and Well St. Father Kavanagh had applied for the lease of land in the area on which to build a church, and in 1866 St Joseph's Church opened there at a cost of £10,000.

Swansea felt the effects of Britain's second cholera epidemic in 1849, and Greenhill was especially susceptible, and in a letter sent by Father Lewis to Canon Wilson [81] he said of Father Kavanagh 'he and the doctor were the only ones to look after the sick. He washed them, combed their hair, made their beds, and put them in their coffins. The relatives and all that had to do with them were panic-stricken.' Within a six-week period he had helped bury 170 victims, often acting as an interpreter to the Gaelic-speaking family members. In December that year, he was presented with a purse of fifty sovereigns by Mayor Christopher Jones in recognition of his selflessness during that period. Doctor Bird commented, "None could have surpassed his exertions, for the simple reason, that none have the physical powers to perform them." [82]

Reverend Kavanagh passed away in October 1856 at the age of 47 yrs. old, and his funeral was nothing like Swansea had seen before, and was attended by Catholics and Protestants alike. [83]

Funeral of the Reverend Charles Kavanagh

'The funeral of the late Rev. Charles Kavanagh, whose death we record in the supplement, took place on Tuesday and it may truly be said that in the respect paid to his memory by all classes—in the thousands of every denomination who followed him to his last resting place— a tribute was paid to him in death that attested the power which the virtues of the man exercised while living. The aspect of the whole scene - the tears that were shed to his memory by those who recognised in him the pastor, guide, and friend of many years standing—and the respectful silence of the thousands who thronged the funeral procession- was a homage to departed worth far more eloquent— more noble-more touching and truthful-than any that rank or fortune could bestow, and which worldly riches in vain would essay to purchase….on the conclusion of the service, the funeral cortege was formed, and proceeded towards the New Cemetery in the following Order of Procession:

Sixteen Bearers in cloaks and hatbands. Tradesmen and other Inhabitants of Swansea—four abreast. Members of the Deceased's Congregation - four abreast.

Undertaker Carriage containing the Mayor of Swansea, J.T. Jenkin, Esq., W. H. Michael, Esq and R. Richards, Esq.

The Hearse Mourning Coach, containing the Right Rev. the Catholic Bishop of the Diocese (Dr. Brown), the Rev. Matthew Kavanagh, Professor Kavanagh, the Rev. P. Malloy, and the Very Rev. Canon Illingworth.

Mourning Coach, containing the Rev. Fathers Marshall, Segnini, Murphy, Nearey Lewis, and Hopkins. Private Carriage, containing the Rev. Father Havard, W. Jones, Esq. (the Hall, Pyle), and Miss Nichol. Carriage containing Messrs. W. Gregor, T. Boundy, and others Carriage containing Messrs. J. Oakshot, G. T. Stroud, G. Harry, &c.

This portion of the line was completed by several carriages containing members of the congregation of St. David's and other Catholic congregations in the vicinity, the whole numbering sixteen carriages. The cortege was closed by the children of the Catholic School, and an immense body of the general public, walking four abreast and preserving the most perfect order, an object much aided by the services of several gentlemen bearing wands, who acted as conductors and regulators of the procession.

The line of route to the Cemetery, it is scarcely necessary to inform our readers, lay over a road which presented peculiar facilities for seeing this immense procession to advantage-lying as it did, along the winding road which leads from the Bridge over the Lock along the skirts of Fabian's Bay to Danygraig. Along the whole route, on every elevated spot, groups were collected to witness the procession. It would be difficult to analyse the feelings with which a beholder would look upon the whole scene—the homage which a whole community paid to the memory of a good and kind man—and its suggestions blended with those called up by the fact that it was not only the first burial in a spot where thousands of the present generation will find their final resting-place but in the completion of which the deceased took the most lively interest.'

Swansea Cemetery was completed in early 1857 however, due to a disagreement over travelling expenses expected by the Vicar of Swansea the Reverend Edward Bernard Squire for carrying out funeral services, the official Anglican consecration was held up, and thus the official opening of the new town cemetery was delayed.

The Vicar had the strong support of Connop Thirlwall, the Bishop of St. David's, who informed the local Burial Board that he refused to consecrate the cemetery, arguing that it would be unfair that Reverend Squire should be expected to travel from his vicarage at White Styles at the top end of Walter road near Mirador Crescent 'all the way to Danygraig', often numerous times a day and irrespective of weather conditions, with a return distance of four and a half miles, 'and without conveyance other than at his own cost'. [84]

Lewis Llewellyn Dillwyn, M.P. for Swansea intervened on the side of Swansea Burial Board and put the blame on the holdup fully on the shoulders of The Bishop of St. David's, and after consulting with the Home Secretary the matter was heard in the House of Commons. [85] The views of Mr Dillwyn were reported in The Cardiff and Merthyr Guardian of 7th February 1857. [86]

'The grounds on which his Lordship refuses to either consecrate or licence for burial are two- first, that the cemetery is at such a great distance from the residence of the vicar that it is absolutely necessary that a conveyance should be provided to carry him to and fro on occasions of funerals; and secondly, that proper respect has not been paid to him by the Board, inasmuch as they allowed a letter to remain unanswered for fifteen months, in which the conveyance for the clergyman was made a 'sille qua non' (an essential) by his Lordship for the consecration of that ground set apart for the church. The Board contends that the conveyance for a clergyman is not necessary, and even were it so, they cannot legally provide the same, inasmuch as a rate would have to be made upon the whole parish for such a purpose, the funds derivable from the cemetery not being sufficient.

With respect to the second point, the Board contends that no disrespect whatever has been shown by his Lordship - that he was consulted upon every step taken, but that when his Lordship alluded to a conveyance being provided for a clergyman some fifteen months ago, the site for the cemetery had not been fixed, and therefore they were unable to reply definitely upon that point. In the meantime the Board of Guardians have passed a resolution; paupers shall be buried in the ground allotted to the church, but by whom the ceremony of burial will be performed we know not, as no clergyman of the Establishment can, of course, bury in the ground not consecrated.'

Mr Dillwyn further stated that there were a number of 'leading articles' in the London daily papers who had also picked up on the Bishop's continued refusal to consecrate the burial ground, noting that the Burial Board had the full backing of Swansea residents. The Bishop of St. David's was appalled that the issue get so much elevated attention and responded in The Times on 27th July and reported on the Cardiff and Merthyr Guardian on August 8th [87] arguing that his actions had been grossly misrepresented and that Mr Dillwyn had portrayed him as 'an obstinate, wrong-headed person', arguing that he was acting only to protect the Vicar of Swansea from 'grievous hardship and injustice…without remedy or compensation.'

The Bishop acknowledged that the Burial Board had engaged legal counsel on this matter who had informed them that from a legal perspective they could neither provide a conveyance nor could they pay for the expense of conveying the Vicar of Swansea in addition to his current fees, but counsel had suggested the problem could be solved if the Burial Board revised the existing level of fees to an acceptable level to both parties, rather than focus on new charges, and this had been deemed acceptable and the matter would have been dealt with some time ago '…had not happened that many of the leading members of the Swansea town-council have been for several months detained in London on business of the utmost importance to the borough in connexion with their new docks.'

The Bishop goes on to say that '…on the 10th of this month, as I learn from a Swansea newspaper, at the monthly meeting of the town council, this committee presented its report, in which it recommends 'That the sum of £100 per annum should be given to the vicar in lieu of his fees.' In answer to a question put by a member of the board, the mayor said that the vicar had agreed to accept this sum if it met with the approval of the bishop. 'That approval, as I have stated, I virtually gave on the 4th of April.'

However, Lewis Llewellyn Dillwyn did not accept the Bishop's response at face value and queried the Bishop's assertion that an agreement had been made some months earlier, as if it had then there was no reason for the Bishop not to take immediate steps to Consecrate the ground, as the inhabitants of Swansea have been obliged to bury their relatives and friends in other districts and parishes to their own or have to enlist the services of Dissenting ministers to perform the last rites of religion over the departed.

Following a conciliatory letter from the Bishop to the Burial Board in September 1857, it was expected that the new cemetery would finally be consecrated in October and officially opened, however further holdups ensued culminating in a letter from the Vicar of Swansea who complained that 'the board had provided no service-books or surplices at the cemetery, and suggested that 'difficulties' were being 'purposely thrown in the way by contentious men', to which the Burial Board responded that ' while repudiating the latter assertion, (they) consented to provide the articles required as an act of grace, and not of right'.

After fourteen months of wrangling, the Burial Board finally agreed on transportation costs for the Vicar of Swansea, and the new Swansea Cemetery was finally consecrated on 7th January 1858 [88] after which the Bishop of St. David's, the Vicar of Swansea and Dissenting ministers dined with the Mayor and corporation at the Guildhall. The Burial Board duly issued a 'Table of Vicar's Fees & Charges', however in November 1860, the Burial Board decided to lower prices 'in view of private competition.' [89]

The Eastside, an area that had for so long been 'on the outside looking in' at Swansea from the other side of the river, was now the final resting place for many of the town's residents, as funeral processions, be they on foot or by horse-drawn coach, made numerous trips per day from homes across Swansea, over the North Dock Lock and New Cut bridges and along the edge of Fabian's Bay towards Cemetery Road and Swansea Cemetery.

Swansea Cemetery, or Danygraig Cemetery as it later became known, quickly became a place where Swansea families could pay their respects to their late relatives, especially during religious festivals, as is evident in the following excerpt from a Palm Sunday report in The Cambrian 23rd March 1894 [90]:

Palm Sunday in Swansea and District: Is the Custom Being Overdone?

'Palm Sunday this year was celebrated in Swansea and district quite as large as previous years...There was a splendid array of flowers, ferns, plants, etc. in the market on Saturday, for which there was a very good demand, and fairly good prices prevailed. The shop of Mr Tom Barron, the Royal Florist, in Oxford Street, attracted considerable attention. The window was filled with a beautiful selection of wreaths, crosses, choice-cut flowers, and ferns.

It is surprising to what an extent the poorer people indulge in the custom of decorating the graves of their dead relatives. Many think they overstep the bounds of good sense and propriety, and that were they to look more after themselves than those "gone on before" them, and whom they can do no possible earthly good, the results would redound to their own credit and benefit and to the credit and benefit of the community in which they live. We know of numerous instances where people have gone without their Sunday dinner and many other things in order to "make a show," and to out-do their neighbours.

There can be no denying the fact that many people decorate graves more for show than anything else. Such conduct cannot be too strongly deprecated, and it very largely contends that Palm Sunday should not be kept up if only to put an end to such sacrilegious conduct…The Swansea Cemetery was visited by thousands of people, the main road between Swansea and Danygraig being alive with pedestrians throughout the day, especially in the afternoon. Fairly good order prevailed, viewed in the light of previous occasions, but it was nevertheless, not the order we expect on the Sabbath, and from people who devote an afternoon avowedly with the object of visiting the graves of their relatives and friends and mourning over their deaths.'

Whilst the article acknowledges the celebration of Palm Sunday, at the same time it questions its level of importance, and one cannot fail to notice the clear social distinction made between 'poorer people' and the "many (people who) think they overstep the bounds of good sense and propriety".

That said, thirteen years later the enthusiasm of the public had not diminished, as described in a Cambrian newspaper of March 1907 [91]:

Palm Sunday Observances - Scenes at Cemeteries - Forty Thousand Visit Danygraig

'Sunday was the festival of flowers. The graveyards of Swansea and district, from early dawn till late at eve, were invaded by flower-bearing crowds, all bent on observance of the usual customs of Flower Sunday, and by visitors inspecting the florally decorated graves. …It was about half-past six in the morning when the gates of Danygraig Cemetery were opened, and there were a few people waiting even then. The stream soon commenced to flow rapidly, and from eight o'clock onwards, the visitors formed a constant and close procession. At nearly every grave there was at least one time or another a little group, planting potted blooms, big carving knives doing the job of trowels.

There have been up to date 30,622 burials at this ground, and the twenty-three acres contain something like ten thousand graves, practically every one of which contained some floral tribute, one dense mass of blooms, decked dozens of graves. It is estimated that about 40,000 visitors entered Danygraig Cemetery through the day. The order was excellent.'

On April 14th 1896, the Earl of Jersey, accompanied by his son Lord Villiers, came to the Eastside to open a new thoroughfare built on land he had gifted to Swansea Corporation a few years earlier. [92] The new road would be an important part of the town's main funeral procession route to Danygraig Cemetery, taking the place of Cemetery Road (renamed Ysgol St) which had been the final stretch of the route for 49 years.

At 12.30 pm, led by two mounted policemen and accompanied by a large group of dignitaries that included the Mayor and Mayoress Mr & Mrs Aeron Thomas and the Chairman of Swansea Harbour

Trust Mr Griffith Thomas, the Earl and his son were driven in 'carriages and brakes' from Swansea Townhall in Ferryside towards the North Dock Bridge. Unfortunately, the bridge was open and the delay caused the Earl to arrive later than planned for the opening ceremony. After the dignitaries had alighted their carriages opposite St. Illtyd's School, the Mayor first addressed the huge crowd assembled before inviting the Earl to officially name the road, which was 'dedicated to public service forever.'

The tree-lined road, initially to be called Jersey Road in honour of the Earl, was officially named Danygraig Road. After the Earl made a short speech, the Mayor reciprocated and took the time to also thank the Earl for the land gifted nearby to the road which the Corporation had since developed as Jersey Park. Alderman W. Lewis seconded the mayor's sentiments, whilst mentioning that he was the son of the oldest tenant in his lordships district. The Chairman of the Streets Committee Colonel W. Pike suggested the Earl also erect a few seats along the northern side of the new road, something supported by Alderman Tutton. After Sir John Llewelyn proposed a vote of thanks to the Mayor for his efforts, his proposal was duly seconded, and at the invitation of the mayor 'refreshments were afterwards partaken of in the schoolroom.'

Since the cemetery's official consecration in January 1858, funeral processions from all parts of Swansea became a part of daily life on the Eastside, passing through St. Thomas and Danygraig on a regular basis, with Danygraig Road taking the place of Ysgol St in 1896, as an official part of the funeral procession route.

Additional municipal cemeteries were opened in Mumbles (1883), Cwmgelli (1896) and Morriston (1915). The last new grave was opened at Danygraig in July 1956, before a decision was made shortly after that the opening of new burial plots would cease at the cemetery (although there have been some new plots opened in 2022).

Bibliography

[1] T. S. &. P. T. D. H. Website, "Bridges over the North Dock and New Cut," [Online]. Available: http://www.swanseadocks.co.uk/docksnewsite/bridges.html.

[2] W. Jones, History of the Port of Swansea, Royal Institute of South Wales, 1922, p. 190.

[3] W. Jones, History of the Port of Swansea, Swansea: Royal Institute of South Wales, 1922, p. 189.

[4] A. Smith, The Wealth of Nations, Vols. Book 5, Chapter 1, Part 3, p. 5.

[5] W. Jones, History of the Port of Swansea, Royal Institute of South Wales, 1920, p. 184.

[6] W. Jones, History of the Port of Swansea, Royal Institute of South Wales, 1922, p. 191.

[7] W. H. Jones, History of the Port of Swansea, Royal Institute of South Wales, 1922, p. 203.

[8] W. Jones, History of the Port of Swansea, Royal Institute of South Wales, 1922, pp. 213-224.

[9] W. Jones, History of the Port of Swansea, Royal Institute of South Wales, 1922, pp. 230-233.

[10] T. Cambrian, "The Proposed New Tramline from Swansea to Port Tennant," *The Cambrian,* p. 8, 13 February 1891.

[11] T. Cambrian, "Cable Connection With St. Thomas," *The Cambrian,* p. 2, 13 May 1904.

[12] T. Cambrian, "Wooden Paving for St. Thomas," *The Cambrian,* p. 5, 23 September 1904.

[13] T. Cambrian, "St. Thomas Tramways," *The Cambrian,* p. 7, 31 March 1905.

[14] T. Cambrian, "Trial Run of St. Thomas Trams," *The Cambrian,* p. 5, 4 August 1905.

[15] T. Cambrian, "Port Tennant Trams Running," *The Cambrian,* p. 3, 25 August 1905.

[16] E. Express, "Lord Jersey's Complaint," *Evening Express,* no. 4, 8 September 1905.

[17] D. H. Beynon, Swansea's Street Trams, Swansea Maritime and Industrial Museum, 1994, pp. 52-58.

[18] T. E. Papers, “Lease for 99 years; George Tennant esq., to (left blank); land at Port Tennant (formerly called Salthouse Point) for building 20 cottages for workmen; also 3 letters from J. Bedford concerning formation of company of Neath gentlemen for above building sch,” West Glamorgan Archive Service, 17 November 1825. [Online]. Available: https://archiveshub.jisc.ac.uk/data/gb216-d/dt/d/dt531/1-6.

[19] 1. Census, 1841. [Online].

[20] 1. Census, 1851. [Online].

[21] 1. Census, 1861. [Online].

[22] 1. Census, 1871. [Online].

[23] 1. Census, 1881. [Online].

[24] 1. Census, 1891. [Online].

[25] E. C. Williams, The Non-conformist Movement in Industrial Swansea, 1780-1914 thesis, Swansea University. http://cronfa.swan.ac.uk/Record/cronfa42655, 1993, p. 44.

[26] H. B. L. A. Robert Ackland, Saints Alive - The History of All Saints Church Kilvey, 1995, p. 13.

[27] G. L. I. A. Society, “Notes and News - October 2008,” [Online]. Available: http://www.glias.org.uk/news/238news.html. [Accessed 2 July 2022].

[28] T. Cambrian, “St. Thomas Parish and Church Work in the East of Swansea,” *The Cambrian,* p. 3, 3 November 1893.

[29] T. E. Papers, “Description of 'Swansea. Plan of lands at Port Tennant included in the canal lease dated 31 Dec. 1817 from the Earl of Jersey to George Tennant Esq., also of the piece of ground and dock at salthouse point included in the lease dated 1 Mar. 1837 from the,” 1817. [Online]. Available: https://archiveshub.jisc.ac.uk/data/gb216-d/dt/d/dt2319/1-4. [Accessed 2 July 2022].

[30] T. E. Papers, “'Correspondence between Charles Lambert and Charles Tennant concerning erection of copper smelting works at Port Tennant; clauses for lease; appointment of

Lambert's son as vice-consul in Chile to protect family's mining interests., 1852-18," 1852-1855. [Online]. Available: https://archiveshub.jisc.ac.uk/data/gb216-d/dt/d/dt1738. [Accessed 2 July 2022].

[31] E. Rowse, In and Around Swansea, 1896, p. 38.

[32] T. Cambrian, "The end of Morris Lane School," *South Wales Evening Post,* 1945.

[33] T. Cambrian, "St. Thomas's Iron Church," *The Cambrian,* p. 8, 21 April 1876.

[34] T. Cambrian, "St. Thomas's New Church," *The Cambrian,* p. 8, 28 April 1876.

[35] T. Cambrian, "St. Thomas's Iron Church," *The Cambrian,* p. 8, 5 May 1876.

[36] T. Cambrian, "New Church for Port Tennant," *The Cambrian,* p. 5, 15 February 1907.

[37] E. C. Williams, The Non-conformist movement in industrial Swansea, 1780-1914.. thesis, Swansea University., Swansea University, 1993, p. 166.

[38] Tennant Estate Papers, "Lease for 99 years; Margaret Elizabeth Tennant of Cadoxton, widow, to the trustees of the Welsh Calvinistic Methodist Society; Chapel or meeting-house at Port Tennant, in the parish of Llansamlet. Endorsed: 28 Mar. 1851; Conveyance (Bargain and Sale); Tru," [Online]. Available: https://archiveshub.jisc.ac.uk/search/archives/c5b71faf-cc50-3f0c-ad50-6d011c2df0ed?component=e2c0b1dd-2ae5-3871-8e5a-8166c785635f&terms=Port%20Tennant. [Accessed 3 July 2022].

[39] G. Hicks, "Glamorgan Chapel Database Project," 2005. [Online]. Available: https://www.genuki.org.uk/big/wal/GLA/Swansea/Chapels. [Accessed 3 July 2022].

[40] N. L. Thomas, The Story of Swansea's Districts and Villages, The Guardian Press, 1964, p. 90.

[41] E. C. Williams, The Non-conformist movement in industrial Swansea, 1780-1914.. thesis, Swansea University.

http://cronfa.swan.ac.uk/Record/cronfa42655, Swansea: Swansea University, 1993, p. 101.

[42] C. C. Church, Centenary of Canaan Congregational Church, Foxhole, Swansea 1940, 1940, p. 16.

[43] E. C. Williams, The Non-conformist movement in industrial Swansea, 1780-1914.. thesis, Swansea University. http://cronfa.swan.ac.uk/Record/cronfa42655, Swansea University, 1993, p. 68.

[44] E. C. Williams, The Non-conformist movement in industrial Swansea, 1780-1914.. thesis, Swansea University. http://cronfa.swan.ac.uk/Record/cronfa42655, Swansea University, 1993, p. 91.

[45] N. Thomas, The Story of Swansea's Districts and Villages, Vols. 1-3, The Guardian Press, 1964, pp. 35-36.

[46] N. Thomas, The Story of Swansea's Districts and Villages, Vols. 1-3, The Guardian Press, 1964, pp. 70-71.

[47] E. C. Williams, The Non-conformist movement in industrial Swansea, 1780-1914.. thesis, Swansea University., Swansea University, 1993, p. 89.

[48] N. Thomas, The Story of Swansea's Districts and Villages, Vols. 1-3, The Guardian Press, 1964, p. 61.

[49] N. Thomas, The Story of Swansea's Districts and Villages, The Guardian Press, 1964, pp. 61-62.

[50] I. Rees, "A Dedicated Couple: David and Elizabeth Williams," *The Swansea History Journal No. 23,* pp. 52-59, 2016.

[51] J. C. Bennett, The English Anglian practice of pew renting, 1800-1960. University of Birmingham. Ph.D.http://etheses.bham.ac.uk/id/eprint/2864, University of Birmingham, 2011.

[52] E. C. Williams, The Non-conformist movement in industrial Swansea, 1780-1914.. thesis, Swansea University. http://cronfa.swan.ac.uk/Record/cronfa42655, Swansea University, 1993, pp. 223-224.

[53] E. C. Williams, The Non-conformist movement in industrial Swansea, 1780-1914.. thesis, Swansea University. http://cronfa.swan.ac.uk/Record/cronfa42655, Swansea University, 1993, pp. 225-226.

[54] E. E. Papers., "Will of Hopkin David Edwards of Swansea, esq., devising and bequeathing to his eldest daughter, Catherine, wife of Walter Thomas, a mansion called Danygraig... GB 216 D/D RE 1/178," 13 September 1626. [Online]. Available: [https://archiveshub.jisc.ac.uk/data/gb216-d/dre/d/dre1/178]. [Accessed 21 July 2022].

[55] P. Moore, "Three Seventeenth-Century Travellers in Glamorgan," *The Glamorgan Historian,* pp. pp. 13–36, at pp. 22–23., 1971.

[56] W. Thomas, The History of Swansea, Gomer, 1990, pp. 206-207.

[57] W. Thomas, The History of Swansea From Rover Settlement to the Restoration, Gomer Press, 1650, p. 200.

[58] G. G. F. Charles Baker, Surveys of Gower and Kilvey and of Several Mesne Manors within That Seigniory / Edited for the Cambrian Archaeological Association, Cambrian Archaeological Association , 1861.

[59] G. G. F. Charles Baker, "Surveys of Gower and Kilvey and of several mesne manors within that seignory," *Archaeologia Cambrensis. Supplement,* 1870.

[60] e. B. M. Gabriel Powell, Gabriel Powell's Survey of the Lordship of Gower 1764, Swansea: Gower Society Publication, 2000.

[61] B. F. E. Records, "Description of 'Counterpart Lease for three lives, in consideration of twenty-seven pounds, of properties specified in No. 210, dated 1806, Mar. 31 ...,, 1810, Mar. 12.. Briton Ferry Estate Records, GB 210 211.," [Online]. Available: https://archiveshub.jisc.ac.uk/data/gb210-brirry/211.. [Accessed 5 July 2022].

[62] F. Green, "Captain Jenkin Jones's Dairy (1819)," West Wales Historical Records, The Annual Magazine of the Historical Society of West Wales V.1 1910-1911, 1912.

[63] B. F. E. Records, "Lease for three lives of Dan-y-Graig Fawr Farm (see No. 211, dated 1810, Mar. 12),, 1839, Jan. 1.. Briton Ferry Estate Records,. National Library of Wales / Llyfrgell Genedlaethol Cymru. GB 210 212.," 12 March 1812. [Online].

Available: https://archiveshub.jisc.ac.uk/data/gb210-brirry/212. [Accessed 5 July 2022].

[64] T. Cambrian, "To Be Sold Or Let By Private Treaty," *The Cambrian,* p. 1, 25 August 1827.

[65] B. F. E. Records, "Grant, in consideration of two thousand nine hundred and ninety-nine pounds, of annuity or yearly sum of three hundred ...,, 1841, Feb. 12.. Briton Ferry Estate Records,. National Library of Wales / Llyfrgell Genedlaethol Cymru. GB 210 213.'," 12 February 1812. [Online]. Available: https://archiveshub.jisc.ac.uk/data/gb210-brirry/213.. [Accessed 5 July 2022].

[66] B. F. Estate, "Lease for 99 years from 25 Mar 1830 for £20 annual rent dated 5 Jan 1835; George earl of Jersey, with Margaret Elizabeth Tennant relict of George Tennant, to Pascoe Grenfell and Charles Pascoe Grenfell esq. of Middle Bank Copper Works, Swansea; Land (9a 1," 5 January 1835. [Online]. Available: https://archiveshub.jisc.ac.uk/data/gb216-d/dbf/d/dbf1783. [Accessed 5 July 2022].

[67] S. Lewis, A Topographical Dictionary of Wales, S. Lewis and Company, 1848.

[68] A. a. e. b. R. C. a. P. Morgan, A Gower Gentleman, The Diary of Charles Morgan, Llanrhidian, 1834-1857, diary entry 24th May 1848, South Wales Record Society, 2021, p. 209.

[69] T. P. H. a. G. Advertiser, "The United County Asylum," *The Pembrokeshire Herald and General Advertiser,* p. 2, 7 September 1849.

[70] B. F. Estate, "West Glamorgan Archive Service," 1851. [Online]. Available: https://archiveshub.jisc.ac.uk/data/gb216-d/dbf/d/dbf701. [Accessed 6 July 2022].

[71] T. E. Papers, "Letter from George Tennant to Lord Jersey concerning a letter from lady Jersey to Lancelot Dent accusing George Tennant of acting to further his own interests. 20 Nov. 1812, 20 Nov. 1812, GB 216 D/D T 1437," 20 November 1812. [Online]. Available:

https://archiveshub.jisc.ac.uk/data/gb216-d/dt/d/dt1437. [Accessed 6 July 2022].

[72] D. R. Fisher, The History of Parliament: The House of Commons 1820-1832, ed.2009, Oxford University Press, 2011.

[73] R. Grainger, "Correspondence relative to the proposed site for a Lunatic Asylum...," Guardian Office, Cardiff, 1852.

[74] T. C. a. M. Guardian, "United Counties Lunatic Asylum," *The Cardiff and Merthyr Guardian Glamorgan Monmouth and Brecon Gazette,* p. 3, 30th October 1852.

[75] G. A. Walker, Gatherings from grave yards ....revolting custom of inhuming the dead in the midst of the living, Longman, 1839.

[76] T. Principality, "Public Meeting fpr the Establishment of a General Cemetery," *The Principality,* p. 5, 11 May 1849.

[77] T. Principality, "The Non-conformist Cemetery at Swansea," *The Principality,* p. 4, 11 May 1849.

[78] G. T. Clark, "Report to the General Board of Health of the Town and Borough of Swansea," Her Majesty's Stationery Office, London, 1849.

[79] T. W. MD, "Report on the Copper Smoke, and the Industrial Diseases of Coppermen.," Herbert Jones, Swansea, 1854.

[80] T. Cambrian, "God's Acre in Swansea - A Visit to Danygraig Cemetery," *The Cambrian,* October 1858.

[81] G. Spencer, Catholic Life in Swansea, St. David's Church, 1947.

[82] G. Spencer, Catholic Life in Swansea, 1947.

[83] M. Merlin, "Funeral of the Reverend Charles Kavanagh," *Monmouthshire Merlin,* p. 5, 1 November 1856.

[84] W. Rogers, A Pictorial History of Swansea, Gomer Press, 1981, p. 156.

[85] H. 1803-2005, " Commons Sitting → BURIAL ACTS AMENDMENT BILL. CONSIDERATION.," 4 August 1857. [Online]. Available: https://api.parliament.uk/historic-hansard/commons/1857/aug/04/consideration. [Accessed 8 July 2022].

[86] T. C. a. M. G. G. M. a. B. Gazette, "The Swansea Burial Board and the Bishop of St. David's," *The Cardiff and Merthyr Guardian Glamorgan Monmouth and Brecon Gazette,* p. 8, 7 February 1857.

[87] T. C. a. M. Guardian, "The Bishop of Saint David and the Swansea Burial Board," *The Cardiff and Merthyr Guardian Glamorgan Monmouth and Brecon Gazette,* p. 3, 8 August 1857.

[88] T. C. a. M. Guardian, "The Swansea Cemetery," The Cardiff and Merthyr Guardian Glamorgan Monmouth and Brecon Gazette, p. 6, 16 January 1858.

[89] T. Cambrian, "The Swansea Burial Board to lower prices in view of private competition," *The Cambrian,* p. 7, 23 November 1860.

[90] T. Cambrian, "Palm Sunday in Swansea and District. Is the Custom Being Overdone?," *The Cambrian,* p. 7, 23 March 1894.

[91] T. Cambrian, "Flower Sunday Scenes at Danygraig Cemetery," *The Cambrian,* p. 8, 29 March 1907.

[92] T. S. Walian, "Earl of Jersey and Lord Villiers at Swansea. the Earl Opens a New Thoroughfare," *The South Walian,* pp. 460-461, May 1898.

PART THREE - The Industrialists that shaped the Eastside

Whenever the subject of Swansea's industrial past is raised, for most people it is the copper industry that inevitably springs to mind. However, whilst it could be argued that Hafod was central to this, it was the Eastside of Swansea, more than any other area, that carried the town's industrial growth on its back, and yet it hardly, if ever, gets a mention. Whilst Hafod was home to both the Morfa Works and the massive Vivian Works, across the river the Eastside had four copper works (Upper Bank, Middle Bank, White Rock and 'Lambert's' Port Tennant Copper Works) and was the destination of two vitally important canals, the Smith's Canal whose southern terminal ended at Foxhole, and the Tennant Canal that linked the mineral wealth of Neath to Fabian's Bay, via Crymlyn Bog.

In order for the town to move to its next stage of growth, a substantial amount of land at Tirlandwr was severed off from the Eastside to form the North Dock, which was developed between the original course of the River Tawe and the New Cut. Thirty years later, Fabian's Bay began disappearing under first the Prince of Wales Dock, then the Kings Dock and finally the Queen's Dock, whilst the town's Patent Fuel business was established and grew around them.

Driving this change were the dreams and aspirations of a small group of industrialists whose determination forever changed the fortunes of Swansea and simultaneously the shape and definition of the Eastside - The Grenfell family, The Tennant family, The Benson family, and the Briton Ferry Estate.

The Grenfell Family

The family name 'Grenfell' can be closely identified with St Jude in Cornwall dating back to the 17th century, and possibly earlier. Pascoe Grenfell of Penzance (1692-1752) was listed as a 'merchant', whilst his second son, Pascoe Grenfell of St Hilary (1729-1810) was a copper and tin ore merchant, who was at one time Commissary to the States of Holland and served a number of times as Mayor of Marazion between 1763 and 1782. However, it was his son, also called Pascoe, that would develop businesses in Swansea.

Pascoe Grenfell (1761-1838) was the son of Pascoe Grenfell of St Hilary and Mary Tremenheere, who, after working for his father as an agent for the business interests of Thomas Williams of North Wales (1737-1802) on a sales trip to France, soon after became a shareholder in Williams' businesses. By 1785 Williams had control of the copper ore found at Parys Mountain in Anglesey (Greenfield Co & Brass Co), the Mona Mine in Anglesey, smelting plants in Middle Bank Swansea and Ravenhead Lancashire (Stanley Co), as well as a rolled copper sheet manufacturing plant at Meadow Mill Holyhead, North Wales. [1]In addition, he also had a non-compete agreement in place with the Cornish Metal Company but by 1787 he had taken that company over too. Thomas Williams was often described as 'The Copper King', but by the end of the decade Pascoe was heading Williams' new London office, and perhaps it was he that merited that title.

In 1786 he married his cousin Charlotte Granville, with whom he had four children, two sons George Granville (1789-1853) and Charles Pascoe (1790-1867), and two daughters, and established the family seat at Taplow House in Marlow, Buckinghamshire. His wife passed away in 1790 shortly after the birth of his son Charles Pascoe, and in 1798 he married Georgina St. Leger, with whom he had two sons, Pascoe St. Leger (1798-1879) and Riversdale William (1807-1871) as well as nine daughters. As an MP he represented Great Marlow from December 1802 to February 1820, and latterly Penryn in Cornwall from March 1820 to June 1826, throughout which time he was a supporter of anti-slave trade advocate William Wilberforce, and also held positions as the Governor of the Royal Exchange Company (1829 -1838) as well as being a commissioner for the lieutenancy of London.

In 1794, he formed a partnership with Owen Williams, son of Thomas, to purchase Cornish ores in order to supply the Swansea smelters at Middle and Upper Bank. [2] In the latter years of Thomas Williams' life his business was restructured, and after his death in 1803 Pascoe and Owen Williams took control of Middle and Upper Bank, [3] whilst Pascoe also took over Thomas Williams' role as MP for Great Marlow. In the following years, he and Owen Williams had either bought out or else were major shareholders in all of the late Thomas Williams' businesses. In 1823, Grenfell, Williams & Fox, a partnership between Pascoe Grenfell, Cornish businessmen John Williams and Lewis Fox took over the Rose Copper Smelting Company [4] which had been in operation since 1780 and had considerably enlarged its smelting capabilities.

However, Pascoe withdrew from the partnership the following year, as did Lewis Fox shortly after that, and with Sampson Foster and Joseph T. Foster of Norwich replacing them, the company was renamed Williams, Foster and Company, who from c1828 built and owned the Morfa Works [5] and from 1870 would own and run the White Rock Copper Works. On the death of John Williams in 1880, the company was bought by metal merchants HR Morton & Co of London, and in December 1888 became a new company, Williams, Foster & Co. Ltd, which in 1892 would purchase the liquidated Pascoe Grenfell & Sons business.

In 1828, Middle Bank and Upper Bank Copper Works had been leased to Pascoe Grenfell, Owen Williams, Owen's son Thomas Peers Williams and Pascoe's son Charles Pascoe Grenfell. In the following year, Owen Williams retired from the copper business, and a new partnership of Pascoe Grenfell & Sons was formed [6] now the new owners of Middle and Upper Bank, as well as retaining many business interests in North Wales. They also ran a small fleet of vessels that travelled between Liverpool, Deeside, Swansea and Bristol, including a clipper, complete with passenger accommodation, known as 'The Taplow', that was used as a family yacht.

In the 1830s two well-documented legal cases were held involving the Swansea region copper works owners, David v. Vivian (1833) and David v. Grenfell (1834), the plaintiffs in both cases engaged Thomas David, a barrister from Merthyr, to argue their case. The first in 1833, later described as 'The Great Copper Trial' [7] was a case brought against the firm of Vivian & Sons by eleven local farmers who had clubbed together to claim 'damages and public nuisance.' John Henry Vivian had previously sought the expertise of eminent scientist Michael Faraday and Professor Richard Phillips, Chairman of the London Chemical Society, to assist with finding a solution to 'the smoke problem'. The company took the matter seriously enough to engage Sir James Scarlett, the leading London barrister of the day, on a retainer of 500 guineas, and the trial was held in Carmarthen rather than in Swansea in case of any perceived bias from either side. The plaintiffs argued that livestock and crops had been severely affected by the copper smoke that engulfed their land, and 'the once fair and productive Kilvey Hill was as barren as the road.'

Scarlett argued that the case had only been brought forward as a money-making exercise, highlighting the fact that Vivian's chimneys were very high and would have had minimal if any damage at all, ignoring the fact that as the chimneys were higher, they actually spread the discharge over a wider area. He also made the argument that if these eleven men were successful, then upwards of 90,000 people would be put out of work. Vivian & Co. were found not guilty and the Cambrian newspaper [8] who had given this 'Most Important Trial' in-depth coverage, announced 'the greatest joy throughout this town and neighbourhood, which has been manifested by the ringing of bells and firing of cannon throughout the day.'

In the second case, David v. Grenfell, the plaintiffs only claimed 'damages', and once again, the evidence put forward from both sides was highly contradictory. [9] The chimney stacks of the Grenfell works of Middle Bank were much shorter than those of the Vivian's Works and this time the jury found in favour of the plaintiffs, but they could not successfully apportion blame between pollution and agricultural mismanagement, and damages of only one shilling were awarded. Even a payment of an insignificant sum such as a shilling was deemed a danger to the copper works owners of Swansea, and in 1835 an appeal was lodged, again led by Sir James Scarlett who claimed a mistrial, and the judgement was overturned. However, in 1836 the appeal decision was subsequently revoked by the 'Court of King's Bench' after it was shown that Scarlett's submission was found to have incorrectly described the evidence.

In 1834 Grenfell and Sons went into partnership with George Frederick Muntz (1794-1857) who in 1832 had started producing 'Muntz metal,' an alloy of approximately 60% copper and 40% zinc with a trace of iron. [10] The metal was already being used to sheath the hulls of ships and was a similar metal compound to that previously invented by James Kier who had patented his material in 1779. Muntz transferred his production facility from Birmingham to Swansea forming 'The Muntz Patent Metal Company', where they manufactured sheathing as well as bolts and fittings used in the marine industry (Muntz's patents 6325 and 6347 respectively). Customers included the British Navy as well as the owners of the many copper barques that brought copper ore to Swansea for smelting. Sheathing the hulls of ships meant they stayed cleaner for longer as it dissuaded marine life from sticking to its surface, and whilst Muntz metal maintained the anti-fouling properties of pure copper it could be produced at two-thirds of the price, and the new company priced its products at a substantially lower level than the equivalent copper products.

Such was their success that the number of ships clad with Muntz metal sheaths grew from fifty in 1837 to over one hundred a year later, and doubled again in 1840, by which time there were over thirty men employed at its production facility producing around two thousand tons of products. By 1843 there were over two hundred men producing up to four thousand tons per year, and by 1844 over four hundred ships were sheathed with Muntz metal. Muntz felt he needed more room to expand the business than the Swansea facility could provide, and after some disagreement, production was moved to Muntz's French Walls facility in Birmingham [11] and Grenfell and Sons left the partnership, but when Muntz's patents expired in 1846, most if not all of Swansea's copper smelters began producing Muntz metal sheathing and bolts.

Company Housing and Schools

Together with John Freeman & Co who owned the White Rock Works, Grenfell & Sons were one of the first companies to invest in housing their staff, and built workers' houses alongside the river at Foxhole and also on the lower banks of Kilvey Hill. The houses were of 'two-up, two down' construction, with little or no amenities. There is no clear evidence that these houses were built for family use only, and it is likely that they were shared by a number of workers. The Grenfell-built houses were in Pentrechwyth to the north of Foxhole, the street names highlighting their Grenfell family connections, whilst the housing in Foxhole was built by Freeman & Co and was known from a legal standpoint as the White Rock Estate. Rows of worker's houses were built including Canaan Row, Freeman's Row, Lamb's Row, Llewellyn's Row, Owens Row, Martin's Row, Prospect Row, Pleasant Row, and Tiger Row, although it is unclear if the properties at Jericho Road, Jericho Row, and Jericho Gardens were so named because of their proximity to the Canaan Church on Foxhole Road, or perhaps in agreement with the landowner or leaseholder.

In 1849 George Clark, the manager of the Dowlais Ironworks was employed by the General Board of Health to come to Swansea to review the conditions in the Lower Swansea Valley [12] and was not impressed by them at all. After reviewing property on the western side of the Tawe he looked eastward and commenting on the Kilvey area he wrote:

'Across the Tawe and upon its steep bank opposite to Swansea, are built the long and irregular villages of Foxhole and Pentre-guinea. The houses are for the most part niched into the hillside, are old, damp, and very dirty, and have no back premises. The water-springs used by the lower cottages are defiled by those living above them on the hill, and the roads and gutters, when I visited them, were in a filthy state. The copper smoke here affects the vegetation and the glass in the windows so that it is not impossible that it may affect the water...'

Clark did not mince his words, and clearly felt that whilst the Industrialists in the Lower Swansea Valley provided worker housing, in reality, they were slum dwellings that they made money from.

Pascoe Grenfell and his eldest son Charles had considerable business interests in the Swansea area and on the Eastside of the river in particular, and in March 1830 (amended in January 1835) they took out a 99-year lease from the Earl of Jersey on a tract of land that sat on the slopes of Kilvey Hill adjacent to the family's business interests, at a ground rent of £20 a year. [13] The land leased is described variously as 'part of Dan y Graig Fach', and also as 'part of two farms (now held as one) known by the names of Dan y Graig Fach (little) and Dan y Graig Ganol (middle), which included 'Graig farm.'

With over nine acres of land that included dwellings, cottages and other buildings, the lease identifies close no. 938 as 'Cae Maes Teague Ychaf' (sic) as well as the neighbouring close no. 955 as 'Cae Maes Mawr'. a 'close' meaning 'an enclosed tract or portion of land with an outer boundary.' Both names are mentioned in the lease as the use of lanes and roads between them became exclusive to the Grenfells, who were expected to maintain them and keep them at 20ft in width. Nearly ninety years later Cae Maes Mawr would become Maesteg Park, and the road would become St. Leger Crescent.

The lease states that the Grenfells':

'...shall and will within the space of 12 months from the date thereof erect and build upon the land hereby derived or same part thereof one or more good and substantial dwelling house or other buildings and substantial improvements and shall and will lay out in such building improvements during the said term hereby demised repair and keep in good and substantial repair the dwelling houses and other buildings erected and built upon the said demised premises and also all other erections and buildings.'

Whilst the above suggests that a 'substantial dwelling house' to be built within twelve months of signing the lease, an earlier document, 'Survey of Danygraig Fach and Danygraig Genol farms' carried out by Adam Murray in 1820 [14] shows an existing property at 'Cae Maes Teague Ychaf' that also utilised much of the land highlighted in the 1830 and 1835 amended lease agreements mentioned above, and whilst a new house could have been built on the site, it is possible that the same building may have been repaired and/or extended, and later became known as Maesteg House.

Pascoe Grenfell passed away in 1838, and four years later, on land provided by Freeman & Co, his youngest son Riversdale William Grenfell began the building of the All Saints Church in Foxhole, the first church on the Lower Eastside of Swansea. The new church, of Anglican denomination, became a chapel of ease to the main parish church of Llansamlet a few miles to the north, until the area of Kilvey became a separate parish in 1881.

Records show that Riversdale, whose 27-year-old wife Charlotte Adelaide Grenfell had passed away in December 1840, was first to take residence in what was known on the 1841 census as simply 'Maesteg' along with his three young children, Georgina, Seymour and Charlotte. The census also shows that two of his sisters, Henrietta Grenfell and Frances 'Fanny' Grenfell were living at (or maybe visiting?) the house at that time. Another of Pascoe Grenfell's sons, Pascoe St. Leger Grenfell, had taken over his father's business concerns upon his death and he moved to Swansea in c1845 to take a 'hands-on' approach to the copper businesses.

Pascoe St Leger Grenfell (1798-1879) was the eldest son of Pascoe Grenfell and his second wife Georgina St Leger, and was born in London in 1798. Educated at Eton College and in France, in 1824 he married Catherine Anne Dupre, with whom he had four sons, Pascoe De Pre, St. Leger Murray, Arthur Riversdale and Francis Wallace, and five daughters, Madelina Georgina, Gertrude Fanny, Elizabeth Mary, Katherine Charlotte, and Eleanor Catherine. He took on the control of Grenfell copper and tin smelting businesses after his father's death in 1838, and two years after the death of his first wife in 1845, he married Frances Madan.

Pascoe St. Leger has been credited in various publications and online sources with the construction of 'Maesteg House' but without any supporting information to confirm this, and there does not appear to be any record of him residing in Swansea before 1845 [15] nor does there appear to be any records of a house being built in this location.

Maesteg House (author's collection)

The census for 1851 shows that Pascoe St. Leger, together with his second wife and five daughters were listed as in residence at Maesteg House, although Madelina is listed as Madelina Llewelyn as she had married Griffith Llewelyn of Baglan the previous year and was likely visiting at the time. In the years after Pascoe St. Leger moved to Swansea until his death in 1879, he became a prominent fixture in both local business and government, becoming a borough councillor, a Justice of the Peace, Chairman and later Treasurer of the Swansea Harbour Trust, Deputy Lieutenant of The County of Glamorgan, President of the Royal Institute of South Wales, and a committee member of the Committee of the Swansea Board of Health. However, his legacy on the Eastside of Swansea may have been triggered by an 1847 commission to assess the level of education in Wales, the results of which also showed how local people, many of whom spoke only Welsh, were viewed by the industrialists that came to Swansea to make their fortune.

The report was commissioned in 1846 after William Williams, a Welshman from Carmarthen, at that time MP for Coventry, tabled a measure in the House of Commons calling for an inquiry into the state of education in Wales following numerous clashes at Chartist meetings in 1839 where more than twenty people were shot and killed by soldiers near Newport, as well as a series of protests between 1839 and 1843 (later known as The Rebecca Riots) against increased taxes and the general conditions in the rural areas of Wales. These well-publicised events caused some consternation in British government corridors, and doubts were raised as to whether the lack of English was a key factor in the problems.

The Government agreed to Williams' request, and in the following July, three commissioners were appointed to undertake the inquiry, ensuring every part of Wales was visited in order to compile the evidence and statistics that would form the substance of the report. Of the many industrialists who came to set up works in Swansea in the 1700s and 1800s, all did their business in English, however, only a small number of them felt the teaching of reading and writing would benefit both their respective businesses as well as their employees, and set up schools for this purpose.

In 1806 Freeman and Company, who owned the Morfa Works on the East side of the river, together with Grenfell and Sons began schooling the children of their workers in Kilvey, whilst across the Tawe, Vivian and Sons had set up a similar school in Hafod. The first school to be built on the Eastside, it was paid for by deducting a penny a week from a workers' wages. Although the schools were non-sectarian in nature they were run in a scripture-based format with lessons in English.

The 1847 'Reports of the Commissioners of Inquiry into the State of Education in Wales' [16] observed and reported on the mostly untrained tutors as well as the conditions of the schools, and the section written on the Parish of Llansamlet describes local people and their jobs, as well as the local environment:

Extracts from the Report relating to 'the Foxhole schools':

- From the sea upwards toward Morriston, there is a succession of enormous copper works. There is not a blade of vegetation to be seen on the steep hills on either side of the river, which seem to have been greatly raised, if not in some places created, by accumulations of slag. This with a whiteish smoke of the furnaces, and the penetrating taste of copper, makes the whole region as dreary and disagreeable as I can imagine it to be.

- There were 15 or 16 public houses between Pentrechwyth and the ferry, about a mile and a half. Drunkenness was the prevailing sin of the district. Wages were good and there was little suffering except by the people's own fault, the masters complained that the children could not come early in the morning because they have to take their parent's breakfast to the works, and that they were removed at an early age from school. The population in the south were coppermen, and in the north of the parish colliers and agriculturists.

- Kilvey Infant and Juvenile Schools – these schools are supported by stoppages upon the wages of the men in the copperworks of Messrs Grenfell & Sons and Messrs Freeman & Co. the cost of accommodation is borne by employers. Mr Grenfell told me that he had contemplation after a time (he had but recently resided in the neighbourhood) to admit no young people to his works that could not read or write, or to at least to make such, at extra hours, attend school.

QUESTIONS	VALE OF SWANSEA, P.S.L GRENFELL Esq
1. Are you acquainted with the Condition of the Mining and Manufacturing Population in any part of Wales?	Of a portion of the manufacturing population engaged in the copper-works near Swansea
2. State your opinion of it under the following heads :	
a. Domestic accommodation	The workmen's houses are generally pretty well built, but small, and deficient in the means of separation
b. Sobriety	I fear among the men with low ebb, to judge from the immense number of public-houses and beer-shops and the number of men who may be seen intoxicated
c. Providence and economy	But little; they spend nearly all they get. They mostly subscribe to sick-clubs, and there is a good clothing-club, but not so well supported as might be, considering their earnings
d. Religious feeling and observances	The Dissenting chapels are very well attended generally; great numbers attend funerals, and there is an outward reverence for religious ordinances
e. Care for their children and sense of parental responsibility	In this they seem deficient; the children exceedingly dirty, playing all day in the road or the street; generally looking well fed and sufficiently clothed, the want of shoes and stockings being no sign of poverty

f.	Feeling towards their employers and superiors	Generally very respectful and willing, staying a long time in the same employ
g.	Capability of forming a judgment on the true interests of their class, and general intelligence	Very little, if any: in general they are very ignorant and narrow-minded, with some cunning and very little appreciation of truth
h.	Whether improving or retrograding and in what respects; and whether likely to continue in the same direction	From my limited residence I can scarcely give a decided opinion, but I should say, rather stationary, owing to imperfect education and their language serving to keep up much ignorance and prejudice
i.	Whether their moral condition is improved, or the reverse, by good times	I think not improved, as good wages do not make them more prudent or comfortable; for if wages increase, they either work less or drink more, and their social and domestic comfort is not increased
j.	Extent to which English is understood	Very limited. Many of the workmen speak none at all, and those that do, scarcely understand anything beyond the common routine phrases applying to their own peculiar station
k.	Position, character and influence of females among them, and how far the duties of mothers and wives are adequately understood and fulfilled	The women seem hard-working and industrious, I have never seen one intoxicated, nor, among the working-classes out of the town, is there much outward evidence of immorality. I am told they are not good managers, dirty in their persons, and careless of the appearance of their children, and generally very ignorant. I believe generally they are good wives.

3.	Whether an improved system of education is required for this population – what means exist for procuring it – the best manner of employing those means	I believe an improved system of education, especially to give the rising generation a good knowledge of the English language, by which their views maybe extended beyond the narrow circle to which their own language confines them, to be the most effective means of raising the exceedingly low and defective tone of principle, morality, and truth of this people. From their great want of order and system, I should conceive a sound Scriptural education, conducted on moderate Church principles, the best adapted for that end. The present means are, or have been hitherto, very defective in this neighbourhood, but the public attention has been roused lately, and many schools are in progress and in contemplation (signed) P.S.L. GRENFELL 10TH April 1847

The report noted that the school was opened in c1806 and was in a poor state of repair, and that the master was an elderly ex-stonemason. It appears that there was no real benevolence being shown by the late Pascoe Grenfell for the nearly forty years the school had been open, and in the accompanying questionnaire, the candour in the responses of his son Pascoe St Leger clearly highlighted the hardships that families endured daily. It is important to note that Pascoe St. Leger's comments in the report were requested of him in his role as a relatively new local captain of industry, having only moved to the area a short time before (his response to question 2h appears to confirm this) so his answers reflect what he saw as the lack of capabilities of the local workforce, as well as highlighting the environment and conditions they lived in.

The combination of both the findings of the 1847 commission coupled with those of the 1849 General Board of Health report, would no doubt have disturbed Pascoe St. Leger, and he and his family responded almost immediately to the inadequacies he saw and began to make improvements in teaching and company-owned buildings in the Kilvey area. In the same year, the Grenfell's purchased two cottages near to the church, one to be utilised as the schoolmaster's house, and the other to accommodate the infants' school, and with attendances of around two hundred, Richard Gwynne was appointed schoolmaster.

Swansea had, administratively speaking, been an English-speaking town since at least the 1400s so by the 1800s most if not all written records and transactions were in English rather than in Welsh, and as the population of the town grew it did so with mostly non-Welsh speakers, although around the outskirts of the town and beyond the Welsh language continued to be used daily.

Schooling, if there was any, was left to the various churches and chapels, often in poor conditions with untrained tutors, and based on religious rather than secular lines. By the mid-1800s, the majority of workers living in the heavily industrialised areas of Swansea were not local people at all but were 'immigrants' who came from West Wales, the West Country, Devon, Cornwall, Ireland and further afield, something that is supported by the names listed on the censuses on the Eastside of Swansea from that time onwards. When technology from outside the U.K. was utilised by local industries such as patent fuel manufacturing equipment or spelter works equipment, nationals from those countries e.g. Belgium and Germany, were also brought to Swansea to ensure successful installation and operation, and the training of local staff would have been in English.

Being bi-lingual allowed people from 'the Welshry' opportunities for upward movement to the position of supervisor or manager within a company, something reflected in Pascoe St. Leger's comments to the questionnaire in the 1847 commission (above), where he stated 'the problems that prevailed amongst the Welsh working class was to give the rising generation a good knowledge of the English language, by which their views may extend beyond the narrow circle of which their own language confines them', a view that was shared by many prominent English and Welsh industrialists of the time. The teaching of English was necessary for Swansea to take its place in the new world as, as stated in the conclusion of the same report '...in his [the Welsh workman] home, his language keeps him under the hatches, being one in which he can neither acquire nor communicate the necessary information. It is a language of old-fashioned agriculture, of theology and of simple rustic life.'

Whether this particular choice of words should be considered somewhat dramatic given that Wales has a culture and language of its own, it never-the-less illustrated that at that time a lack of spoken English meant an area or group of people was either not capable, or perhaps more accurately, not ready to embrace the rapid changes the Industrial Revolution had brought with it. Swansea was now viewed as the copper-smelting capital of the world and a key part of Britain's industrial leadership. It was a place where industrial ideas, methods and processes were in abundance and were documented in a language seen as progressive, and one that was able to easily absorb new words and phrases, something that has played a big part in the fact that English remains the business language of the world until this day. Teaching English was therefore deemed absolutely essential in order to ensure a capable local workforce for the future.

By 1850 the children of other employers were allowed to attend school, albeit at a slightly higher weekly rate. In 1856 the church was extended, and four years later a Girl's School was added. In addition to the school and church in Kilvey, in 1858 Pascoe St. Leger agreed to the 80-year lease of land at Pentrechwyth, north of the Maesteg Estate, for the sum of £18 10s. a year, building Grenfell Town, Taplow Terrace, and Rifleman's Row, as well as a school. Whilst there is little or no documented interface between Pascoe Grenfell and his workforce, the positive interaction between Pascoe St. Leger's family and the local population appeared to be far in excess of any other industrialist family in the region at the time.

The final reading of the Elementary Education Act was passed on 25th July 1870, with the aim of providing a consistent level of education throughout Wales, irrespective of social class, with compulsory attendance until the age of 10 years old. All teaching was to be done in English, and in some schools across the country 'the Welsh Not', a piece of wood with 'WN' inscribed, was hung around the neck of children who were heard to speak Welsh in class, passed from one child to another until the end of the day, at which time the unlucky recipient of 'the WN' would be punished. Given that in many places in Wales children only spoke Welsh, the Act is still viewed by many as a major setback to the Welsh language.

The Demise of Grenfell & Sons

By the middle years of the 1860s, Grenfell & Sons employed about 800 men at Middle and Upper Bank, however in 1867 co-founder, senior partner and Pascoe's eldest son Charles died and his shares were split amongst the remaining partners, and thus the effect of his personal and long-standing support to the business was diluted. After the death of Riversdale in 1871 and then the passing of Pascoe St. Leger in 1879 [17] outwardly it appeared that the two deaths affected little if any change to the Grenfell business, however, control was now in the hands of a new generation of Grenfell family members who seemed to have no real interest in the copper business or in Swansea, preferring instead to manage it from the company's Upper Thames St offices in London, and by 1892 the business was in serious trouble.

Chairman Charles Seymour Grenfell, son of Riversdale, and managing director Claud Grenfell, grandson of Charles, fell out over an overpayment of 25 shillings on a consignment of copper, and as a result, Seymour wanted Claud to travel to Swansea, fire the existing manager, and then take his place in running the Swansea business. However other family shareholders rejected Seymour's proposal, and he resigned from the company. Claud then visited Swansea and compiled a report on the business for the board of directors to review, and voluntary liquidation of the company followed soon afterwards in October of the same year. The headline in The Cambrian [18] was to the point, and the newspaper offered its own opinion as to why the company was closed down:

"THE RETIREMENT OF MESSRS. PASCOE GRENFELL AND SONS FROM THE COPPER TRADE. THE TOTAL STOPPAGE OF THE MIDDLE BANK AND UPPER BANK COPPER WORKS. A SUDDEN AND STARTLING DECISION. NEARLY 600 MEN THROWN OUT OF EMPLOYMENT."

- "Mr Claud Grenfell some time ago resided for a few months at Maesteg House, and paid considerable attention to the works and the processes carried on within" when "not the slightest hint or suspicion that any thought of discontinuance was entertained. The notice came like a thunderclap to all concerned".

- "These works have now fallen into the hands of the fourth generation of the copper-smelting Grenfells, and this generation, chiefly composed of young men under the age of 30, have decided to entirely sever themselves, and such others of the family as are now in it, from the smelting and manufacture of copper and yellow metal"

Grenfell and Sons had traded in Swansea for nearly one hundred years, many families had three or four generations of men that worked for the company, and under Pascoe St. Leger Grenfell's stewardship, there had been no strikes or disputes. Records later showed that the company had had financial problems for some time, something that was likely been behind the 5% reduction in wages imposed on workers twice in the previous ten years. The current workforce had become unionised, and far from expecting closure of the company, they were looking for parity of wages with the Vivian Works, so its sudden closure with the loss of six hundred jobs had a devastating effect on the Eastside.

Rumours that Vivian & Sons, the Cape Copper Company or perhaps Rio Tinto would step in and buy the company circulated, as did the possibility of a mercantile bank buyout as had happened with the Morfa Works The valuation of the business as a going concern 'including works and machinery' was thought to be between £150,000 to £200,000, however, the figure would be much less should the business be broken up, so it came as a shock to many when in November, The Cambrian announced that Grenfell & Sons had been purchased, but not by any of the companies that they had earlier speculated over. The Purchase of the Grenfell Copper and Spelter Works by Messrs. Williams, Foster, and Co. Ltd. [19]

The business was bought for only £40,000 by Williams, Foster & Co. Ltd, who at this time were also owners of The White Rock Works, and a new company formed, Williams, Foster & Co and Pascoe Grenfell and Sons. Councillor George Nancarrow of 'Trefula', Mackworth Villas, St. Thomas was appointed as the company's new manager. Mr Nancarrow was held in high regard, and both his father and grandfather had previously been Grenfell employees.

In 1924 a further merger with Vivian and Sons formed a new company called British Copper Manufacturers, which in 1927 was bought by Imperial Chemical Industries Limited (ICI). In 1957 the works became the home of the newly formed Yorkshire Imperial Metals, a joint venture between ICI and Yorkshire Copper Works, which remained in Swansea until 1980.

A list of 83 'two up-two down' cottages was provided to the Receivers by Frederic Bishop, the Grenfells manager at Middle Bank at the time of liquidation in 1892, the majority in Pentrechwyth, plus properties in Llysnewydd, Middle Bank, Spelter Row and Upper Bank. Valued at a total of £8300, each house was rented out at 6d a room. In addition, they owned the Foxhole Music Hall and the adjacent Foxhole Cottage on Foxhole Road from which the family expected a decent return, but Briton Ferry Estates records showed that they had been sublet by the Grenfells in 1853 [20] and again in 1886 [21], and with only thirteen years left remaining on the lease from Lord Jersey, the music hall was valued at only £54, and both music hall and cottage were sold for only £100. The previous year the Grenfells had auctioned off their other St. Thomas housing, a total of four properties on Pentreguinea Road, and one on Mackworth Terrace.

On discovering that the school buildings were on the asset list of the liquidated company and therefore up for sale, Mary Grenfell worked hard to keep them out of the hands of the Swansea School Board, as she feared that under their control the religious content would lessen and Sunday school would not be compulsory. She implored her older sister Madelina Llewellyn to lend her the £2000 needed to retain them, and the school buildings were subsequently bought by Mary, although shortly after her death in March 1894, the Grenfell schools were taken over by the Corporation, and when the new St. Thomas School opened in 1898, all children attending the Kilvey Schools were transferred to it.

The Grenfell Legacy

In 1850, Pascoe St. Leger's eldest daughter Madelina Georgina married Griffith Llewellyn of Baglan Hall in Briton Ferry, whilst under the guidance of his second wife Frances, his four younger daughters took active participation in the family's charitable works that included the religious education of local children, 'Gertrude' Fanny at Pentrechwyth, 'Eleanor' Catherine at Kilvey and Foxhole, Elizabeth 'Mary' at St. Thomas, and 'Katherine' Charlotte at Port Tennant. His two youngest daughters also married, Katherine to Nottingham banker Edward Thornton, and Eleanor to the Reverend Henry Trotter of St. Mary the Less, in Cambridge.

Of Pascoe St Leger's nine children from his first marriage to Catherine Anne Dupre, three of them had lives that directly or indirectly impacted Swansea and the East Side specifically; his daughters Madelina and Mary, and his youngest son Francis.

'Madelina' Georgina Llewellyn, nee Grenfell (1826-1903) married Griffith Llewellyn of Baglan Hall in Briton Ferry, whose family fortune came from a business interest in the Rhondda coal fields, and whilst she did not have the same 'hands-on' approach to benevolence that her younger sister Mary possessed, together with her husband she was responsible for many significant charitable endowments that funded the building of Alms Houses in Neath as well funding the building of churches at St. Catherine's in Baglan and the restoration of St. Mary's in Aberfan. The Llewellyn's were regular benefactors of the Swansea Eye Hospital, and Madelina was also rumoured to be the anonymous donor of £2,000 that went toward the building of a new wing of the Nurses Home at Swansea

Hospital. At the request of her sister Mary, she also provided the funding to add the tower, spire, and chancel at St. Thomas Church, built in honour of their father, Pascoe St. Leger, and when Grenfell and Sons went into liquidation, and it was Madelina Llewellyn who continued to pay the rent on Maesteg House, thus protecting the Grenfell family from the indignity of losing their family home.

Francis Wallace Field Marshal Lord Grenfell GCMG (1841-1925), the fourth and youngest son of Pascoe St Leger who, whilst born in Lambeth in London, spent much of his younger years at Maesteg House before being educated at Milton Abbas School in Dorset. On leaving full-time education he purchased a commission as an ensign in the 3rd Battalion of the 60th Rifles (later The Kings Royal Rifle Corps) in August 1859 and served with them in Ireland, Malta, Canada and India. He purchased a promotion to lieutenant in July 1863, and in October 1871 purchased his captaincy, shortly before the abolition of the sale of commissions [22].

In 1873, he accepted the role of Assistant Deputy Commissioner to Sir Arthur Cunynhame in South Africa, and it was during his time there that he took part in the claiming of Griqualand West for Britain that years later would be the site of the Kimberley diamond fields. He was also involved in the recovery of the body of the French Prince Imperial, son of Napoleon III, who was killed whilst serving with British forces during the Zulu War of 1879, before leaving South Africa for Egypt in 1882 where he took part in the British occupation of Egypt.

In April 1885, he succeeded Sir Evelyn Wood as 'Sirdar', or Commander In Chief, of the Egyptian Army, which was to be totally rebuilt after their 1882 defeat. An amateur archaeologist with a keen interest in Egyptian history, he was visited by his sister Mary, who encouraged his interests, and in 1888, with the help of eminent Egyptologist, Orientalist and philologist Sir E.A. Wallis Budge, Francis purchased the mummy 'Tem Hor', its coffin and numerous other funeral items that, to be known as The Grenfell Collection, were gifted to The Royal Institution of South Wales, now better known as Swansea Museum. After leaving Egypt in 1892 to work at the War Office, he received The Knight Grand Cross of the Order of St. Michael and St. George (GCMG), and represented the British Army at the Coronation of the last Tsar of Russia in 1896.

He returned to Egypt in 1898, and Grenfell's rebuilt Egyptian army fought under Lord Kitchener at the Battle of Omdurman, although Grenfell actually out-ranked the more famous Kitchener. In 1899 his first wife of 12 years, Evelyn Wood died, and in 1903 he married Margaret Majendie and had two sons and a daughter. He became Governor of Malta in 1899 and became a Freeman of Swansea in the same year. He received a peerage in 1902, and as Baron Grenfell of Kilvey, headed the newly created Fourth Army Corps. On promotion to full General, he moved to Ireland as Commander-in-Chief where he stayed until 1908. He was promoted to become Field Marshall on his retirement and devoted himself to work on behalf of both the Church Lad's Brigade and the Royal Horticultural Society.

He was likely an inspiration to five of his nephews who followed him into military service, all of whom were sons of his brother Pascoe De Pre. Pascoe St. Leger was killed in 1896 at the second war of Matabele (part of what is now Zimbabwe), Robert Septimus was killed at Omdurman in Sudan on 4 Sept. 1898, and Reginald died "of illness caused by service in India". Twin brothers 'Francis' Octavius and Riversdale 'Rivy' Nonus Grenfell both served with honour in the First World War.

Francis became the twins' guardian after the death of their father. Riversdale was killed in action on the 14th of September 1914 at the beginning of the Battle of the Aisne, whilst Francis was the first British officer to be awarded a Victory Cross (VC) in the First World War "For gallantry in action against unbroken infantry" at Audregnies, Belgium on the 24th August 1914, before he was mortally wounded by shrapnel at Hooge, east of Ypres in Belgium, on the 24th May 1915.

The twins did not have a direct local connection to Swansea but nevertheless were included on a war memorial at All Saints Church Kilvey, unveiled by Baron Grenfell in 1920. Field Marshal Lord Grenfell died on 27th January 1925 and was buried at Beaconsfield in Buckingham Estate.

Mary Grenfell

Elizabeth 'Mary' Grenfell (1836-1894), one of Pascoe St. Leger's two unmarried daughters, dedicated her life to the service of others, and it was she that had the most direct effect on the lives of the people of the Eastside of Swansea. Able to converse in several languages and a capable musician proficient with a number of instruments, she trained as a nurse with the intention of serving in the Franco-Prussian War but instead returned to Swansea to work with the poor and disadvantaged. She is said to have pressured her father into giving her land on which to build a new school, and when he (allegedly) asked "where can you raise the money to build it?", her response was to raise over £30 in three weeks, and in 1862 the school was built and used as both a day school and a Sunday school.

In 1879 she opened an Anglican mission house in Benson St (later Pinkney St) and extended it by purchasing the house next door. From there she ran mothers' meetings, friendly and clothing clubs, prayer meetings and weekly women-only Bible classes. Such was the success of the mission house that she purchased an Iron Church from Cheltenham that was installed at the top of Sebastopol St. After the opening of the current stone-built St. Thomas Church at the top of Lewis St in 1890, the Iron Church was relocated to the junction of Tymawr St and Danygraig Rd and became St. Stephen's Church.

On Tuesdays, she ran a weekly mother's meeting in Pentrechwyth, and three days a week she would visit the local Patent Fuel Works during their lunch hour to give young workers free lessons in reading, writing and mathematics. Her support for the railwaymen in the area involved running Sunday afternoon bible classes for the men, their wives and friends, their singing often supported by Mary on the harmonium that had been presented to her by a grateful congregation, and she organised an annual tea party for local railwaymen and their families, held under a specially erected marquee on the lawns of Maesteg House.

A follower of the Temperance movement, she opened the 'Golden Griffin' coffee tavern near the entrance of the St. Thomas Railway Station, a golden griffin/gryphon being a feature of the Grenfell family crest. On Thursday afternoons she held meetings for dockworkers there and every Sunday morning ran a young men's Bible class. She later added an adjoining library and reading room to the tavern. She was also an ardent supporter of the YWCA, and purchased and furnished property for them in Grove Place, Swansea, where she offered regular support and assistance. It was at this property that she organised and ran a regular bible class for the local policemen, so well attended that she became known as 'The Policeman's Friend'.

Similarly, she offered the same consideration to the spiritual welfare of Swansea's postal and telegraphic staff, at all times embracing the teachings of the Anglican church. She was also active in Landore, where her fund-raising efforts helped in the construction and furnishing of a church house, as well as paying its weekly expenses, which included the caretaker's wages.

Mary was also active at the opposite end of the social spectrum and ran a school 'for girls of good birth' in the Uplands area of Swansea as well as at Maesteg House. Up to eight girls between the ages of six and eighteen years old, 'who are privately recommended by friends' were boarded at Maesteg House and taken daily by carriage to the Uplands House school where another twenty girls, daughters of friends of the Grenfell family, also attended.

A December 1900 article in 'Baby: The Mother's Magazine' [23] described the school as '…a model educational institution…not a school in the ordinary sense of the word, as it is not intended to make it a source of financial profit, but the pupils have all the advantages of a refined home and training suitable to enable them to take their place in society, as well as those of sound teaching.'

The school was run by two governesses and had a staff of servants. Pupils were taught pen and letter writing skills, needlework, French, German, Italian, Music and Art, and afternoons were spent on country walks in order to 'awaken interest in natural history.' The article further noted that 'sensible and modern, but not 'faddy' teaching methods were used', and that 'the religious tone was Evangelical and not High Church.' At Maesteg House, Mary Grenfell, together with a certified teacher of cookery, taught Domestic Economy, and if pupils were old enough, they spent time with Miss Grenfell in the drawing-room where they obtained 'excellent social training.' Pupils were often sent to London in the spring 'where special masters gave them lessons in special arts or sciences.' Young ladies could also learn and practice photography, cycling and horse riding.

She visited her brother Francis during his time as Sirdar in Egypt where she collected artefacts, and on her return to Swansea produced a set of lectures about her visits. On 2nd November 1888, she opened an Egyptian display that featured the mummy 'Tem Hor' and other items that were gifted to the RISW by her brother Francis. She also visited Palestine, and on her return carried out a series of lectures and slide shows on the subject of the Holy Lands for various local charities.

Mary Grenfell died on 12th March 1894 and was fitting that the dedication and commitment she had shown to others was recognised by a substantial eulogy in The Cambrian newspaper [24] who reported:

'Miss Grenfell has led amongst us so vigorous, so devoted, and so self-sacrificing a life, that comparatively few suspected she suffered from any ailment at all. She was so reserved, so resigned, and so deeply interested in promoting the well-being, religiously and socially, of the people round about her, and of whom she had taken a much more than sisterly care for so many years, that she almost forgot herself in her labours of love for others.

Quite a gloom has been cast over the whole of the district known as Kilvey, Pentrechwyth, St. Thomas, etc. You can speak to no one who does not bear a sad face, and who has not a regretful voice for the good lady who is gone As a mark of respect, and in token of the esteem in which the deceased lady was held, most of the shops in St. Thomas have shutters up, whilst a very large proportion of the dwelling houses have had the blinds drawn all the week', and the bells of St. Mary's Parish Church have been solemnly tolling every day. Indeed, the inhabitants of Swansea in general, and the East Side in particular, fed the irreparable loss they have sustained very keenly, and are frequently heard exclaiming that "they will miss the kindly and familiar face of a very dear benefactor and friend for a long time to come.'

…Miss Grenfell proved herself to be an earnest, thoughtful and capable educationalist. The young men of Kilvey, St. Thomas, &c., owe much to her in this respect, and many gentlemen who now hold important positions in Swansea and elsewhere, speak in the highest praise of the beneficent teacher of their early days. Many, also, were the kindly letters of recommendation and friendly counsel she gave to young men and women who were on the point of leaving home to take situations in strange and distant towns, corresponding with them and imbuing them with hope and strength to pursue an upright and honourable career through life, and the recollection of her teaching has often been the means of enabling them to obtain and retain positions in the world.'

In the same article, The Cambrian also highlighted 'a brief sketch' previously featured in 'The Railway Signal' of May 1888:

'Miss Grenfell stood by the Railway Mission work from its commencement in the western counties, and has borne a large share of the expenses in many places…in connection with other work her name is alike familiar; we know that not a movement in the South Wales district is carried on without her sympathy. Policemen as well as railwaymen, navvies and boatmen, all sorts and conditions of men, have been befriended by her.'

'…every effort on behalf of girls, young women, and mothers, postmen, railwaymen and policemen, hails her as a helper. As a visitor to the sick, too, our dear friend is well-known. For her, no sickness or disease had any terror, she waited for hours by bedsides ministering comfort and consolation. In fact, Maesteg House, St. Thomas, the family residence, has always been known as a resort for help in times of sorrow, need, sickness or other adversity. Her untiring zeal and anxiety for the spiritual welfare of all grades of humanity was proverbial, and no movement, having for its end the improvement for the masses, ever appealed to her generosity and liberality in vain. She was as ready with her purse as she was with her person and her accomplishments.'

After her death in London, her body was returned to Swansea and was met at High St Station by large crowds who accompanied it to St. Thomas Church where her funeral service was held the following day, and the local press estimated that 10,000 people lined the streets as the coffin made its way to Danygraig Cemetery for internment. A stained-glass window in St. Thomas Church is dedicated to her memory.

The last member of the Grenfell family to live at Maesteg House was Katherine Madelina 'Kate' Grenfell, daughter of St. Leger Murray Grenfell. Whilst the annual rent of the house had continued to be paid by her aunt Madelina Llewellyn, from whom she had received a legacy of £6000 in 1904, she had closed the Uplands House school four or five years earlier on expiry of its lease but continued to run Mary Grenfell's mission houses as well as opening her own school at Maesteg House. Alas, Kate Grenfell had no business acumen nor did she have a grasp of the running costs of Maesteg House, and she filed for bankruptcy in 1907, owing nearly £5000, her average income being only £220.

Whilst her total assets amounted to nearly £1,436, which included £575 for leasehold houses, £200 for furniture sold from Maesteg House, and £127 from investments, her gross liabilities were nearly £4690. Much of the deficit was due to money lenders who were owed £2664, and the balance attributed to ground rent and local taxes. A list of seventy-eight unsecured creditors included drapers (owed £566), fish and poultry dealers (owed £119), butchers (owed £99) and grocers (owed £490 [25] whilst the nearly £1000 owed to the various 'clothing clubs and penny banks' in St. Thomas, Kilvey, Pentrechwyth and at Grove Place in the town, were settled by friends of Miss Grenfell. There was no debt attached to the Golden Griffin Coffee Tavern, as that had previously been settled out of Miss Grenfell's own pocket, but it would close shortly after the bankruptcy case was dealt with. The three properties that Kate had inherited from Mary Grenfell were sold in auction, and the Mission House at No. 1 Grove Place in the town centre and the Church House in Landore sold for £305 and £300 respectively. The third property was No. 17 Phillips Parade which sold for £290.

Maesteg House was also to be auctioned but had only twenty-one years left on its lease. The auctioneer stated that whilst 'he was not sure that the late Pascoe St. Leger Grenfell had built the mansion…at any rate, he had lived there for many years.' Bidding for the house began at £500 but the property was withdrawn when bids only reached £650 [26]. Two years later in September 1910, Field Marshal Lord Grenfell returned to Swansea to inspect the Swansea United Service Brigade and to attend their anniversary dinner at the Hotel Cameron. 'Eastside Notes' in the South Wales Daily Post [27] mentions his visit and notes: 'Alas! The glories of Maesteg House have departed. Lord Grenfell on this occasion has been a guest of Colonel Wright at West Cross.'

During the First World War, Maesteg House was used by Swansea Council to accommodate Belgian refugees [28] and in 1919 the Earl of Jersey made it known to the council that he was prepared to let the house and outbuildings with grounds totalling over five acres at £50 per annum for 20 years and proposed that the house and outbuildings to be converted into eight flats, which would 'do something appreciable in the relief of congestion' [29]. The proposed work did not take place and Maesteg House was demolished, and both house and grounds became part of a new public housing development programme. Its main thoroughfare was named Grenfell Park Road, and the streets and highways adjoining it were given names associated with the Grenfell family.

Shortly after the council housing was approved, a new private estate was proposed, to be sited above Windmill Terrace on what was once Ty Gwyl. The land was owned by Briton Ferry Estate and whilst previously leased by Freeman & Co., the new development was named the Grenfell Park Estate.

The Tennant Family

George Tennant was descended from a family of lawyers, his grandfather Christopher Tennant of Dent in Yorkshire, and his father Thomas Tennant of Standishgate in Wigan, who married Alice Latham of Wigan in 1759, who gave birth to their only son George in 1765. George was to follow in his family's footsteps, and at the age of 12 he moved to London to 'take up articles'. In 1792 he married Margaret Beeston and by 1796 was in partnership in a law firm in Greys Inn Square with Mr Thomas Green. During this period he began representing the fifth Earl of Jersey, George Child-Villiers, who owned substantial estates as well as other interests in South Wales, and during visits made on behalf of the earl, he realised the potential of developing his own interests in the area. He purchased the Rhyddings Estate and Colliery near Neath from the Earl of Jersey, and then bought Cadoxton, adjacent to Rhyddings, to add value to his new assets.

The Neath Canal

After gaining parliamentary approval in June 1791 work began on the Neath Canal in August of the same year. The canal was to run from Abernant (Glynneath) to Brickfield near Melincryddan Pill, Neath, where it reached the river Neath, however, a year later the canal had only reached Ynsybollog when engineer Thomas Dadford Snr. resigned to take up a new position on the construction of the Monmouth Canal. He was replaced by Thomas Sheasby, with the goal and target of completing the construction of the canal by the following year at a budgeted cost of nearly £15,000.00 Unfortunately Sheasby was arrested and subsequently imprisoned for accounts irregularities on the Glamorgan Canal project he had previously worked on. After two major hold-ups due to changes in engineers, the Canal was subsequently completed in 1795 although the planned river lock was not built.

Following a second parliamentary act in May 1798, a further extension to the canal was made from Melincryddan Pill to Giants Grave (which also included Lord Vernon's Penrhiwtyn Canal) plus three private extensions, Glynneath Maesmarchog (1800), Cwm Sart (1812) and Cnel Back (1817). Another extension was added in 1842 which linked the canal to Briton Ferry. The Neath Canal regularly handled coal, iron ore, gunpowder, silica, limestone, fire clay, fire bricks, building stone, and once transported cannons made at Abernant and Llwyncoed Foundries, destined for the Napoleonic War in 1812. Tennant reasoned that he could build his own canal system, and after constructing the Rhyddings Canal and building an inclined plane from his colliery to a wharf on the River Neath, he proposed crossing the river via an aqueduct to its west bank to link it to Red Jacket Pill, and then utilise the disused Glan-Y-Wern Canal to reach the River Tawe in Swansea via Fabian's Bay.

Glan-Y-Wern Canal

Richard Jenkins wanted to transport coal from the Glan-Y-Wern Colliery on Kilvey Hill to the River Neath by moving canal boat cargo onto river barges at Red Jacket Pill (then known as Trowman's Hole), but after successfully obtaining a lease to carry out the work from Lord Vernon of the Briton Ferry Estates on 14th August 1788, Jenkins died on the same day. The three-and-a-half-mile-long canal was completed in May 1790 by Edward Elton who had taken over management of the colliery.

In Oddisworth's Guide of 1802 [30] the Glan Y Wern Canal, also known as the Elton Canal, is described as follows:

'About 2 miles from Swansea, on the northeast side of Kilvey Hill, is Burley Hill, or Kilvey Mount, one of the seats of Herbert Evans Esq, but at present in the occupation of Edward

Elton Esq a mile beyond it is Llanywern Colliery, the property of the last-named gentleman. Binding coals of very superior quality, and sold for exportation on the river of Neath, at a place called Trowman's Hole, whither they are conveyed from Llanywern by means of a canal, which in many respects is worthy of observation, and particularly as being the first that was ever made in Wales. Before this canal was cut, the coals were taken to Swansea river by a tedious and expensive land carriage and shipped at Foxhole. It was found necessary to take the canal for nearly two miles through the midst of Crymlyn, or Crumlin bog or morass, the soft spongy ground of which rising up repeatedly after the surface was cut away, seemed to present an insufferable obstacle to the completion of the undertaking. The work was finished in the year 1790, and may be looked upon as not the least striking instance which this country affords of spirit and perseverance successfully exerted; the length of the canal being somewhat more than three miles, and the whole cost of the undertaking defrayed by a single individual.'

In the process of preparing the canal, Elton's men discovered the skeleton of an old boat in what appeared to be an even older canal or ditch known as 'Clawdd-y-Seison' ('the English Ditch'), likely used in early times for the conveyance of coal from the ancient collieries of Kilvey. The Glan Y Wern Canal was used for about 20 years, during which time Elton was declared bankrupt, passing away in 1810, however, by then it was disused as Lord Vernon had placed distraint on wharves and barges against Elton's unpaid debt.

The Tennant Canal

After the construction of his Rhyddings Canal which ran to the River Neath, Tennant set his sights on the acquisition of the Glan-Y-Wern and Red Jacket Pill with the aim of linking the River Neath to the River Tawe, so as to enable transportation of the mineral wealth of the Neath Valley to the fast-growing port at Swansea. W.H. Jones [31] observed that Tennant held the opinion that the 'great merchants of London, Liverpool, and Bristol' would soon Swansea as a port 'superior to that of Bristol', and that they would then establish 'branch-houses' in the town to reflect its importance. However unlike the canal development in Neath which was the result of a number of parliamentary acts that allowed for a compulsory purchase of any and all land deemed a requirement to develop the project, in 1817 Tennant opted instead to use private funds to develop what would be a four-mile-long canal beginning at Red Jacket Pill and ending at a sea lock at his own port on Fabian's Bay, close to the mouth of the River Tawe.

In 1823 Tennant came to an agreement with the Neath Canal Company to provide a junction with their canal, and in 1824 a navigable waterway of nearly 14 miles was completed that linked Aberdulais, via the Aberdulais Aqueduct and the Neath Canal, to the port of Swansea. Neath Valley minerals could now reach world markets and Tennant's port would become a vital part of the region's economic growth, as reported in The Cambrian [32] on 15th May 1824:

'We yesterday witnessed with much satisfaction, in which we were heartily joined by some thousands of spectators, the opening of Mr Tennant's Junction Canal. Ten barges fully laden with coal, accompanied by a brass band, were safely conveyed from the colliery of Mr Protheroe, in the Vale of Neath, and delivered at the shipping place in our harbour… 'the health of George Tennant, Esq, and may his canal return him a large interest for all the capital expended on it' was drunk with great enthusiasm accompanied by three times three.'

Seven weeks later the same newspaper commented on the immediate success of the canal, and noted that 376 barges with 5930 tons of coal and timber have already 'passed over its line', and 49 ships have cleared 4484 tons of culm from what the traders now call 'Port Tennant'. In addition, an 'inconsiderable number of passengers have used the canal as 'the inhabitants of Neath and vicinity are allowed to navigate it with their families, servants, shop goods and parcels, free of all charge.

In October 1823 an anonymous proposal was published in the local press to further develop Swansea's port, and on 10th January 1824, George Tennant's signed 'Prospectus' was promoted via the pages of The Cambrian to build two docks on Fabian's Bay adjacent to the Tennant Canal [33]

Prospectus the Proposed Docks at Swansea. The Docks may be of any required dimensions, those now proposed are as follows:

First: A Dock SCO yards in length on the Northside of the New Canal, and to communicate therewith by a stop-gate. This dock to be at the distance of 60 yards from the Canal, and to run parallel therewith. The Wharfs may range on both sides (as each will be equally accessible), for its whole length - each Wharf 60 yards in depth. Centre of the Dock 40 yards wide, slightly reduced towards each end, so as to give each wall the form of an arch.

Second: Another Dock on the Southside of the Canal, and also parallel therewith, of similar shape, but not quite so wide as that to the North-distance from the Canal 40 yards. Wharfs to oil both sides as in the former case, and equally accessible.

Thus there may be a frontage for Wharfs' of 1200 yards, with a depth of from 60 to 40 yards; and there will be water in each Dock, from 30 feet to any less depth. Ordinary spring tides rise to within two feet, extraordinary tides to within a few inches, of the surface of the Canal, and they have now and then risen to the towing path. The land on the north, through ten miles of country, inclines towards the Canal, and every stream and spring necessarily flows into it, so that it can never want water. The water in each Dock may when required be level with that of the Canal and if necessary, a communication for vessels might be made between them by crossing the Canal; but each will have access to the sea by a separate gate. Ship-building and Graving-docks may be easily added and timber may be had in abundance, with water carriage through 40 miles along the country where it is produced.

The flat ground adjoining the Docks contains ample space for all sorts of buildings, and conveniences applicable to Trade; and the rising ground behind, sheltered from the North and East Winds, commands Swansea Bay, the Mumbles Point and Light-House, with the finest scenery in South Wales. If this proposal meets with suitable encouragement, the Proprietor of the Land will grant long leases of the Wharfs at Nominal Rents, for moderate fines, or at reasonable Rack Rents—and undertake to employ the money thus to be raised, or so much thereof as shall be necessary, in finishing the Docks, without any additional charge on the Trader for entering them, the first applicants will have the first choice of situation. Other Grants or adjoining Lands may be obtained for Building purposes.

GEO. TENNANT. Cadoxton Lodge, 10th Jan. 1824.

As 'the Proprietor of the Land', the above prospectus did not gain the necessary support that Tennant had hoped for, and in 1827 another plan was mooted in the local press for a new floating dock at Port Tennant, but that also went no further than the drawing board. Local industrialists on the Swansea Harbour Trust acknowledged that the port did need further development to support its growing industrial needs and perhaps with their own vested interest in mind favoured a different plan, one that involved making a 'new cut' to redirect the river, with the land in between the 'new cut' and the old route of the river becoming a 'floating' dock.

The opening of the canal meant that Tennant could also utilise the adjoining land leased near his port, and a series of leases were taken out by Swansea and Neath coal shippers. The first was taken out in 1825 by Edward and Phillip Protheroe who were using the canal to transport stone, coal and culm to the port, and they leased a coal wharf at Salthouse Point. Other companies followed and the Bristol Iron Company (1827), Fox and Price (1829), Perkins & Morgan (1831), and Penrose & Starbuck (1831) were all operating their own wharves at 'East Pier Docks, Port Tennant' over the next few years.

RED-LION INN, SWANSEA FERRY.

Cheap CONVEYANCE by Canal.

ROBERT DAVIS respectfully informs the Public, that a commodious COVERED BOAT, neatly fitted up for Passengers and light Goods, will leave Port Tennant for Neath at half-past nine in the morning on Mondays, Wednesdays, and Fridays, and every Sunday at nine; and will return from Neath to Port Tennant at six o'clock in the evening of the same days.

N. B. Parties wishing to engage the Boat to proceed along the Canal up the Vale of Neath to Melincourt Waterfalls, on any of the intermediate days, may be accommodated by applying as above.

Swansea to Neath Return Trips via the Tennant Canal, August 1833

The canal was popular with traders and the public alike, and soon there was a daily canal packet boat travelling from Port Tennant to Neath every afternoon, whilst the same vessel made the Neath to Swansea trip every morning, with the markets in both Swansea and Neath seeing the benefit of this link. Tennant also opened a hotel close to the canal, and an 1830 letter from him to William Jenkins regarding a plot of land near the bridge at Danygraig suggests it may have been the Burrows Inn. [34] Tennant planned to expand his access to Swansea's port and also took out 1000-year leases on shorefront land owned by Francis Pinkney [35] as well as on land at Salthouse Point owned by The Duke of Beaufort. [36]

George Tennant became Deputy Lord Lieutenant of Glamorgan in 1828 and passed away four years later on 27th February 1832 whilst visiting Reverend George Pickard of Warmwell in Dorset, and such was his standing locally, that over 5,000 people attended his funeral service at Cadoxton. The Cambrian newspaper [37] posted an obituary on 3rd March that:

'Our obituary this week announces the lamented death of George Tennant of Cadoxton Lodge, in this county, whose name is inseparably connected with that spirited and beneficial undertaking of the formation of a canal connecting the rich Vale of Neath with the flourishing port of Swansea, and effecting a junction between the rivers Neath and Tawe. Mr Tennant's enterprising spirit furnished employment to numerous workmen and was constantly eliciting new and extended objects of speculation or practical interest. His talents were of the first order, and his manners eminently courteous and attractive. He was a kind and generous master, and a benevolent friend to the poor: his death is consequently a serious loss to the neighbourhood, as well as to his own affectionate family and near connexions.'

Alas, what could have been viewed by many as an overtly entrepreneurial approach to business during George Tennant's lifetime, soon became a liability to his sons. Henry and Charles Tennant took over their father's legal firm at Grey's Inn in London, whilst his youngest brother William took control of the estate in Neath that included the canal. They quickly found that much of the land utilised to develop his canal was purchased from Lord Jersey and financed via the Childs Bank, owned by the family of Lord Jersey's wife Sarah.

By 1830 a figure of £60,000 was owed, secured against George Tennant's estate, an amount equivalent to over £7.6 million in 2022. The pressures of an exceedingly complex canal business proved too much for William, and he passed away in October 1833 only eighteen months after his father and was buried with him at Cadoxton Church, after which Charles Tennant, together with his mother, Margaret Tennant, took charge of all of his father's South Wales business interests.

Distrust between the Briton Ferry Estate and the Tennant family continued for many years after the passing of George Tennant, and Charles Tennant's interference in the County Asylum issue in 1852 likely did not help matters. In 1855 he and his family were accused by the Earl Of Jersey of falsifying Estate Accounts as well as of acquiring Estate property under false pretences, [38] reflected in the Tennant family's own records on the same issue [39] as 'Notes made by Charles Tennant of 'false and slanderous communications made by earl and countess of Jersey…'.

In October 1872, after years of legal issues, by order of the High Court of Chancery in London, the Tennant Canal and the Port Tennant Works were put up for auction [40] as were Red Jacket, the Briton Ferry Works, Cadoxton House and numerous other properties in Swansea and Neath, although, the canal still remains in the ownership of the Coombe-Tennant family to this day.

The Benson Family

Thomas Starling Benson (1775-1858) was an industrialist from Camberwell in London, although his family had its roots in North Yorkshire, and he moved to London in 1790 to be apprenticed as a surveyor. He was a vinegar and mustard manufacturer in 1802, and by 1806 he had been accepted into the Worshipful Company of Drapers, who listed him at various times as a timber merchant, iron merchant and latterly a copper smelter. He married Elizabeth Newbury in 1800 who passed away in 1803 leaving two children, Thomas and Elizabeth, and married her sister Hannah in the same year. Thomas and Hannah had 4 children – Starling (1808), Sarah Jane (1812), Emma (1813) and finally, Florance John (1815) however Hannah passed away shortly after his birth.

The following year he married again, this time to Elizabeth Meux, and had 3 more sons, Richard Henry (who died as an infant), Henry Roxby and Richard Meux. Thomas and Elizabeth also had two daughters, Margaret Sanderson and Elizabeth Meux, both of whom also died in infancy. At the age of thirty-two he was appointed the Deputy Lieutenant of Surrey and five years later in 1812 became High Sheriff of the County.

He first took an interest in South Wales in the 1820s, and in 1827 formed Usborne, Benson & Company with brothers Henry and Thomas Usborne, with offices on Broad St. London. Thomas Usborne, whose son had married Benson's daughter Emma, left the partnership in 1825. In 1830, Usborne Benson & Company bought the Fforest Copper Works near Morriston from Nicholas Troughton, a business that recovered copper from slag and rolled rather than stamped it into sheets, a common process at that time.

Within a short period it was evident that access to more coal was required to be able to realise the company's potential, and two farms (Tyr Eynon and Noyadd Wen) were leased in order to gain access to the nearby Graigola coal seams. Wenallt Colliery and Ynsygerwn Copper Works were also leased from George Tennant who had various business concerns in the Neath Valley area.

Following a survey, they built a tramway that connected the mine to the copper works, a line that would later become the origins of the Swansea Vale Railway. Works supervisor William Hart Logan Edmonds had a positive influence on the business, and in April 1833, after Henry Usborne sold his interest in the company, a new company was formed known as Benson, Logan & Company. Thomas' son Starling acquired part of his father's shareholdings, and Logan's nephews William and Henry Logan were given part of his.

Swansea Vale Railway

Note: In the following paragraphs the acronyms are used so as to simplify the text:

SVR - Swansea Vale Railway; SWR - South Wales Railway; WMR - Welsh Midland Railway; MRC - Midland Railway Company; GWR - Great Western Railway

For many years John Smith's Canal was the route of choice for Swansea Valley companies to get their goods to the port of Swansea, the main product being the highly prized anthracite coal from Graigola. Smith's Canal ran from Hen Noyadd in Ystradgynlais to Brewer's Bank north of the strand in Swansea, and companies connected to it via their private wagonways, however, there was a general agreement between company owners that a link to a steam-driven railway service would drastically speed up transportation links.

The west bank of the river was heavily industrialised with the adjacent infrastructure geared up to the smooth operation of the copper smelting companies, whilst by comparison, infrastructure on the east side of the river was underdeveloped, although there was an existing tramway that ran from Gwenllwynchwyth to the White Rock wharf. Known as 'Scott's Tramroad', it was named after John Scott who built it in c1817. Scott sold it in 1828 to Charles Henry Smith, who worked 'Scott's Pit' as well as a number of others he owned locally.

By 1835, the Bensons had taken ownership of Tyrlandwr [41] and knowing that linking the Swansea Valley companies to the proposed 'Float' offered great opportunities, they engaged engineer William Kirkhouse to carry out a survey to assess the Vale of Swansea as to the viability of developing a new railway that would run on the east side of the River Tawe. By the end of 1844 an agreement between Starling Benson, Joseph Martin of Glyncollen, John Nicholas Lucas of Stouthall and C.H. Smith amongst others had, by a combination of lease and ownership, control of lands that enabled the group to construct a railway line from Tyrlandwr via Pentrechwyth and onto the tramroad leading to Graigola colliery, and in April 1845, a tender announcement was placed in the

Cambrian by SVR for contractors to extend and develop Scott's Railway. [42]

The new company was called the 'Swansea Vale Railway Company' (SVR) and initially Starling Benson and Joseph Martin took the role of provisional directors [43]from which point shares were allocated to other directors, who included CH Smith, Starling's brother Florance John Benson, and his half-brother Richard Meux Benson. With the board of directors in place, the company requested an Act of Parliament to allow the purchase or lease of the land to further extend the line from Tyrlandwr to Ystradgynlais as well as the purchase of the land for five branch railways, so SVR decided to purchase Lord Jersey's interest in 'Scott's Tramroad' as well as buy out CH Smith's interest in the White Rock Company. The bill failed at its second hearing when it was pointed out that the railway crossed three watercourses claimed by the Duke of Beaufort.

The company were in negotiations with Welsh Midland Railway (WMR) and with the South Wales Railway (SWR), who had agreed to buy their undertaking for £74,516, the negotiation handled by Florance John Benson. SWR applied for a new bill in Parliament for the purchase and development of a new railway to run on the east side of the Tawe that they named 'The Swansea Valley Railway', but due to a breakdown in internal communications involving SWR advisor Isambard Kingdom Brunel, in December 1846 SWR rescinded their earlier agreement. Starling Benson responded and advised that SWR would be expected to pay compensation for the loss and delay incurred by SVR since entering into the now-rescinded agreement.

In July 1847, the new Swansea Valley Railway Act was passed that allowed for the building of a new railway from Ystradgynlais to Swansea, although the Act made clear that construction included the purchase and utilisation of the Swansea Vale Railway 'as may have been agreed on with the proprietors of said Railway.' The SWR resolved to purchase SVR, and offered the sum of £70k, with the new railway to be called the Swansea Valley Railway. Richard Meux Benson disputed the valuation based on the then valuation of SWR shares, and an impasse was reached. SVR continued its operation between Tryrlandwr and Llansamlet, and for the next three years, both they and SWR operated independently of each other, although they clashed over a section of rail at Llansamlet where the South Wales Railways service line crossed SVR lines. In 1850 SWR extended their 'Swansea Valley Railway' power to purchase for an additional year, however in August 1851 it had lapsed, and now free of any SWR options, in 1852 Swansea Vale Railway extended its line to Graigola.

Pursued under the chairmanship of Starling Benson, new Parliamentary Acts [44] allowed them to further extend the line in 1855 'and work the same as a Passenger Railway' from Graigola to a new station in Pontardawe, as well as from the terminus near Tyrlandwr to a point further south near the mouth of the New Cut on Fabian's Bay in St Thomas. It linked to Llanelly Railway, extended further from Pontardawe to Ynysygeinon, added loop lines at Morriston and Clydach, and opened a goods shed on the East Dock via an extension from St Thomas Station that ran, in an agreement with Great Western Railway, via an overhead line across Fabian Street. In the following year SVR had approval for an extension to Claypon's Wharf in Ystradgynlais, the three branch lines to Ystalyfera Ironworks, Palleg or Cwmtwch Railway, and a third to Ynyscedwyn Branch Canal.

In 1869 SVR began discussions with MRC and in a shareholder meeting held on March 25th 1874, the board approved the MRC to SVR Lease, which passed on July 30th 1874, and MRC took possession on September 1874, an agreement that finally gave them direct access to Swansea. SVR remained as a financial entity until 1876 at which time, as a result of an Act and it was absorbed into MRC. The Great Western Railway (GWR) opened its Swansea District Line in 1913, a route that bypassed Swansea and interacted with the MRC line north of Morriston and extended on to Clydach and Trebanos. Although all services were affected by WW1, the GWR line, together with the introduction of bus services in 1918, had a detrimental effect on MRC's services. The Railways Act of 1922 saw the compulsory merging of railway companies into four new companies, and the MRC became a major part of the London, Midland and Scottish Railway (LMS), whilst some of its lines moved to the London North West Railway (LNWR) resulting in the discontinuation of the MRC's Swansea to Birmingham route.

Over the following 20 years, many of its Welsh routes were either re-routed to old LNWR lines, passed to GWR, or closed down completely, although the old SVR network remained active thanks to its Graigola links. British Railways were nationalised in 1948 and both the Upper Bank Station and the Swansea St Thomas Station, which had opened on 21st February 1860 and was known locally as 'The Midland', finally closed on 25th September 1950.

Further to their Swansea Valley interests, Thomas and his son Starling also had business concerns on the Gower Peninsula, specifically in the Penclawdd area (outside the remit of this book), but in addition to the Swansea Vale Railway, it is their direct involvement in the development of the new 'Floating Harbour' at Swansea port that would forever change the shape of the east side of the River Tawe.

The New Cut

The Neath Canal, via the Aberdulais Aqueduct, had been linked to the Tennant Canal since 1824, running between Red Jacket Pill and ending at George Tennant's own wharves on Fabian's Bay, resulting in Swansea exporting substantial amounts of coal and minerals from Neath. However following an 1827 Parliamentary bill amendment to the Glamorgan Turnpike Act of 1823, the approval of the building of bridges at Briton Ferry and Swansea, plus a new road through Crymlyn Burrows that offered a more direct road route between Swansea and Neath, and for the first time a bridge built at the River Tawe would link the rural east side of Swansea to the town, to that point only manageable by a two-boat arrangement known as the 'The Swansea Ferry', where one boat carried people, and the other carried livestock, horses, carriages and larger items.

Founded in 1791, the role of the Swansea Harbour Trust (SHT) was to 'repair, enlarge and preserve the Harbour of Swansea' and the board of trustees was made up of local businessmen and industrialists. Keen to take advantage of his recent success, George Tennant proposed a new 'Public Docks' at Swansea, to be built at Fabian's Bay, and linked directly to his canal, and promoted his plan directly to the public via the pages of The Cambrian, however, his proposal for docks, wharves and supporting facilities was not acted upon and instead Trustees put forward a number of other ideas as to how to best further develop the port before a consensus was reached.

The proposal to make a 'new cut' to redirect the river was favoured, which would involve the purchase of land on the east bank at the mouth of the River Tawe. At a Trustees meeting In April 1831, the concept of a Floating Harbour was finally agreed upon, something that depended upon making a navigable 'new cut' waterway through Reverend Henry Sharpe Pocklington's Tyrlandwr estate that ran adjacent to the eastern bank of the Tawe, from the mouth of the river up to the end of Pentreguinea Road.

A competition was organised for the best-engineered plan for a Floating Harbour 'to be built for not more than the budget of £60,000' with a prize of 200 guineas [45] and Mr Jesse Hartley was deemed the winner. His plan was approved, and the Trustees set about the purchase of Tyrlandwr, accepting Reverend Pocklington's asking price of £13,000, but noting that an Act of Parliament would first be required to allow for work to be carried out before any purchase could be completed. However, due to a combination of poor stewardship and short-sightedness of the Swansea Harbour Trust coupled with a reluctance of the local copper barons to pay additional taxes to fund 'The Float', the purchase was not made.

In 1827 Tyrlandwr was let and four years later, after Pocklington had married and left Swansea, it was put up for rent or sale on multiple occasions between 1828 and 1830 [46]. In October 1834, after Thomas Benson had finalised the sale of a property from the estate of his wife's family, he purchased Tyrlandwr, paying only £11,000, substantially less than that offered previously by the Trustees a few years earlier, and on completion of the purchase, the property was immediately made available to rent. [47]

The Swansea Harbour Act of 1836 subsequently came into force, which allowed for the various purchases to be made to make the New Cut, as well as build a Wet 'Floating' Dock that linked to both the New Cut and to a Half-Tide Basin. The Act also covered the deepening and improvement of the river bed to enable navigation of shipping to reach as far as the Fforest Works near Morriston, in the Parish of Llangyfelach. Given the importance of such a project, the number of Trustees was increased to twenty-four, most of whom were businessmen with a vested interest in the success of the project, and this included both Thomas Benson and his son Starling, who had become a town councillor a year earlier.

Discussions between Swansea Harbour Trust and the Bensons over the purchase of Tyrlandwr began amicably but turned sour when Thomas Benson made it clear that he intended to retain the eastern side of the estate with the aim of developing wharves on the east bank of the New Cut, to be linked via a new railway to his businesses in the Lower Swansea Valley. His ambitious plans were thwarted however when the Trustees voted to make the New Cut a waste-water cut only.

Thomas had been willing to sell the land required for New Cut and float at the price he paid for it, but instead informed SHT that he required an additional £5,000 severance payment because of the various disjointed resolutions tending to the injury of the property in adjoining lands', addressing this directly in a letter to The Cambrian on 13th February 1841 [48]. Outraged at his request, SHT evoked section 33 of the 1836 Act in order to get an independent valuation of the land in question, and the case was heard on July 14th 1838 at the Glamorgan Quarter Sessions. Expert witnesses were called on both sides and a valuation of between £19-21,000 was estimated for the whole estate of Tyrlandwr. The jury awarded Thomas a total of £10,341 broken down as £2,865 for the land to be utilised by the New Cut and 'Float', and a further £7,476 as a severance payment, an amount totalling nearly 50% more than that initially severance payment requested. [49]

This result did not sit well with the Trustees, who applied to the Court of the Queen's Bench to overturn the decision, however, the Bensons had already applied to the Court of Bail to support the jury's award and this was subsequently granted, and the SHT application was neutered. In April 1839, SHT reluctantly agreed to pay Thomas the full amount awarded but added a caveat that should it later become navigable, Thomas should return some of the payment awarded plus renounce all his shipping rights, a condition that was refused outright.

Henry Tennant, the eldest son of the late George Tennant, was long aware of the ill-feeling voiced by certain Trustees who felt excluded from the big profits to be made on port trade via Port Tennant and addressed his frustration at the continued delays to the New Cut project in a strongly worded letter in The Cambrian on May 9th 1839 [50]. After first taking aim at Mr John Henry Vivian for his perceived lethargy on the matter, he set upon the rest of the trustees for their reluctance to act in the best interests of the town before themselves, something he likened to the attitude shown towards his late father over the construction of the Tennant Canal and its wharfage.

He highlighted the contents of a letter he had sent to the Clerk of Trustees in strong support of the Bensons, in which he directly challenged the complacent attitude shown by the Trustees and urged them to ensure compliance with the award of the Court of Queen's Bench award to pay to Mr Benson the several sums of money therein mentioned, without further delay. He urged that work begins 'at full speed' on 'The New Cut', and that the cut be 'navigable' and not a 'waste-water cut' as some Trustees had asked for. He requested a Financial Committee be formed to ensure regular and proper financial reports are available to Trustees, and if the above actions were not taken in the manner he stipulated then, he moved that 'there ought to be appointed in the place and stead of the present Trustees of Swansea harbour, an entirely new set of Trustees.'

Tennant also blamed Swansea Harbour Trust for the delay in building a Tawe Bridge, and whilst mentioning John Henry Vivian's lip-service to the issue tied the matter to the recent loss of lives from the Swansea Ferry:

'…when I reflect upon the late lamentable loss of lives at Swansea ferry, and the charge contained in the letter written by the Agent of His Grace the Duke of Beaufort, relating to that most disastrous occurrence, which, as he states, (and I fear but too truly) never would have happened "but for the senseless squabbles of the

Trustees of Swansea Harbour", in as much "a good bridge would have been long since substituted for the inconvenient ferry, I feel it to be my bounden duty to do all that in me lies to assist Mr Vivian in his laudable "object of inducing the Trustees to decide on some definite plan of proceeding"

I remain, Sir, your obedient servant, HENRY TENNANT.'

By May 1840 work had finally begun on the excavation of the New Cut, and by the end of 1843, although still not complete, it could be traversed as a waterway. In January of the same year, Starling Benson was elected as Mayor of Swansea. Although vessels used the New Cut from March 1845, by early 1848 the New Cut was completed and the Float, later known as The North Dock, opened officially on January 1st 1852.

The South Dock

Swansea had earned the title of 'The Brighton of Wales' complete with promenade, bathing machines and spas, but a wet dock 'to be built on corporation land' and initially suggested in 1839, was to be built on Burrows Square, part of Swansea's health and wellness beachfront. Bordered on two sides by the upmarket properties of Gloucester Place and of Cambrian Place, which included the newly constructed Assembly Rooms, Burrows Square was also a stone's throw away from the nearby Town Hall. The potential loss of one of Swansea's most prestigious residential areas was a major concern to those who opposed the plan, but a new Swansea Docks Act was passed in July 1847 that included plans for a new wet dock that would later be known as The South Dock. The Swansea Dock Company Ltd, supported by Lewis Dillwyn, JH Vivian and George Grant Francis amongst others, had successfully reached the stage of a ground-breaking ceremony, held on February 26th 1852, when the Duke of Worcester was invited to 'cut the first sod'.

However, the project was fraught with financial problems, and Swansea Corporation had to intervene and buy many of the company's shares. By 1857 the Swansea Dock Company was no more and the task of completing the construction of the dock was passed to the Swansea Harbour Trust, now led by Starling Benson who was made Chairman a year before, at which time proposals were being discussed for developing yet another new dock, to be built on the east side of the Tawe.

A railway link to the South Dock was a major issue, and George Grant Francis put forward a plan to construct a line from Landore that would run via the Graig quarries near Heathfield [51] and then on to Oystermouth Road, where it could link to the Oystermouth line, and from there head east to the new dock, but his proposal was not accepted. A railway connection was finally agreed on and a high-level line was constructed, supported by a series of railway arches that ran from a junction at the South Wales Railway Station (later known as High Street Station) and ended at the north-western corner of the South Dock.

A broad-gauge track of seven feet was to be laid, and WH Jones, in his History of Port of Swansea [52] commented that 'For this purpose much property and wharfage had to be acquired; transformed by the erection of the substantial arches; the canal wharves, the Brewery premises, Richardson's dry dock and repairing yard, the Landore Cameron's and Swansea wharves, and particularly the Corporation quay, suffered considerable encroachment. Some ancient houses on the east end of the Strand were removed, as to, was the western side of Quay Parade, where stood the Ship Inn, one of the rendezvous of the press-gang, a great many old houses on the east side of Little Wind-street (formerly Watchet-row, significant of a good deal of trade which had been carried on between the two ports), including another press-gang resort, the Beehive public house, and the spacious gardens of these houses, which reached to the present line of the Victoria-road front of the Sailors' Home, paid a heavy toll to the great mass of masonry which formed the viaduct upon which the railway was to be laid.'

The line passed between York St and Victoria Road, and cut through the ground of the Royal Institution of South Wales and onward to the South Dock, narrowly missing the premises of 'the familiar sculptor's shop of Mr Levison, wherein had long been carved the attractive and highly coloured figure-heads which, to the pride of generations of gallant seamen, adorned the prow of many a wind-jammer whose well-set-up lines had been fashioned upon the banks of the Tawe.'

The South Dock (author's own collection)

Both the South Dock and its connecting railway line were opened on September 23rd 1859 by the daughter of CRM Talbot, Lord Lieutenant of Glamorgan by operating a lever Miss Talbot opened the lock gates that allowed the steam tug 'Beaufort' the honour of being the first vessel to officially enter the South Dock with SHT chairman Starling Benson and other Trustees onboard [53] followed by the steamer 'Cornelia', the barque 'Hampshire' (towed by the 'Tartar'), and lastly the yacht 'Bluebell'.

The opening of the dock meant the end of Swansea's plans to be a resort town, and the beginning of a sharp decline of the Burrows as a residential area, and within a few years most buildings there had become offices of the various companies serving the South and North Docks.

The East Dock (later renamed The Prince of Wales Dock)

Whilst a dock on the east side of the river had first been put forward by George Tennant in 1824, by 1858 there was a recognised need for even more docking facilities to handle Swansea's port trade. Amongst the schemes put forward was a proposal by Trustee councillor Frank Ash Yeo that both the North Dock and New Cut should 'be floated' with wharfage on either side of both waterways. However a proposal for a new dock to be built on Fabians Bay was accepted and preparation was made to apply to Parliament for a Bill to cover the construction, and in 1872 Engineer-in-Chief James

Abernethy was asked to produce a report on the most effective ways to deepen the approaches to the docks as well as advise on the best way to increase wharfage to the port 'having regard to provision for railway access and arrangements for the shipping of minerals and goods [54] In his report [55] Abernethy stated:

'For the purpose of maintaining a channel of the wide and depth proposed, it is necessary not only to give all possible effect to the direction of the ingoing and outgoing current, but also to the tidal volume flowing into and out of the river, and therefore in approaching the question of dock accommodation, it is obvious that the closing up of the great indent of Fabian's Bay will tend to accelerate the tidal flow into the upper reaches of the river, and give a better direction and greater force to the outgoing current. I have, therefore, for this reason, together with the questions of facility of access and the best means of affording railway communication, selected as the site of any future dock, the whole of Fabian's Bay and the greater portion of Port Tennant.

As regards the entrance to the dock, I propose the construction of a lock 400 feet in length and 60 feet in width, divided into two compartments of the respective lengths of 150 feet and 250 feet, the outer cill to be laid at the level of 28ft. 6in. below high water average spring tides, or 21 feet at neaps, being the same depth of 25 feet below high water average spring tides; the water in the dock being maintained at that minimum level, the bottom to be 2 feet below the cill level, or 27 feet below high water average spring tides. The dock at its greatest length will be 2330 feet, with a maximum width of 500 feet, having an area of 22 ½ acres, communicating at the east end by a small lock with Port Tennant canal, from which by proper arrangements a supply of water may be obtained.

With respect to the important feature of railway communication, I propose in the first place the construction of a quay with sidings on its north side. The space occupied by the quay being 80 feet, and for the sidings, 280 feet in width, the latter to be on the level with the Great Western and Swansea Vale Railways and admitting of extensive siding accommodation in connection with the coal drops, eight in number, each siding being 1000 feet in length, and capable of accommodation complete rain of coals. Each drop will be capable of loading on an average of 1000 tons per day.

For the accommodation of ores, iron, patent fuel, and general traffic, I propose a low-level connection with the Great Western and Swansea Vale Railways; the quays are of great width, and there is ample provision for storing and the construction of warehouse and sheds. In addition to the quays, which are 300 feet in width, an extensive space of ground may be formed from excavation, dredging, and ballast between the quay and the new line of the eastern pier, 15 acres in extent and of great value for general and commercial purposes.'

The purchase of land required to develop the East Dock lacked the protracted drama that surrounded the proposal and construction of both the North and South Docks, and an agreement with the Tennant Estate granted the Corporation their required facilities on the condition that, instead of payment, they be given a dedicated wharf on the proposed docks for which the Tennant Estate would receive dues. Dealings with the Duke of Beaufort were amicable and dealt with acquiring land actually formed by the 'spoils' of the New Cut, which were deposited and spread on Fabian's Bay. At the time of excavation, the Duke gave the Trustees an option of paying £5,000 for his ground needed for the New Cut project, or alternatively a £500 payment plus the depositing and spreading of the spoils on the foreshore of Fabian's Bay. The Earl of Jersey also understood that such a development would be to his advantage and withdrew objections he had previously raised.

The link to a railway system was now vitally important, and whilst there was some concern that the bigger railway companies had begun to monopolise routes, an agreement was reached with the Great Western Railway with respect to the land required by the Trust, in line with the Swansea Harbour Act 1874, and shortly afterwards the Midland Railway applied for an Act to lease the Swansea Valley Railway, fully supported by the Trustees, who recognised its potential for further dock growth. In July 1879 excavation work on the new East Dock began on an informal basis, formally commencing in March 1880.

The Prince of Wales Dock (author's own collection)

After reducing the planned shutting out of tidal water from twelve to three months, the official opening of the dock was carried out on 18th October 1881 by the Prince and Princess of Wales, at which time the dock was renamed 'The Prince of Wales Dock' in honour of Prince Edward's attendance.

Figure 1 A Commemorative Coin issued to guests at the official opening of the Prince of Wales Dock. (author's own collection)

During the same royal visit a new Swansea highway, for a short period known as Yeo St after the twice-mayor of Swansea and current Harbour Trust chairman Frank Yeo, was renamed 'Alexandra Road' in honour of the Princess. An extension of the

Prince of Wales Dock, designed by Joseph Abernathy, was approved by the Swansea Harbour Act 1894 and work commenced in February 1896, its official completion commemorated by the laying of the last coping stone by The Marchioness of Worcester on the 14th March 1898.

Starling Benson would not see the opening of the new East Dock as on January 16th 1879, he died tragically at his estate at Fairy Hill, on the Gower peninsula [56]

Whilst out rabbit shooting with his gamekeeper William Lewis, he stumbled about 12 feet down a bank, but whilst both barrels of his shotgun discharged during his fall, they were not the cause of any injury, and it was understood that he had struck his head on a rocky outcrop. His gamekeeper stated: 'it is a very rocky place, and one large stone projects very sharply at the edge, almost like a knife. I looked at the stone afterwards and saw some hair on it. This makes me feel sure he must have struck against it falling.'

Semi-conscious, he was taken to Fairy Hill where he was attended to by Doctor Henry Vaux Ellis of Reynoldston, who confirmed that there was 'a fearful scalp wound, extending from the right eyebrow, taking a course up to the top of the head and back down to the nape of the neck…and the skull was fractured.'

Starling Benson died just a few hours later. He was 70 years old.

The Briton Ferry Estate

Note: For simplification of text, the acronym BFE is used for the Briton Ferry Estate.

Originally part of the lands of Margam Abbey, you would be forgiven if you thought that the Briton Ferry Estate (BFE) was to be found to the east of the River Neath. Whilst the estate encompassed land in Aberavon, Baglan, Briton Ferry, Neath, Cadoxton-juxta-Neath, Margam, Michaelston-super-Avon and beyond, it also included lands to the west of the river, including land in Gower, Llangyfelach, Llansamlet, Swansea St Mary's, St John-juxta-Swansea, Kilvey and St Thomas.

In the early 1600s, the BFE was owned by the Price family of Briton Ferry, and when Jane Price, the daughter of William Price (died 1627) married Arthur Mansel the son of Sir Thomas Mansel of Margam (died 1631), their third and only surviving son Bussy Mansel was in line to inherit the estate. Born in 1623, Bussy Mansel supported the Royalist cause, as did the rest of Thomas Mansel's family. His sister had married William Thomas of Danygraig, Sheriff of Glamorgan, son of Walter Thomas of Swansea and Danygraig, both of whom were also prominent Royalists in Swansea.

The Mansel Family

The Mansel family of Oxwich had invested in monastic lands following Henry VIII's Dissolution of the Monasteries and owned the estates formerly belonging to Margam Abbey, and in 1595 Sir Thomas Mansel inherited the family mansion, which had been built on the site of the Abbey. A Member of Parliament for Glamorgan in 1597, 1604 and 1614, he bought a baronetcy in 1611, shortly after James I had created the hereditary order, and became the 1st Baron Mansell of Margam.

After Oliver Cromwell's success in the First Civil War of 1642, whilst many of Sir Thomas's grandson Bussy Mansel's friends had their estates sequestrated, he changed sides and his brother-in-law William Thomas's estates were passed to him, and although he regained them after he was pardoned, Bussy inherited them after his death. Now a fervent Parliamentarian, in 1645 Bussy was appointed Commander-in-Chief of the parliamentary forces in Glamorgan at only 22 years old. Two years later he was made High Sheriff of Glamorgan, and in 1650 together with John Price, he was tasked with the supervision of Cromwell's Survey of Gower.

His rise within the Parliamentary governance of Wales was dramatic, and on 25th June 1651 he was added to the High Court of Justice, and in 1653 was on Cromwell's 'Barebones Parliament' as one of six members selected to represent Wales. In 1654 he was made a Militia Commissioner for South Wales, and in the following year, he was made a Justice of the Peace for Glamorgan. After acting as a Commissioner for Safety of the Protector, in 1659 he was given the command of all militia forces in South Wales, horse and foot, "to lead them against the enemy if need be". During the Restoration period, he changed his allegiances from Parliamentarian back to Royalist again, seemingly without any loss to either his assets or reputation, and was described at the time as 'concerned in the late times, but early repenting', and in 1660 he was elected Member of Parliament for Cardiff in the Convention Parliament.

He was High Sheriff of Glamorgan in 1677, and was elected MP for Glamorgan in 1679 until 1681, and again in 1689 until his death on 25th May 1699. He was succeeded by his eldest son, Thomas Mansel (c1646 –13th December 1684), who on his death was buried in Westminster Abbey, and he, in turn, was succeeded by his son, also Thomas Mansel (c1688 -15th January 1706) who was Member of Parliament for Glamorgan (1701) and of Cardiff (1702- 1706), and at the time of his death was Constable of Cardiff Castle. He died without issue and was buried next to his father at Westminster Abbey. The Briton Ferry Estate was bequeathed to his godson Bussy Mansel, who would later become the 4th Baron Mansel of Margam.

The second Bussy Mansel (c1699 - 29th November 1750) inherited the BFE in 1706. He was the Member of Parliament for Cardiff between 1727 and 1734, and for Glamorganshire between 1737 and 1745, and succeeded his brother Christopher Mansel as the 4th Baron Mansel of Margam in 1744. On 17 May 1724, he married Lady Elizabeth Hervey, the daughter of John Hervey, 1st Earl of Bristol, and after his wife died without issue, on 13th March 1729 married his second wife Barbara Villiers, daughter of William Villiers, 2nd Earl of Jersey. They had one daughter, the Hon. Louisa Barbara Mansel, who on 16th July 1757 married George Venables-Vernon.

Drawn by Swansea's readily-available coal supply, in 1717 the Llangyfelach Copperworks in Landore was opened by John Lane of Bristol (taken over by Morris, Lockwood & Co in 1726), and in 1720 a Quaker named James Griffiths opened a second copper works in Swansea, this time very close to the town, where the Burlais Brook met the Tawe. This marked the beginning of what would make Swansea the copper-smelting capital of the world, and in 1736 Bussy Mansel saw an opportunity to be part of the growing copper industry, and to that end acquired a 1000-acre estate known as Cnapcoch on the western slopes of Kilvey Hill, previously owned by the Popkin family.

After the death of John Popkin in 1730, the land remained in the hands of his mother Elizabeth Popkin who had a life interest, however on her death in 1732 Bussy Mansel, aware that the land was now worth a considerable amount of money, approached John Popkin's son and heir Morgan, and advised him of his intention to take ownership of the Cnapcoch estate due to unpaid loans made by Lord Mansel to John Popkin in 1723, and secured against his land. By 1736 Bussy had for 'fifty pounds paid in hand' acquired the equity of the redemption of a mortgage from the young man. [57]

The land reverted to the BFE, and a lease was agreed with a group of Bristol businessmen led by Thomas Coster for six acres of riverside land for the construction of the White Rock Copper Works, plus a nearby piece of land called Morfa Carw, which would be used for laying down cinder and slag. Bussy paid £1500 for the rights to supply coal to the new works, brought directly to White Rock via the 'Great Coal Road' from Llansamlet, that had been built some years earlier by the first Bussy Mansel and his partner Hopkin Jones, who had together mined in Bonymaen and Llansamlet.

The Elizabethan 'Cnapcoch House' was converted into workers housing some years later. After the closure of their Llangyfelach Works in 1748, Lockwood, Morris & Co opened the Fforest Copperworks in 1749, and in the following year one of Bussy's last pieces of business only weeks before his death was to agree on the 99-year lease of land dated 7th Nov. 1750, 'for rent £600 yearly and duties on coal' to Chauncy Townsend, who wanted to build a waggon way to carry coal from his Llansamlet pits to wharves on the eastern side of the River Tawe, from where it could be loaded directly onto ships. [58]

Following his death on 29th November 1750, the Briton Ferry Estate passed to his sole heir, his daughter Louisa Barbara Mansel, at which time the Mansel barony and baronetcy became extinct, and on 16th July 1757 Louisa Barbara Mansel married George Venables-Vernon, who assumed control of the Estate.

The Vernon Family

George Venables-Vernon, 2nd Baron Vernon of Kinderton (9th May 1735 –18th June 1813) was educated at Westminster School, Westminster, London before he graduated from Trinity Hall, Cambridge University, with a Master of Arts. A Whig Party politician, he held the office of Member of Parliament for Weobley (1757 and 1761), Bramber (1762-1768) and Glamorgan (1768-1780). He became 2nd Lord Vernon, Baron of Kinderton, on the death of his father on 21 August 1780.

In 1755 Chauncey Townsend established the Middle Bank Works on BFE land on the eastern bank of the River Tawe, located between the White Rock Copper Works and the Upper Bank Works being constructed further north. The Middle Bank Works was set up to smelt lead but moved to copper in 1765. The Upper Bank Works, also owned by Chauncey Townsend in partnership with his son-in-law John Smith, had opened in 1757 as a zinc works, but by 1765 it too was used to smelt copper. Townsend later sold his interests in the copper smelting industry, and his descendants the Smith family played a leading role in the success of the local coal industry, and opened the Smith Canal in the mid-1780s, replacing Townsend's waggon way.

In 1777, John Popkin, the son of Morgan, began civil proceedings against the BFE and Lord Vernon via a Chancery bill and alleged that the late Bussy Mansel had bullied his father, and began legal action against him in order to regain control of his father's land. He argued that the mortgage redemption payment made was only a third of its true worth, and that his father was also promised a further payment based on coal cleared under the estate. Alas with no such agreements mentioned in the deed of surrender of the mortgage equity, John Popkin had to drop the case.

The Harbour Improvement Act was passed in 1791, but much of the Eastside of Swansea remained a rural area, reflected in the often lifetime leases being issued to individuals who wanted to both live on and work on the land or else keep animals on it, with the land reverting back to its owner on death or forfeiture. Although many leases were surrendered and reissued as new leases to the leaseholder or his relatives, they ensured all mineral rights remained with the landowner. However, leases issued in relation to industrial usage were often short-term in nature and reflected the potentially volatile business environment of that time, and allowed the landowner an opportunity to issue more favourable agreements to themselves should tenants require additional land or services.

An example of one such 21-year lease agreement was made between George, Lord Vernon of Kinderton with John Freeman and a group of Bristol merchants in January 1796 [59] covered:

'Buildings, furnaces and smelting houses called White Rock copper and (brass) works, with all houses, garden, lands, mills, millponds, stanks, waters, watercourses, slagbanks, wharves and rights on Crymlin Morass…Part of Crwmlyn Morass or Crwmlyn Bog, adj. S. land called Crwmlyn Burrows in occ. of George, lord Vernon, E. and N. tow path of canal through said morass, W. said morass…'

'Right to smelt copper and brass and to convert buildings for this purpose; right to deposit slag, cinders and rubbish on land called Morfa'r Carw and adj. waste land, with right of demolition for this purpose; use of dock and quay at White Rock; use of springs and streams on lands at Graig Tyle Brown, Llannerch Clydir, Graig Knap Coch, Tir y Gwl and Graig y Foxhole, and all other waters and water courses, with right of diverting said courses, and landing rights.'

'Quarry rights at Cwm Skethan quarry and other quarries of George, Lord Vernon, right to extract earth, clay, sand and loam; Veins, mines and seams of coal, culm, tin, lead, copper, and iron, and quarries of slate and stone, and springs of salt, brine, copperas and allom, at Graig y Gwl and Crwmlyn Morass.'

These examples show that whilst land on the east bank of the Tawe was being utilised for new works and facilities, the agreement appears to sanction the use of the Crymlyn Bog as the dumping ground for any and all waste produced.

When Lady Vernon died in 1776, her last will and testimony showed that she had disinherited close relations from her family estate due to their 'lack of support to her in her troubles' and had also excluded her husband because of his unfaithfulness. [60]

She left her Newick Park Estate in Sussex to her friend Lady Fortescue, and the Penline Castle Estate in Glamorgan was given to Miss Emily Gwinnett of Cottrell. Gifts of money were left to her god-daughters, and a part of her estate also passed to her paternal aunt Mary Mansel who had married John Ivory Talbot, whilst her money, stocks and the 'residue of her estate' was left to her uncle Thomas, the Earl of Clarendon. The Briton Ferry Estate was passed to the Earl 'for his life' after which it would pass to the second son of George Bussy Villiers Earl of Jersey and his heirs on the condition that they 'take on themselves the name of Mansel', and on George Vernon's death in June 1813, the estate passed to **William Henry Augustus Villiers (1780–1813).**

In line with the proviso in Lady Vernon's will, William took the additional surname Mansel in order to inherit the estate, however, he passed away a month later without issue, and the BFE passed to his elder brother's son, George Child Villiers, the 5th Earl of Jersey.

On the death of Lord Vernon in June 1813, BFE papers [61] note that 'correspondence relating to proposed leases, legacies from the Will of Lady Vernon was enacted, and a circular letter sent out on 28th September 1813 to the leaseholders who received their leases from the late Lord Vernon, requiring them to quit and deliver up possession to George, Earl of Jersey, Edward Ellice and Alexander Murray, the new owners of the estate.'

The Villiers Family

George Child Villiers, 5th Earl of Jersey (19th August 1773 – 3rd October 1859). Born at the family's country seat Middleton Park in Oxfordshire, he was the elder son of the fourth earl George Bussy Villiers and succeeded in the earldom on his uncle's death in 1813.

He attended Harrow School, and before being awarded a Masters of Arts degree from St John's College, Cambridge, and was A Gentleman of the Bedchamber to the Prince of Wales in 1795.

On 23rd May 1804, he married Sarah Sophia Fane, with whom he had five sons and three daughters. Sarah was the sole heir of John Fane, the 10th Earl of Westmorland, and the granddaughter of the banker Robert Child of Osterley Park in Middlesex, and inherited her grandfather's substantial wealth that included his interest in Child's Bank. On 1st December 1819, the earl assumed the name of Child Villiers under royal license.

Lady Jersey was regarded as one of the great hostesses of English society and considered a leader of 'The Ton', a rigidly class-conscious social hierarchy, many of whom were from the gentry, aristocracy and royalty. [62] The term 'Ton' was shortened from the French phrase 'haut ton' meaning 'high fashion' or 'people of high fashion', something held in high regard by the 'beau monde' or rich and fashionable, of Britain. She was also a well-known patron of 'Almack's Assembly Room'[63], an exclusive London venue utilised by ladies and gentlemen of quality. Lord Jersey was untroubled by his wife's social life and when asked why his wife's numerous love affairs never troubled him and, why he had never fought a duel in her honour, he replied that he 'could hardly fight every man in London'. [64]

One of the most celebrated fox-hunters of his time, 'Nimrod' (Charles James Apperley) wrote that the 5th Earl was 'not only one of the hardest, boldest, and most judicious, but perhaps the most elegant rider to hounds the world ever saw.' [65] The Earl was also a successful racehorse owner, breeding and training his own horses at Middleton, and had many celebrated winners in his stables, including an Oaks winner ('Cobweb' in 1824; and three Derby winners - 'Middleton' (1825), 'Mameluke' (1927) and 'Bay Middleton' (1836). He was appointed a Privy Councillor in 1830 and a Knight Grand Cross of the Guelphs of Hanover in 1834 and twice held the position of the office of Lord Chamberlain of the Household of William IV (in 1830 and 1834–5). He also held the position of Master of the Horse to Queen Victoria in 1841–6 and

1852 and was awarded the honorary degree of Doctor of Civil Law by the University of Oxford.

The 5th Earl inherited an estate with a mortgage that dated back to 1693 and in order to clear the long-outstanding debt, where practical began to sell off or else swap isolated areas that included lands in Gower, other parts of Glamorgan, and in Brecknockshire, and ensured all existing leases on the estate were renewed. Forestland was cleared and substantial quantities of timber were sold, all of which resulted in reducing the physical size of the estate by half, whilst at the same time ensuring its financial stability.

The rapid development of canals, docks and railways networks across the UK meant that the BFE-owned farmland, marshes, uplands, mudflats and rivers at and around Foxhole, Pentrechwyth, Gwernllwynchwyth, Port Tennant, Pentreguinea, Morfa, Upper Bank, Middle Bank, White Rock and Crymlyn Bog, offered the necessary acreage to companies wanting to build new facilities within easy access to the raw materials found locally, ample space to dump their waste materials, as well as land to build housing for the influx of workers that would be required, and with longer leases than previously offered, this was something that Pascoe Grenfell and his partners took advantage of [66] [67] as did Charles Smith [68], both taking out 99-year leases.

The abundance of coal in South Wales was a major factor in the growth of the copper refining business in the region, and the establishment of patent fuel manufacturing plants soon followed, much of which was built on BFE land. Made by blending and heating waste small coal and the residue from distilled coal tar (pitch), the resulting mix was pressed into various size moulds that produced patent fuel blocks between 7lbs and 56lbs.

A local trade directory of 1851 directory [69] noted that Warlich's Patent Fuel Works had been established on a plot of nearly four acres on the east bank of the New Cut in St Thomas; it also produced naphtha, a by-product otherwise lost in the emissions, and utilised as a fuel used in 'Patent Lamps'. Warlich's process of manufacturing uses steam presses, so a location near a canal or river was necessary as a source of water. A second patent fuel manufacturer in Port Tennant was 'in full operation' producing fuel 'under Lyn's patent'. The Port Tennant works were on a smaller scale and it is not known if the naphtha was extracted in the Port Tennant works, but the works must have been a source of considerable pollution in the area and more companies were drawn to the Eastside, including a Cornish gunpowder manufacturer company headed by Messrs. Benjamin Sampson and Richard Lanyon obtained a 21-year lease in 1853 to set up a gunpowder magazine at Crymlyn Burrows [70]

An 1830 lease (updated in 1835) on land on the southern slopes of Kilvey Hill known as Cae Maes Teague Ychaf, with accompanying farms and buildings on 'Dan y Graig Fach and Dan y Graig Genol' was issued to Pascoe Grenfell and Charles Pascoe Grenfell [71]. It is unclear whether the existing house on Cae Maes Teague Ychaf was enlarged or was demolished and replaced with a new building known as Maesteg House, although the 1919 notes of WH Jones in the Cambrian newspaper, suggest work on a house was carried out for the Grenfells by Samuel Lewis, who had previously built houses in Morris Lane, although this could also have been related to the building of lodges, outbuildings or even on the neighbouring Danygraig Farm.

To the east of Danygraig Farm was an abundance of mineral resources, and by 1851 one Thomas Miles held leases for mining and quarrying at Danygraig Colliery and Stone Quarry 'for the mining and removal of all coal, culm and ore' as well as stone, with a caveat that the builders of the soon-to-be-built lunatic asylum at Danygraig could obtain stone from the quarry 'at a fair market price.' [72]

The plan to locate a lunatic asylum on the Eastside did not come to fruition, but due to the growth of the town, Swansea Corporation required a larger burial ground, which resulted in the development of land for Swansea Cemetery (aka Danygraig Cemetery) which officially opened in 1858.

The 5th Lord Jersey died aged 86 at 38 Berkeley Square, London on 3 Oct. 1859, and was buried at Middleton Stoney. He was succeeded by his eldest son George, Viscount Villiers. His wife Sarah, the Countess of Jersey died in January 1867, aged 81.

George Augustus Frederick Child Villiers (4th April 1808 – 24th October 1859), was better known as Viscount Villiers. A Member of Parliament for the constituencies of Rochester from 1830 to 1831, for Minehead (1831 - 1832), Honiton (1832 - 1835), Weymouth & Melcombe Regis (1837 - 1842) and for Cirencester (1844 to 1852), He also served as a Lord-in-waiting to the Duchess of Cambridge at the coronation of Queen Victoria in 1838. On 12th July 1841, Viscount Villiers married Julia Peel, the daughter of Prime Minister Sir Robert Peel, and they had three children. After his father's death, on the 3rd October 1859, he became the **6th Earl of Jersey** but only held the title until his own death three weeks later on 24th October 1859, at the age of 51 years old.

Victor Albert George Child-Villiers (20th March 1845 – 31st May 1915) succeeded his father George Augustus as **7th Earl of Jersey in 1859** and became the 7th Earl of Jersey at only 14 years old. Born at Berkeley Square in London, one of his godparents was Queen Victoria, who had accepted her role as a token of friendship to the infant's maternal grandfather, Prime Minister Robert Peel. Educated at Eton and Balliol College, Oxford, he became the principal proprietor of the family banking firm of Child & Co. On 19 September 1872, the Earl married the Hon. Margaret Elizabeth Leigh, daughter and eldest child of William Henry Leigh, 2nd Baron Leigh, with whom he had six children.

THE RIGHT HONOURABLE THE EARL OF JERSEY.

A Conservative in his political life, he served as a Lord-in-waiting between 1875 and 1877 in the government of Benjamin Disraeli, and as Paymaster-General in 1889/90 under Lord Salisbury during which time he was sworn as a member of the Privy Council, and was made a Knight Grand Cross of the Order of St Michael and St George (GCMG). In August 1890 the Earl was appointed Governor of New South Wales and commenced his role in January 1891 however to the consternation of the Colonial Office in London, he resigned in November 1892 citing pressing business affairs and returned to Britain in March 1893.

As Swansea's copper industry grew, other industries soon followed. Ambitious plans for new docks and railways were being acted upon, and with the need for more housing than ever before, the BFE was best placed to accommodate the town's needs. The 7th Earl had clearly benefited from the astute management of the 5th Earl, and it was under his stewardship that the shape of Kilvey, St. Thomas, Danygraig and Port Tennant would change forever. BFE records show that in 1873 the Earl of Jersey owned an estimated 7,110 acres of land in Wales (all in Glamorgan), with an estimated rental of £36,928, and that he was a 'great landowner (owing more than 3,000 acres with a rental of more than £3,000) in respect of property outside Wales'. [73]

Aside from the Tennant Canal that ran roughly parallel with the shoreline, the Crymlyn Bog was still undeveloped and had only been used to drop the 'spoils' from excavations elsewhere on the Estate, but this soon changed with the signing of new leases as well as the sale of land to businesses keen to manufacture such as arsenic and zinc, as well as support the growing rail industry. Companies that moved to the area over the next twenty years included Jennings Arsenic Works [74], Bristol and South Wales Railway Waggon Co. Ltd [75], Shackleford & Ford [76], Pritchard's Chemical Works [77] The Swansea Zinc Co [78], English Crown Spelter Company Ltd [79] British Wagon Company Ltd [80] and Baldwins Ltd [81].

Government-ordered compulsory purchases meant selling BFE land to Great Western Railway as the GWR would have to cross Estate lands on its way to Swansea town in Landore [82] and via Briton Ferry. [83] Similarly, following the 1883 Act that authorised the Rhondda and Swansea Bay Railway Company 'to extend their Railway to Swansea and for other purposes', they too wanted to run their networks into Swansea through the Eastside. [84] BFE land was also in demand for the building of various docks and ancillary services, with the Swansea Harbour Trust, Swansea Bay Graving Dock and The Prince of Wales Dock some of its active partners. [85] [86] [87] [88] [89] [90]

Industrial development continued at a pace as did the influx of workers, and as 'immigrant' workers from West Wales, the West Country, Ireland and elsewhere were drawn to Swansea and to the Eastside in particular by work opportunities the inevitable local housing boom followed, often at the request of local industry or railway companies, and nearly all constructed by locally based companies or by private builders. With limited schooling options available for local children, more schools were needed to serve the community, and leases were issued to accommodate this between 1868 and 1904. [91] [92] [93] [94]

Prior to the 1880s the only stone-built church in the area was All Saints Church in Kilvey, and a number of leases relating to the building of new Churches and Church houses were issued between 1884 and 1890 including a gift of land for the Vicarage at St. Thomas Church. [95] [96] [97]

The growing need for public leisure spaces was also acknowledged and acted upon, and apart from leasing land for public access roads and leisure, the BFE also donated land for the area's parks [98] as well as leased land [99], and on 30th June 1899, the Earl of Jersey gifted land 'to the north of Maesteg House' for a reservoir. [100]

On Friday 7th February 1907 it was announced that the Earl of Jersey had purchased 'the whole of the foreshore down to the low-water mark, from the new King's Dock to Neath River,' from the Duke of Beaufort [101], with the exception of a small strip of land previously acquired by Cammell, Laird and Co., who had 'proposed to build a works.' In making this purchase Lord Jersey became 'the sole possessor of all the land on that side of St. Thomas, thus facilitating any developments that may take place in the future, as sites are required for works and buildings.' The proposed Cammell Laird works failed to materialise.

After suffering a stroke in 1909, the 7th Lord Jersey died on 31st May 1915, aged 70, at the family seat Osterley Park in Middlesex, the funeral took place on Friday 4th June at Middleton Stoney, Oxfordshire, and memorial services were held at the same time at the Parish Churches of Briton Ferry, Llansawel, and at St. Thomas Church and St. Stephen's Church on the Eastside.

The St. Thomas service was officiated by the Reverend William Evans, Vicar of St. Thomas, in the congregation were Sir Griffith Thomas, Mr William Law and Mr Schenk (General Manager and Engineer of the Swansea Harbour Trust), whilst the service was held at St. Stephen's Church. Danygraig, which was conducted by the Curate-In-Charge Rev. William Evans.

The 7th Earl was succeeded by his eldest son, George Henry Robert Child Villiers.

The Countess of Jersey passed away at Middleton Park in Oxfordshire in May 1945, aged 95.

Bibliography

[1] M. K. Davies PhD, "The Nineteenth Century Copper Industry in the Greenfield Valley," *Transactions of the Honourable Society of Cymmrodorion,* p. 79, 1988.

[2] "Grace's Guide to British Industrial History - Grenfell Family 1794," [Online]. Available: www.gracesguide.co.uk/Grenfell_Family.

[3] K. P. M. Davies, "The Nineteenth Century Copper Industry in the Greenfield Valley," *Transactions of the Honourable Society of Cymmrodorion,* p. p84.

[4] "Grace's Guide to British Industrial History - Grenfell Family 1823," [Online]. Available: www.gracesguide.co.uk/Grenfell_Family.

[5] "Grace's Guide to British Indsutrial History - Williams, Foster & Co - 1829," [Online]. Available: www.gracesguide.co.uk/Williams_Foster_and_Co..

[6] "Grace's Guide to British Indsutrial History - Grenfel Family - 1829," [Online]. Available: www.gracesguide.co.uk/Grenfell_Family.

[7] R. Rees, "The South Wales Copper Dispute, 1833-95," *Welsh History Review,* p. 484.

[8] T. Cambrian, "The Most Important Trial - Indictment of Messrs. Vivian's Copper Works," *The Cambrian,* pp. 3-4, 16 March 1833.

[9] T. Cambrian, "Copper Smoke Trial," *The Cambrian,* p. 4, 9 August 1834.

[10] T. Cambrian, "Muntz's Patent Yellow Metal Sheathing, Bolts, etc for Vessels.," *The Cambrian,* p. 4, 25 October 1834.

[11] "Grace's Guide To British Industrial History - Muntz Metal Co. 1842," [Online]. Available: www.gracesguide.co.uk/Muntz.

[12] G. T. Clark, "Report to the General Board of Health...of the Town and Borough of Swansea. p56," Her Majesty's Stationery Office , London, 1849.

[13] "West Glamorgan Archives - Cae Maaes Teague," 1835. [Online].

[14] W. G. Archives, "Tennant Estate Papers - Survey of Danygraig Fach and Danygraig Genol farms by Adam Murray. c. 1820," [Online].

[15] H. B. L. A. Robert Ackland, A History of All Saints Church 1845-1995, 1995, p. 11.

[16] "Reports of the Commissioners of Inquiry into the State of Education in Wales - Part 1.," 1847.

[17] S. W. D. News, "Death of Mr Pascoe St. Leger Grenfell," *South Wales Daily News,* p. 4, 28 March 1879.

[18] T. Cambrian, "The Retirement of Messrs. Pascoe Grenfell and Sons from the Copper Trade.," *The Cambrian,* p. 5, 23 October 1892.

[19] T. Cambrian, "The Purchase of the Grenfell Copper and Spelter Works by Messrs. Williams, Foster, and Co. Ltd.," *The Cambrian,* p. 5, 25 November 1892.

[20] B. F. Estate, "Assignment of leasehold premises dated 1 Feb 1853," 1 February 1853. [Online].

[21] B. F. Estate, "Assignment of Lease for residue of term of 60 years," 24 May 1886. [Online].

[22] D. M. E. Chamberlain, "Grenfell (Family) Swansea industrialists.," in *Dictionary of Welsh Biography*, 2001.

[23] U. (. h. a. c. o. t. article), *Baby, The Mother's Magazine,* December 1900.

[24] T. Cambrian, "The Death of Miss Elizabeth Mary Grenfell of Maesteg House, St. Thomas, Swansea.," *The Cambrian,* p. 6, 16 March 1894.

[25] E. Express, "Affairs of Miss Grenfell - Swansea Philanthropist's Failure.," *Evening Express,* p. 3, 31 January 1908.

[26] T. Cambrian, "Maesteg House," *The Cambrian,* p. 9, 25 September 1908.

[27] S. W. D. Post, "Eastside Notes," *South Wales Daily Post* , p. 6, 17 October 1910.

[28] T. C. D. Leader, "Refugees at Maesteg House.," *The Cambria Daily Leader,* p. 4, 16 October 1919.

[29] T. C. D. Leader, "Maesteg House - To Be Converted Into Eight Flats.," *The Cambria Daily Leader,* p. 4, 16 October 1919.

[30] Oddisworth, "Swansea," *Oddisworth's Guide 1802 - Swansea,* 1802.

[31] W. Jones, History of the Port of Swansea, 1922, p. 150.

[32] T. Cambrian, "Opening of Mr. Tennant's Junction Canal.," *The Cambrian,* p. 3, 15 May 1824.

[33] T. Cambrian, "Swansea New Dock," *The Cambrian,* p. 3, 17 January 1824.

[34] B. F. Estate, "Copy of a letter of 1830 from George Tennant to William Jenkins, regarding a plot of land near the bridge at Danygraig, for the purpose of building a house, with covering letter dated 1902, headed "Burrows Inn, Port Tennant" GB 216 D/D BF/E478," [Online].

[35] T. E. Papers, "Lease for 1000 years; Francis Pinkney of Covent Garden, bookseller, to George Tennant, esq.; cottages in the hamlet of St. Thomas, Swansea. 29 Sep. 1824 GB216 D/DT," 29 September 1824. [Online].

[36] T. E. Papers, "Lease for 1000 years; Charles, Duke of Beaufort, to George Tennant, esq.; land at Salthouse Point within the Manor of Kilvey. 1 Mar. 1827 GB216 D/DT 537," 1 March 1827. [Online].

[37] T. Cambrian, "Deaths 'Our obituary this week...'," *The Cambrian,* p. 3, 3 March 1832.

[38] T. E. Papers, "Jersey V Tennant, 1855 (Earl Of Jersey Accused Tennant Family Of Falsifying Estate Accounts And Acquiring Property From Him Under False Pretences) GB 216 DD T/5/112/HUB," 1855. [Online].

[39] T. E. Papers, "Notes made by Charles Tennant of 'false and slanderous communications made by earl and countess of Jersey, accusing him of embezzling Briton Ferry estate accounts. 1855 GB 216 D/D T 1553/1-3.," 1855. [Online].

[40] T. Cambrian, "to Be Sold...in a Cuse of Tennant v Trenchard...at the Auction Mart Tokenhouse Yard, London," *The Cambrian,* 10 October 1872.

[41] J. N. h. Dorothy M. Bayliffe, Starling Benson of Swansea., D. Brown & Sons, 1996, p. 12.

[42] T. Cambrian, "Swansea Vale Railway - Notice to Contractors," *The Cambrian,* p. 2 , 26 April 1846.

[43] J. N. H. Dorothy M. Bayliffe, Starling Benson of Swansea., D. Brown & Sons, 1966, p. 182.

[44] J. N. H. Dorothy M. Bayliffe, Starling Benson of Swansea, D. Brown & Sons, 1996, pp. 199-200.

[45] T. Cambrian, "To Engineers, Contractors and Others," *The Cambrian,* p. 3, 23 April 1831.

[46] T. Cambrian, "To Be Let or Sold with Immediate Possession," *The Cambrian,* p. 4, 23 February 1828.

[47] T. Cambrian, "to Be Let - Tyrlandwr House," *The Cambrian,* p. 2, 4 October 1834.

[48] T. Cambrian, "To the Editor of The Cambrian," *The Cambrian,* p. 4, 13 February 1841.

[49] J. N. H. Dorothy M Baycliffe, Starling Benson of Swansea, D. Brown & Sons, 1996, pp. 36-37.

[50] T. Cambrian, "Letter to the Editor," *The Cambrian,* p. 4, 9 March 1839.

[51] W. Jones, History of the Port of Swansea, Royal Institute of South Wales, 1922, p. 180.

[52] W. Jones, History of the Port of Swansea, Royal Institute of South Wales, 1922, pp. 201-202.

[53] W. Jones, History of the Port of Swansea, Royal Institute of South Wales, 1922, pp. 203-204.

[54] J. N. H. Dorothy M. Bayliffe, Starling Benson of Swansea, D. Brown & Sons, 1996, pp. 208-210.

[55] W. Jones, History of the Port of Swansea, Royal Institute of South Wales, 1922, pp. 208-210.

[56] T. C. Times, "The Death of Starling Benson, J.P. of Swansea," *The Cardiff Times,* p. 2, 25 January 1879.

[57] B. F. Estate, "Release, in consideration of fifty pounds paid in hand to the said Morgan Popkins and of other monies owing to ... GB210 48," 3 September 1736. [Online].

[58] B. F. Estate, "Lease for 99 years, for surrender of former Lease, dated 7 Nov. 1750, rent £600 yearly and duties on coal (details not extracted) GB 216 D/D BF 380-381," 7 November 1750. [Online].

[59] B. F. Estate, "Lease for 21 years, on Surrender of Lease dated 20 Aug. 1785, rent £270, and £5 on Crymlin Morass, yearly, 30 Jan. 1796; George, lord Vernon of Kinderton (co. Chester), to John Freeman. GB 216 D/D BF 335," 30 January 1785. [Online].

[60] B. F. Estate, "Will of Louisa Barbara, Lady Vernon, wife of the Hon. George Venables Vernon, devising and bequeathing: GB 216 D/D BF/E 754," 23 November 1813. [Online].

[61] B. F. Estate, "Bundle of correspondence relating to proposed leases, legacies from the Will of Lady Vernon, a circular letter to the leaseholders who received their leases from the late Lord Vernon GB 216 D/DBF/E 765," 23 November 1813. [Online].

[62] R. Knowles, "What is haut ton?," 20 December 2014. [Online]. Available: www.regencyhistory.net.

[63] R. Knowles, "Regency History's guide to Almack's Assembly Rooms," 1 November 2011. [Online]. Available: www.regencyhistory.net.

[64] J. Ridley, Lord Palmerston, London: Constable, 1970, p. 42.

[65] Nimrod, Hunting Reminiscences: Comprising Memoirs of Masters of Hounds, Notices of The Crack Riders, 1843, p. 209.

[66] B. F. Estate, "Description of 'Lease (copy), for 99 years...in occ. of Owen Williams, Pascoe Grenfell, Thomas Peers Williams and Charles Pascoe Grenfell. GB 216 d?d BF378," 1833. [Onlinc].

[67] B. F. Estate, "Lease (copy), for 99 years, rent £133 6s. 8d. yearly, 25 Mar. 1828; George, earl of Jersey, to Pascoe and Charles Pascoe Grenfell of Upper Thames Street, London, merchants (co-partners in Pascoe Grenfell & Co.). GB 216 D/D BF 379," 28 March 1828. [Online].

[68] B. F. Estate, "Item Lease for 99 years, for surrender of former Lease, dated 7 Nov. 1750, 3 Apr. 1833; George, earl of Jersey to Charles Henry Smith of Gwernllwynwith, Llansamlet, esq.; Wharf land, at the Foxhole... GB 216 D/D BF 380-381," 16 May 1838. [Online].

[69] J. Lewis, The Swansea Guide ...1851, William Mathias Brewster, 1851, pp. 41-42.

[70] B. F. Estate, "Lease for 21 years from 29 Sept 1853 ... Building used as a gunpowder magazine at Crymlyn Burrows near Swansea. GB 216 D/D BF 1784," 29 September 1853. [Online].

[71] B. F. Estate, "Lease for 99 years from 25 Mar 1830 for £20 annual rent dated 5 Jan 1835; George earl of Jersey, with Margaret Elizabeth Tennant relict of George Tennant, to Pascoe Grenfell and Charles Pascoe Grenfell esq.GB 216 D/D BF 1783," 5 January 1835. [Online].

[72] B. F. Estate, "Agreement (draft) for Lease for 10 years, rent £10 yearly, royalty of 41/2d. per ton of stone,... 1851; George, earl of Jersey, with Tho. Miles of Dan y Graig colliery, contractors; Stone quarry; at Dan y Graig, in St. Thomas, Swansea GB 216 D/D BF 701," 1851. [Online].

[73] B. F. Estate, "Briton Ferry Estate -GB 216 D/D BF - Administrative / Biographical.," 1679-1960. [Online].

[74] B. F. Estate, "Lease for 99 years from 25 Mar 1859 for £70 annual rent dated 27 June 1859; George earl of Jersey to Joseph Jennings and Nicholas Jennings GB 216 D/D BF 1785," 27 June 1859. [Online].

[75] B. F. Estate, "Lease (copy), for 60 years, rent £140 yearly, 3 Mar. 1865; William Child Villiers ...with Sarah Sophia Child, countess of Jersey, to Bristol and South Wales Railway Waggon Co. Ltd.. GB 216 D/D Bf 450," 3 March 1865. [Online].

[76] B. F. Estate, "Lease (copy) for 60 years, rent £300 yearly, 12 Feb. 1866; Hon. ..Child Villiers to Wm. Copley Shackleford and en. Wm. Ford of Swansea, manufacturers of rolling stock; Land (12a.), at end of Crymlyn Burrows GB 216 D/D BF 918," 1866 February 1866. [Online].

[77] B. F. Estate, "Lease (copy) for 99 years, rent £62 10s. yearly, 17 Sep. 1867; Victor Albert George Child Villiers, earl of Jersey, to John Daniel Pritchard of the Chemical Works ...Bristol; Land (2a. 2r.), adj. road parallel with Tennant canal. GB 216 D/D BF 166," 24 April 1875. [Online].

[78] B. F. Estate, "Mortgage for £7327 8s 7d, dated 30 Nov 1868; The Swansea Zinc Co....Land (12a) containing a spelter works at the end of the Crymlyn Burrows, in Llansamlet and St Thomas parishes. GB 216 D/D BF 1590," 30 November 1868. [Online].

[79] B. F. Estate, "Assignment of leasehold premises dated 28 July 1883; John Crow Richardson of Swansea merchant, with John Crow Richardson, John Richardson Francis and Arthur Henry Richardson, all of Swansea,...to the English Crown Spelter Company Ltd; GB 216 D/D BF 1796," 6 June 1907. [Online].

[80] B. F. Estate, "Lease for 60 years from 29 Sept 1906 for £250 annual rent dated 6 June 1907; Victor Albert George earl of Jersey to the British Wagon Company Ltd.GB 216 D/D BF 1796," 6 June 1906. [Online].

[81] B. F. Estate, "Lease for 109 years from 25 Mar 1909 for £937 10s annual rent dated 30 July 1909; Victor Albert George earl of Jersey to Baldwins Ltd.; Land (25a) on the Crymlyn Burrows, not further described. Includes plan. GB 216 D/D BF 1677," 30 July 1909. [Online].

[82] B. F. Estate, "6p of land beside the railway opposite the Landore Siemens' New Steel Works, part of Llysnewydd Farm, Llansamlet, 1884 GB 216 D/D BF/E 543," 1884. [Online].

[83] B. F. Estate, "Correspondence relating to the winding up of the Briton Ferry Dock Company and the sale of the dock

to the Great Western Railway Company, 1871-72. GB 216 BF/E 582," 1871-72. [Online].

[84] B. F. Estate, "Notice of Briton Ferry Estate property required by the Rhondda and Swansea Bay Railway Company for the expansion of their railways, in preparation for a proposed Bill of Parliament, 1896. GB 216 D/D BF/E 619," 1896. [Online].

[85] B. F. Estate, "Schedules of lands sold by the Earl of Jersey to the Rhondda and Swansea Bay Railway Company, 1895-1901. GB 216 D/D BF/E 651," 1895-1901. [Online].

[86] B. F. Estate, "Conveyance (copy), for £200, subject to Lease for 1,000 years dated 31 Dec. 1817, 11 Sep. 1903...to Swansea Harbour Trustees; Canal, works, lands and S. foreshore lands ...GB 216 D/D BF 662," 20 December 1898. [Online].

[87] B. F. Estate, "Papers relating to the Swansea Bay Graving Dock, including a prospectus for the Swansea Bay Graving Docks and Engineering Company Ltd. GB 216 D/D BF/E 866," 1884. [Online].

[88] B. F. Estate, "Conveyance (copy), for £6-265, 13 Mar. 1888...with Victor Albert George Child Villiers, earl of Jersey, to SHT; Lands (29a, 2r. 21p.), part of docks, works and railways, in occ. of said trustees; in St. Thomas, Swansea, except mining. GB 216 D/D BF 714," 2 March 1888. [Online].

[89] B. F. Estate, "Conveyance (copy), for £2-996, 11 Jan. 1897)...to SHT; Land (6a. 3r.), land (2r. 4p.), with rights to use buildings, furnaces and machinery; land, on foreshore on S. side of above, with right to convey goods; in St. Thomas GB 216 D/D BF 721," 1 December 1879. [Online].

[90] B. F. Estate, "Reports of the inspections of the Directors at the Prince of Wales Dock and St Thomas, Swansea, in relation to the price to be paid for the land, 1890. Gb 216 D/D BF/E 657," 1890. [Online].

[91] B. F. Estate, "Conveyance, for £250, 10 Oct. 1873; Lord John Thynne of Hawnes Park...esq., by direction of Victor Albert George Child Villiers, earl of Jersey, to the School

Board of Swansea; Land (2454 sq. yds) part of Dan Y Graig Fawr..GB 216 D/D BF 708," 10 October 1873. [Online].

[92] B. F. Estate, "Conveyance (copy) for £750, 9 Apr. 1885; Rich. Arkwright... esq., Alfred Walter Thynne ...with Victor Albert George Child Villiers, ...to the School Board of the United School District of Swansea; Land (1/2a.) at Dan y Graig.GB 216 D/DBF 713," 9 April 1885. [Online].

[93] B. F. Estate, "Deed of exchange (copy), of lands for school...Victor Albert George, Child Villiers..School Board of the United School District of Swansea; Land (164 feet N. to S., 10 feet E. to W.), part of Dan y Graig Fawr; in St. Thomas.GB 216 D/D BF 720," 9 September 1892. [Online].

[94] B. F. Estate, "Conveyance (copy), for £100,000, 2 Mar. 1904...Victor Albert George Child Villiers, earl of Jersey, to the School Board of the United School District of Swansea; Land (3-311 sq. yds.), part of Dan y Graig Fawr; in St. Thomas GB 216 D/D BF 725," 2 Maarch 1904. [Online].

[95] B. F. Estate, "Lease for 99 years from 25 Dec 1883...Victor Albert George... to the Rev. John Lewis of Swansea...Building land at Dan-y-Graig, St Thomas, on Dan-y-Graig road and Ysgol Street, with covenant to build a Baptist Chapel and schoolroom.GB 216 D/D BF 1788," 25 December 1883. [Online].

[96] B. F. Estate, "Deed of exchange (copy), in trust to establish mission, 21 Dec. 1888...Land (20p.), at Port Tennant, adj. NE., NW., and SW. land (1a.), at Port Tennant; in St. Thomas,...In exchange for: Land (580 sq. yds.); part of Dan y Graig Fawr GB 216D/D BF 715," 21 December 1888. [Online].

[97] B. F. Estate, "Gift (copy draft) free from Mortgage ... 27 Oct.1890...dj. N. Delhi Street, E. Lewis Street, ...for construction of a parsonage; triangular piece of land...part of site of St. Thomas's Church GB 216 D/D BF 716-717," 27 October 1890. [Online].

[98] B. F. Estate, "Deed of gift...with Victor Albert George earl of Jersey, to the Swansea Urban Sanitary Authority of Swansea; Land (4a 3r) at Danygraig Farm between

Danygraig Fach Farm Lane, Margaret Street...or the purpose of a recreation ground GB 216 D/D BF 1570," 30 June 1899. [Online].

[99] B. F. Estate, "Lease for 10 years from 25 Mar 1908 for £25 annual rent dated 28 Dec 1908; Victor Albert George earl of Jersey...Land (4a 2r 9p) beside Farm Lane for a sports field at Dan-y-Graig. Includes plan.GB 216 D/D BF 1790," 25 March 1908. [Online].

[100] B. F. Estate, "Deed of gift, dated 30 June 1899; Alfred Walter Thynne ...with Victor Albert George earl of Jersey, to the Mayor, Aldermen and Burgesses of the Borough of Swansea; Land (1a 3r) to the north of Maesteg House, for a reservoir GB 216 D/D BF 1519," 30 June 1899. [Online].

[101] T. Cambrian, "Lord Jersey and St. Thomas - Foreshore Bought Outright," *The Cambrian,* 1 February 1907.

[102] B. F. Estate, "Briton Ferry Estate -GB 216 D/D BF - Administrative / Biographical.," 1679-1960. [Online].

PART FOUR - Compendium

Eastside by George Herbert Wilkins

(with thanks to Joanne Clegg)

From Kilvey's tall green, I survey
A view that fair takes breath away.
Familiar landmarks, spires tall,
And there below best view of all.

This sight it stirs, it overwhelms.
This Eastside is my kingdom, realm.
As thoughts now drift to days long past,
How swift times flown, so brief, too fast.

The quiet Churchyard by the hill
With jar-jars, pots, drooped daffodil.
No palette brush could true portray
The work of art that's now displayed.

The lines of washing, shirts snow white,
The last bus home, they'll cram tonight.
A shout goes up, drowns mongrels' bark
The home team's scored at Maesteg Park.

Vast docklands stand, in sad decline,
Where once I swam, a pool all mine.
No Leisure Centres, wave machines,
But Cowboys, Indians, flickering screens.

And over there, by weed grown track,
Once chimneys stood, smoke belching black,
And though the dirt, it stunted green,
At least the wages they were clean.

Down there I see it, my old school,
Tall gates through which came scholar, fool.
Where teachers knew each boy by name,
And most found routine, few found fame.

Three score and ten, this place I've known,
Seen old friends pass, young children grown.
As darkness now, the light it steals
It comes to me, how old I feel.

But in my mind's eye, from this hill
I see myself, a young boy still
With patched up trousers, canvas gyms,
The carefree daydreams foolish whims.

Street lights below me, flicker, dance,
Across Port Tennant one last glance.
With cautious steps back down the hill
Remembering jam jars, daffodils.

***

The Old Kilvey Windmill Conundrum.

Growing up on the Eastside in the 1960s, it was regarded as a badge of honour amongst your peers to have climbed to the top of Kilvey Hill and reached the 'Old Windmill', where on a clear day you could view the coast of Devon, but was it really once a windmill, or was it some other long-forgotten structure?

Whilst today there is very little if any evidence left of a summit-top construction, the pile of stones that I remember climbing over as a young boy has been the subject of heated debate for over 150 years in the local press as well as by some of Swansea's most eminent historians, including Welsh antiquary and civic leader Colonel George Grant Francis in the 1870s, and albeit over 90 years later Swansea County Borough Estate Agent and Valuer W.C. Rogers, who had a conflicting view on the subject.

'The Old Kilvey Windmill' c1980 (c) Russ Thomas

To try and better understand the confusion, a good place to begin is the 1688 Survey of Gower & Kilvey [1] which states that 'about six years ago' local landowner Bussy Mansell Esq 'erected a Windmill on Kilvey Hill within the said Manor, and hath also erected a Watermill there called New Mill', however it does not say specifically where either mill was built, and the term 'on top of Kilvey Hill' is not used. At the time of the Survey, the Manor of Kilvey was of a considerable size, and Kilvey Hill was only one small part of it. The southern slopes of Kilvey Hill ran down to the sea, the western slopes ran down to the River Tawe, and the eastern slopes ran toward the Crymlyn Bog, and whilst the lower slopes of the north side of Kilvey Hill included what is now known as Bonymaen, the Manor ran even further north to include Glais, so a lack of awareness of the size of the Manor of Kilvey may be at the root of the ongoing debate as far as the location of the windmill is concerned. By the 1800s, the Manor of Kilvey was listed as part of the Parish of Llansamlet, and since the establishment of the Parish of All Saints Kilvey in 1881, from a residential perspective, the area formerly known as Foxhole was recognised as 'Kilvey'.

Nearly two hundred years after the 1688 survey, an unsigned article entitled "The Kilvey Windmill' appeared in The Cambrian on 22nd October 1875 [2] describing an event that occurred nearly 65 years earlier on a long-neglected structure and seemed to have sparked off some debate:

'KILVEY WINDMILL. Of Kilvey Hill, near whose top the ruins of the old windmill stand, the present inhabitants of Swansea seem to know little and care less. The side of it which the Tawe bounds is denuded of vegetation, scarred by clefts, deformed by slag-heaps, made lurid by furnaces and begrimed with smoke. The wind howls over it without a friendly tree to give it shelter, and the hail and rain storms pelt its bare brow with merciless severity, leaving it as furrowed as a criminal's back to which "the cat" had been applied. It obtains no kindly recognition from lovers of landscape, and can scarcely awake interest in anyone except the geologist and miner. Yet there is one object on it in which many feel an interest. It is the old windmill stump by which local mariners coming into Swansea Harbour steer more steadily than they could by the North Star.

Its blades were in dust long ago. A portion of its ruined wall is all that is now to be seen of it; and here is an account of the catastrophe which caused its overthrow 65 years ago, taken substantially from the Cambrian of that period:— On Sunday, July 1st. 1810, Swansea and its neighbourhood were visited by a tremendous thunderstorm. One of the vanes of a windmill belonging to Morgan Evan of Llansamlet had been broken by a gust of wind, and several people had been attracted to the spot—some by curiosity, and others to assist in getting the machinery into order. About three o'clock a very heavy shower of rain fell and drove between twenty and thirty persons into the mill for shelter. When they were thus collected, lightning struck the roof of the building and penetrating through it, set the whole in a blaze. The scene at this moment was of the most shocking description. The owner of the mill in company with two other men was in the loft. The two men were killed, the owner was much injured, and the remaining persons lay in a promiscuous heap on the ground floor apparently lifeless.

However assistance speedily came to their aid, and, when they were removed from their sad position, it was found that one of them only was dead—no doubt destroyed by the electric explosion -the others giving gratifying evidence of speedy recovery. But the fire which the lightning had thus kindled burned fiercely till all the combustibles about the mill were consumed. Bare, scorched, walls alone remained as a monument of the calamity which befell it, neither corn nor flour having been spared by the devouring element. Nevertheless, though thus shorn of its usefulness in one department of industry, the old maimed mill was turned to no base use, nor was it deprived of power to render valuable assistance to the lords of creation in another. If this benefits it confers upon those who go down to the sea in ships are not so highly esteemed as those of the lighthouse, they are of a more homely and kindly description.'

The article noted the date and approximate time that the storm occurred, the name of the owner of the mill, stated that two men had died there, and that 'between twenty and thirty persons' sheltered in the mill. It established the size of the structure and that it was an operational mill prior to the storm, and states that the windmill was not repaired and that its remains became a beacon, and a letter from 'A. Shipowner' printed the following week [3] pointed out that the 'rapidly perishing structure' is 'one of the special points indicated for sailing into Swansea in the Admiralty and all other 'Sailing Instructions for the Port of Swansea.'

In the early months of 1878, 'The Old Windmill of Kilvey' was again the topic of discussion, and The Cambrian featured the correspondence of Colonel George Grant Francis [4] amongst others, on the same subject:

'18th January 1878 THE OLD WINDMILL OF KILVEY. TO THE EDITOR OF THE CAMBRIAN

Sir, some year or two ago a correspondent in your columns made enquiry as to the date of the erection of the Windmill on Kilvey Hill. At the time, I was unable to put my hand on a reliable authority but, I now have the pleasure to -annex 'The return at a Court Baron, Manerinm de Kilvey, he'd the seven and twentyeth of September 1686 before Commissioners of the Duke of Beaufort.

To item 13:—What watermills, windmills, steel mills, or other sorts of mills are there within this Manor. Who built and enjoyed such Mills? They replied—" To the thirteenth Article, the said Jurors doe say and present—that about six years ago, Bussy Mansell, Esq, one of the Freeholders of the said Manor, hath erected a Windmill on Kilvey Hill within the said Manor and hath also erected a watermill there, called New Mill." Therefore the date of the erection of the Windmill was anno 1680. This Bussy Mansell, of Briton Ferry Esq, was the same person as co-operated with good Bishop Gore in the founding of our Grammar School by giving it a site on Goat-street in 1682.

Speaking from memory only, I think the Windmill was destroyed by lightning on a Sunday morning, late in the last century. It was never restored, probably on account of the inconvenience of conveying corn to an elevation of 625ft. (above the sea level); but its lower has remained a well-known and valued Beacon to the ships frequenting our Bay and Harbour.

Being so noted, in the Admiralty instructions and maps to the present day, its dilapidated state and constant decay should commend the subject to the consideration of the Superintendent of the Harbour, the Trustees of which could doubtless readily obtain permission of the descendant of Bussy Mansell—the Earl of Jersey—to restore it to its ancient form and later use, by a small expenditure of labour and mortar only, as the original stones remain at the foot of the old walls, constantly increased by the trespass of rollicking folk, who not content with the grand sight to be obtained from it, cooperate in its destruction by casting down the loose stones of its weather-worn unprotected walls.

I remain, yours faithfully, GEO. GRANT FRANCIS, F.S.A. Swansea, Jan. 1878.'

The Colonel's letter began a flurry of responses on the subject, which offered a combination of conflicting assertions of dates, locations and occurrences. [5]

'8th February 1878 THE "OLD WINDMILL" ON KILVEY. TO THE EDITOR OF "THE CAMBRIAN"

Sir, Mr G. G. Francis, in a letter published in a recent impression of your journal says that he believes the "old windmill" was destroyed by lightning towards the close of the last century. If Mr Francis had made this statement on the authority of any historical record there would be a strong presumption that so able an antiquary and archaeologist would not have arrived at a mistaken conclusion; but as he seems to rely in this matter on common report only, it may not be improper to question his accuracy.

I have a strong impression that the occurrence took place in the first decade of the current century, in as much as my parents were at that time living at Mile End, and had reason to remember and to relate to their children the fearful tempest which resulted in the disaster in question. My father was at sea in the channel on an attempted voyage to Bristol, and my mother was therefore in a state of dreadful anxiety on his account.

When staying at my native town about five years ago, I met on the road to Morriston a woman under 80 years of age, who not only knew my father and his family well when living at Mile End but remembered the house in which he lived being built. If I am correct in each of these recollections, there must, considering the special longevity of your district, be persons now living who could inform Mr Francis as to the date of the occurrence in which he is interested.

But my memory less clearly suggests a more audacious doubt still on the subject of Mr Francis' letter, and that is whether the existing beacon was ever a windmill at all. There is an indistinct impression on my mind that the old windmill was situated on a lower point of the hill in the direction of Landore. The same old inhabitants who could give information as to the date of its destruction could of course determine whether my latter position is anything more than a myth.

Yours faithfully, WILLIAM RIGG. Luton, Feb. 2, 1878. P.S.—The historical work of the late Mr Dillwyn is silent on the subject.'

Two weeks later, the Colonel responded [6] :

'15th February 1878 THE OLD WINDMILL ON KILVEY - TO THE EDITOR OF "THE CAMBRIAN"

Sir, I thank Mr Rigg of Luton, not for the irrelevant matter connected with his own family, which I take it few of your readers can have any sympathy for, but for the material aid, it has brought respecting the period of the actual destruction of the Mill by lightening, on a Sunday—not at the end of the last century but at the commencement of this century. A friend informs me that his father (Mr John Cawker of Cross Street) has a very distinct recollection of the year 1808, on a very stormy Sunday afternoon, the old Mill on Kilvey was struck by lightning and everything in and upon it destroyed by fire —that his attention from the end of Frog-street, Swansea, was drawn to the conflagration, which, he says, was the more remarkable from the arms or fans continuing to revolve until they were consumed and fell to the ground. The news soon came across the Ferry, with the melancholy addition that two men in the mill had been struck and killed by the flash that had fallen on the premises and caused its destruction.

I am not disposed to follow Mr Rigg's 'audacious doubts' or 'strong presumptions" (as he is pleased to term them), for it would be wasting your space and your reader's patience were I to super add everything "for the record" which I did last month showing that twelve men, on their oaths, that it was erected as and for "a windmill" in 1680; or the veracity of a most respectable eye witness who avers that he saw it burnt down in 1808! I shall, however, take the opportunity of adding that, if the Harbour Trustees desire to continue its utility as a beacon for the shipping of our Port, I have reason to believe that the Earl of Jersey would be advised to himself restore it for such a purpose. The Trustees would then be able to return the compliment by calling the new structure the "Jersey Beacon" on their charts and maps.

I remain, Sir, yours faithfully, GEO. GRANT FRANCIS P S A Swansea, Feb. 12, 1878.'

I suspect Colonel Francis, indulged by his friends at The Cambrian, may have been enjoying a spot of one-upmanship with regard to 'William Rigg', as later that month the newspaper printed a letter correcting the name printed earlier to that of 'Mr William Bigg', a Swansea man who was at that time Mayor of Luton, and I think it very unlikely that Colonel Francis would not have been aware of this fact, and on 22nd February 1878, the Cambrian printed a letter from 'one that has the privilege of knowing Mr William Bigg of Luton' that endorsed his credibility.

On the same day, a second letter published [7] put further doubts on the various assertations of Colonel Grant:

'22nd February 1878 THE LLANSAMLET WINDMILLS. TO THE EDITOR OF "THE CAMBRIAN".

Sir, The letters which appeared lately in the Cambrian on the "Kilvey Windmill," caused the subject to be brought under the notice of a literary meeting at the Cwm, and the following remarks, gleaned from two of the treatises sent in, are offered as additions, and, in some degree, as corrections, to what was stated in the above letters. There are the remains of two Windmills, one on Kilvey Hill (in Welsh called" Y Bigwrn"— the Cone), and the other at Cefn Hengoed (the Old Wooded Bank), near the hamlet of Bonymaen. The more ancient of the two, the one on "Y Bigwrn," has not been used for grinding purposes within the memory of anyone living. The other was built about eighty or ninety years ago.

If the wind sufficed, the work of grinding was carried on Sundays as well as on other days. On one Sunday, in the year 1810, when many, according to custom, were gathered together in the mill, and whilst riotous drinking was going on, the building was struck by lightning and took fire, and two or three of those present were killed. The name of one is given Will Pit; Pit being a nickname. It is said that Will had presumptuously declared that he would have his corn ground on that day unless the d----- were there."

An old woman was heard to say that her father was one of the company and that he was struck by the lightning, but afterwards recovered. Still, throughout his life, whenever a thunderstorm occurred, he felt the old pains return, and from which he suffered acutely during the storm.

On the Sunday the building was struck, the Rev. Hopkin Bevan, of Llangyfelach, was preaching at the Cwm Chapel, and among his hearers were many of those who had been at the mill that day. Several of them became members of the church at that service, and among them was the owner of the mill, who afterwards became a preacher among the Methodists. The mill was repaired and was worked for about thirteen years but the miller having neglected to fasten the door on leaving, a heavy storm carried away the roof and did so much damage, that since then, it has ceased been used as a mill. The building was remarkable for its height and solidity and was so well furnished within, that it continued, after being struck by the lightning, to burn for a week.

The fields surrounding the mill, once well hedged and tilled, are now open and uncared for. One is still called "Cae'r Felin," another Cae'r Glowty," and another, Cae'r Brigos." An old man, ninety-three years of age, was heard to say that a bull once committed some ravages in the road leading to the mill, and upon a house in the road since which, the road has been called "Heol-y-Tarw" (the Bull's Road), and the house "Ty'r Tarw" (the Bull's House).
Yours, Cwm Cottage, Llansamlet. EDWARD HUGHES. '

A few weeks later a number of letters were printed in the Cambrian that extended the debate on the subject, the first relating to the 'beacon', the second clarifying that the windmill that was struck by lightning was actually at Cefn Hengoed in Bonymaen, and in the third Colonel Francis was again adding to the confusion with a combination of his doubts and assurances. [8] [9] [10]

'8th March 1878 - KILVEY OLD WINDMILL. TO THE EDITOR OF "'THE CAMBRIAN."

Sir, as an old Swansea shipowner and master, I too would ask the Harbour Trust to try and save this point of beacon for our port, in the sailing directions to which we were often referred by chart and descriptions. Although the new Tide Table of this year is in some matters an improvement on those gone before it, I cannot think that it is wise to altogether omit 'Sailing Directions from its pages. I hope these remarks will be kindly accepted from an A.B. SEAMAN. St. Thomas, Swansea. March 1878.'

'8th March 1878 HISTORY OF LLYSNEWYDD, AND A WORD OR TWO ON THE WINDMILLS

……….And now for a few words on the windmills, that the windmill near Bonymaen, and not the one on Kilvey Hill, was the one struck by lightning and set on fire in the first decade of the present century, is affirmed by some of the oldest people living in its immediate neighbourhood—persons aged 73, 83, and one nearly 100, I have myself spoken to one of them, who witnessed the fire and was able to confirm most of the facts given in my first letter. Yours respectfully, Cwm Cottage, Llansamlet. EDWARD HUGHES. '

'8th March 1878 TO THE EDITOR OF THE "CAMBRIAN"

Sir, though individually loath to ask more space in your columns, I am in continual receipt of fresh points and facts which prove beyond doubt the general interest in this subject. Considerable difficulty, I find, is caused by there having been two windmills on the Kilvey ridge, both said to have been destroyed on a Sunday by lightning! I don't say that was impossible, but I aver it to be very improbable. Clearly, to ascertain the facts, more time is necessary to elucidate the real state of the case. To facilitate the enquiry, I will quote from the columns of your valuable paper, preserved from

1804 (No. 1) to this day in our Royal Institution library the following contribution to the subject matter in hand:

Ex Cambrian. No. 337, July 7, 1810.- "Violent Storm. "On Sunday last we were visited by a tremendous thunderstorm, the dire effects of which will be long remembered in this neighbourhood. One of the vanes of a windmill, belonging to Morgan Evans, in Llansamlet, about three miles from home. having been broken in the morning by a gust of wind, several labouring people were attracted to the spot, some by curiosity, to assist in patting the machinery in order.

About three o'clock a very heavy shower of rain fell and drove between 20 and 30 persons into the mill for shelter, when almost immediately on their being thus collected, the electric fluid struck the roof of the building and penetrating through it, set the whole in a blaze! The scene at this moment was of the most shocking description. The owner [tenant?] of the mill was in "the loft with two other men, both of whom were killed and he much injured; the remaining persons, more than 10 in number, lay in a promiscuous heap on the ground floor, apparently lifeless, but assistance being instantly procured, they were taken out, and only one was found dead; the others were all happily recovered and are doing well.

The names of the unfortunate sufferers were David Jenkin, William Hopkin and David Thomas, the latter leaving a pregnant widow and six children. Nothing remains of the mill but bare walls. A quantity of corn and flour was destroyed." The question is- Does this evidence relate to Mill (No. 1) at Bonymaen, or to Mill (No. 2) on Kilvey top, both in Llansamlet? Waiting yet further information.
I remain, Sir, respectfully yours, GEO GRANT FRANCIS, F.S.A.
Swansea, 7th March 1878.'

From the information and opinions put forward it seems clear that in 1878 the structure at the top of Kilvey Hill was being utilised as a beacon, and that it had been in use for some years, something that is endorsed in the letters of both A.B. Seaman, and Mr Gibb/Bigg who questioned whether 'the existing beacon was ever a windmill at all', whilst Colonel Francis said of the ruins: 'its tower has remained a well-known and valued Beacon to the ships frequenting our Bay and Harbour. Being so noted, in the Admiralty instructions and maps to the present day'. In addition, there now appears to be a consensus as to when the violent storm that had caused the death and destruction had occurred as well as the date it occurred.

Colonel Francis' understanding of things had initially moved from the storm taking place in the late 1700s to a Sunday afternoon in July 1808 that Mr Cawker had assured him was correct, a date that was also supported by his 'most sincere old friend' Benjamin Hill, but he had since settled on it occurring in July 1810, a date mentioned in the original article, and one that Mr Hughes had also confirmed. Mr Hughes's assertion that there were in fact two windmills on Kilvey Hill - one at the top, and one in Bonymaen - only added further complexity to the topic.

If the incident had occurred at the Cefn Hengoed Mill in Bonymaen as Mr Hughes' version of events had asserted, it would have been impossible for Colonel Francis's 'most respectable eye witness' Mr Cawker to have seen 'the arms or fans continuing to revolve until they were consumed and fell to the ground' on a 'very stormy Sunday afternoon' whilst standing at the end of Frog St in the town centre, given that you cannot see Bonymaen from the town centre, even on a clear day. In a violent storm, it would have been more likely that the beacon on Kilvey Hill had been lit in line with its purpose as a warning to shipping, and that Mr Cawker had actually spotted a beacon burning. Mr Hughes' comments offered more food for thought on the matter. He stated that on top of Kilvey Hill stood the remains of 'Y Bigwrn' (the Cone) that had not been used as a mill 'in the memory of anyone living,' whilst the second windmill was at Cefn Hengoed (the Old Wooded Bank), and was built 'about eighty or ninety years ago;' his correspondence made no reference to a beacon at all irrespective of location.

If Mr Bigg's statement that the 'old windmill' of his memory was 'situated on a lower point of the hill in the direction of Landore' is also taken into consideration, then we are now offered three locations, unless he was actually recalling the mill in Bonymaen. Colonel Francis noted the improbability of two windmills 'on the Kilvey ridge' before then going on to endorse much of the information first laid out by Mr Hughes, but he left open the question of which 'old windmill' was actually hit by lightning.

The Bonymaen Windmill c1930 (unknown)

In line with the pleas of some of the respondents, it appears that the beacon on Kilvey Hill was later rebuilt, as in the Cambrian of 25th June 1897 [11] when describing activities in the town relating to the Queen's Jubilee, the following was noted:

'**THE JUBILEE BEACONS**. The scene from the top of Mumbles Hill on Tuesday night will not soon be forgotten by those who gazed upon it. Breconshire, Devonshire, Cornwall, Somerset, and Glamorganshire, showed us their beacons — that on the top of Kilvey Hill towering above all. As we waited for the fires to be kindled, our thoughts reverted to the beacon fires of long ago. For although Macaulay has made us most familiar with them, they were used centuries before Spain's Invincible Armada inspired his martial muse. Sacred writers testify to their antiquity…'

There is much to consider in the above correspondence, not least Colonel Francis's willingness to retrofit much of the information to suit his narrative, but in sharp contrast to his views, W.C. Rogers, in his 1966 Gower Society Journal article 'The Windmills of Kilvey' [12] is in no doubt that the 'Kilvey Windmill' was in fact erected in Cefn Hengoed in Bonymaen, and also clarifies that the location of the Watermill mentioned in the 1688 Survey, known as Felin Newydd, was 'where the Dyffryn Steel and Tinplate Works came to be built', the area today better known as Swansea Enterprise Park in Llansamlet.

Rogers states: 'Few of the public at large will yet have missed a landmark, which the Swansea Corporation removed in September 1966, from the greatly growing suburb of the Borough which is called Bonymaen. I refer to the remains of the tower of the old Kilvey Windmill. It stood in the Cefn Hengoed recreation ground, half a mile East North East of "Handover" (today called Hanover Square) and 600 yards north of "the Sarnau" or "Llydiade Sarne", where the ancient roads-from Foxhole via the Gwyndy; from the ancient Chapel of St. Thomas via Morris Lane; from Briton Ferry and Neath via the Crymlyn ford, and from the ancient church of St. Samlet via Nantyffin and Pentrecawr all met together.

He goes on to say that the windmill was: 'on the narrow Cefn bye road which went over the ridge (Cefn Henvod) on which "the old house stood, and so made its way to the Trallwng and the Stadwen... Its site was beyond the wastes of the Llanerch heath and recent generations may not have regarded it as being on Kilvey Hill, but the farm on its south side is still known as Kilvey Mount or Mountain, and if one is to distinguish its site from the next big eminence-"the Goppa", where the Talychobau farms lay, one must regard it as part of Kilvey Hill.'

Rogers states that the Bonymaen Mill, was not repaired after the fire and that 'it had served its purpose for but 122 years, and then was to lie in ruin for 156 years more.' Whilst calling the structure atop Kilvey Hill both windmill and beacon, he writes that the last notices of 'the Bigwrn' occurred in October and November of 1850, when to mark the marriage of Pascoe St. Leger Grenfell's eldest daughter Madelina married Griffith Llewellyn of Baglan Hall, flags were flown 'on the isolated ruined windmill on the summit of Kilvey' accompanied by the firing of guns from the ships in the harbour, and that in the following month strong gales had reduced the beacon in size and it was no longer visible to mariners, to which Lord Jersey's agent stated 'It is a mark that appears in all the charts of the world, and in the sailing directions of the Bristol Channel', and that it would be renovated so as to be visible 'to masters and pilots from Lundy up'.

Many old maps refer to the construction on top of Kilvey Hill as 'the Old Windmill', and Rogers explains this away as follows:

'What has led to the confusion is that the ruined stump (now scarcely visible) on Kilvey's summit near Carn Nicholas farm has long been called the Kilvey Windmill. Mariners could observe it from the Tuskar Rock to Lundy when weather conditions suited, and it was marked upon most charts in the last century and a half. I remember playing in it as a boy when perhaps fifteen feet of its height remained. Having impressions of only the tiniest space within its walls I went up there about twelve years ago, and its internal diameter convinced me that this was no tower in which milling and grinding operations took place.'

He further notes that a farm nearby the structure was called Dan-y-Bigwrn, which he translates from Welsh to English as 'Under the Beacon cone', although it is perhaps more accurately translated as 'under the cone' (or peak). When comparing the estimated windmill dimensions offered by Rogers with the details offered in the Cambrian regarding the windmill fire and its aftermath, it seems highly unlikely that the Bigwrn was the location of the accident described, especially given the number of people supposedly inside the building when lightning struck.

Rogers dismisses the hill-top structure as one that had once been a mill, however, a paper by Jane Jo F. Roberts called " The Windmills of Glamorgan" [13] directly challenges his assertion. Ms Roberts' paper clarifies that whilst the Bonymaen and Kilvey Windmills had often been grouped together and confused with each other they are two distinct structures. Whilst WC Rogers argues that the ruin on top of Kilvey Hill is too small to have been a working mill, Roberts counters that it was likely a sloped-sided 'post mill', and many such mills were known to have had similar dimensions to the ruin, whilst the Bonymaen Mill was a straight-sided 'tower mill'.

Roberts points out that a 1759 map by English cartographer Thomas Kitchen shows a windmill marked in this position with a post mill symbol, and adds that an 1844 tithe map shows an adjacent field as 'Caer Felin Wynt' (Windmill Field).

Swansea from Kilvey Hill (unknown artist) SM1989.486, Swansea Council: Swansea Museum Collection

She adds 'an old and rather unrealistic' drawing of Kilvey Windmill (above) that shows a pent-shaped cap and four sails were in place' [14] although this would have to have been completed with some artistic license involved, as if we accept the information offered above, it would have been a ruin at that time. She also references an 1813 'picture'(engraving) by J.G. Wood [15] that illustrates a sloped-sided windmill in the same location, and finally, she refers to a c1930 painting by K.S. Wood [16] that shows 'most of the bottom part of the tower on the point of falling.'

In 'Memories - Swansea Eastside' by T. Quirk [17] the 'old windmill' on Kilvey Hill is referred to in a local tale known as 'The Whitewash Men'': 'In the summer of 1913 several men called at number 2 Dan-y-Beacon and borrowed a ladder. This they took to the old windmill. Here they set to work with brushes, whitewash, and paint.

The result of their labours was a printed text in black letters six feet high "Christ died for the ungodly". The remainder of the building was whitewashed. With the aid of glasses, this text could no doubt be read from ships anchored in the bay. As long as the walls remained intact, they were whitewashed each year and the text repainted.'

("Leader" Sketch.)

The remarkable building on Kilvey Hill, Swansea, used as a landmark for ships at sea, a description of which appears in another column. Note the lettering, "Christ Died For The Ungodly."

Newspaper Cutting from Cambria Daily Leader August 1913

This story aligns with a front-page article in the Cambria Daily Leader of 29th August 1913 [18] complete with an accompanying photograph, and a second photograph in the same newspaper on 13th November 1919 [19] both of which show a large structure on the summit of Kilvey Hill with painted lettering on its walls. Whilst the details in the article confuse the Kilvey and Bonymaen Windmills when describing the destruction on the day of the storm, the article states that the building on top of Kilvey Hill was 'reconstructed' c1893 as a 'landmark for boats', so given the close proximity of dates, it is possible that this was the structure used as part of the Queen Jubilee celebrations in 1897.

If by 1878, the structure on the top of Kilvey Hill had 'not been used for grinding purposes within the memory of anyone living' it could not possibly have been the windmill that was struck by lightning, and in which men perished. This would also explain why the term 'old windmill' was used on old maps and charts showing the summit of Kilvey Hill.

If Mr Hughes's 1878 assertion that the second windmill at Bonymaen was built 'about eighty or ninety years ago' in c1790 is correct, and that it was a large working windmill that was 'remarkable for its height and solidity', then it clearly could not be the hilltop windmill, and given its location on the lower north side of Kilvey Hill, it would not have been used as a beacon. In addition, there are photographs available of the Bonymaen Windmill to assess its condition and size up until it was demolished in 1966.

After taking all of the above into account I believe the following can be gleaned:

a) **The Kilvey Windmill:** It is likely that Bussy Mansel's c1680 windmill was a 'post mill' positioned on top of Kilvey Hill, but by 1780 it had ceased operating as a mill and had been utilised as a beacon. W.C. Rogers writes that the 'the Bigwrn' was used to celebrate Grenfell wedding in October and November of 1850 yet this is not noted by either Colonel Francis or any of the other Cambrian correspondents in 1878. The same correspondence lamented a structure on top of Kilvey Hill that was in very poor condition and needed rebuilding, but remained on various maps and nautical charts as 'The Old Windmill.'

b) **The Bonymaen Windmill:** A 'tower mill' likely built in c1790, it was struck by lightning during a violent storm in July 1810, during which time there was serious structural damage done to the mill as well as loss of life. The building was subsequently repaired and continued working as a mill until c1824, and the structure was finally removed by local authorities in 1966.

c) **The Kilvey Beacon:** Newspaper reports in 1897 state that the ruins of an old beacon on the summit of Kilvey Hill had been rebuilt and that the 'Kilvey Beacon' played an active part in the town celebration of Queen Victoria's Diamond Jubilee. In 1913 and 1919 a substantial cone-topped building is shown on the summit of the hill in newspaper photographs, however, we cannot ascertain from these reports if this particular building (a) included the remains of the earlier structure as part of its construction, (b) retained the old ruins within its walls, or (c) if it is a completely new building. It must also be noted that there is no mention of this structure at all in WC Rogers' notes.

For those of us who can still remember the ruins on the top of Kilvey Hill, the structure will always be "The Old Windmill", but over 340 years after the original windmill was built, were the ruins we all remember really the remains of a long-gone windmill, an old beacon, or the remains of the building that stood on the hill that is shown in the photographs of 1913 and 1919?

Horse Racing on Crymlyn Burrows

Although the term has its origins in war and has also been attributed to hunting, horse racing in Britain is often called 'The Sport of Kings', no doubt due to the fact that the owning and breeding of racehorses was associated with royalty and other affluent families who had both the time and money to develop the sport. By the end of the 18th century, there were a number of race tracks set up across the country that although run by and for the benefit of the landed gentry, made the sport more accessible to the wider population. Annual races soon became a regular part of a town or county's social calendar, normally accompanied by various social functions such as balls and dinners for the benefit of the owners and their friends.

Held on land owned by the Briton Ferry Estate, the Crymlyn Burrows race track first appeared on the Racing Calendar in 1803 [20] held over three days, the events attended by the local gentry, dignitaries and industrialists. 'The Swansea Races' of 1804 [21] were run over two days on 12th-13th July, with various prizes of £50 and Fifty Guineas on offer; horse proprietors/owners paying one guinea per day on entry to the course to cover 'Weights. Scales etc. or Double at the Post', Race Stewards were Robert Jenner, Esq and John Morris Jun. Esq. The meetings were regarded as an opportunity for the working classes to attend what amounted to a county-fair environment that they had never seen before, and the event would have been a cause of great excitement at the time in both Swansea and Neath, given the racetrack's proximity to both towns.

In 1813, on the death of his uncle without issue, the Briton Ferry Estate passed to George Child Villiers, 5th Earl of Jersey, who was a successful racehorse owner, breeding and training his own horses at Middleton, and who would go on to have many celebrated winners in his stables, including an Oaks winner ('Cobweb' in 1824), and three Derby winners ('Middleton' (1825), 'Mameluke' (1827) and Bay Middleton (1836). Races continued on the Crymlyn Burrows until 1815, although after an eight-year hiatus, they began again in 1823, before once more interest waned. By the mid-1830s there was renewed interest in reviving the annual Swansea Races, and in August 1834 [22] was led by local industrialists and gentry, and supported by local tradespeople.

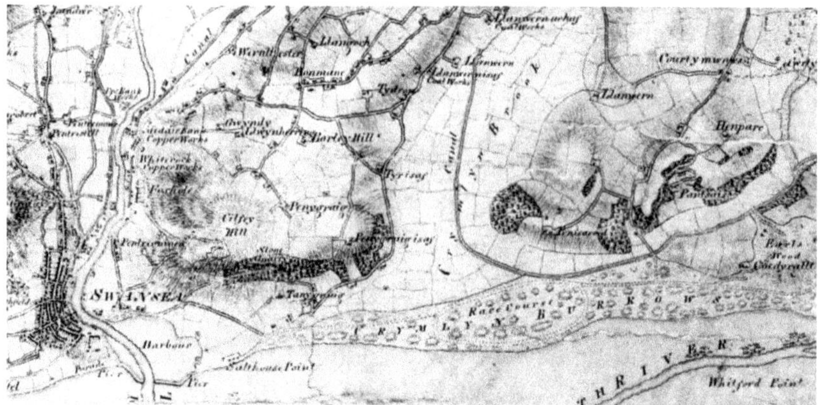

Map showing Crymlyn Racetrack (authors digital collection)

The two-day 'Swansea and Neath Races' took its place on the local social calendar, with John Henry Vivian, Swansea's leading copper works owner, and Frederick Fredericks owner of the Duffryn Estate in Neath, acting as Stewards. The racing was enjoyed by all and the races were well documented in The Cambrian which reported that the festivities sent up to accompany the races were a great success:

'SWANSEA AND NEATH RACES. These Races, on Wednesday last, were well attended by the principal families in the neighbourhood, and the day proving very fine, the sports attracted a vast concourse of spectators of all classes. There were upwards of sixty carriages and vehicles ranging from the Stewards' Stand to the distance post, and the number of persons on the ground, on a moderate computation, exceeded five thousand. The running was very good, and the arrangements by the Stewards, J. H. Vivian, Esq M.P., and F. Fredericks Esq. gave great satisfaction. The weather on Thursday was very unfavourable, notwithstanding the attendance on the race ground was numerous, and the sport afforded much gratification.

Organised around the dates of the races were 'Ordinaries' held at the Mackworth Arms on Wednesday, and at the Bush on Thursday, both of which were well attended, as well as a 'Public Breakfast' hosted by J. H. Vivian, Esq M.P., at the Mackworth Arms, which was attended by over one hundred dignitaries - 'ladies and gentlemen of the town, neighbourhood, and different parts of the County'. In addition, The Stewards' Ball, held at the Assembly Rooms, drew a crowd of 'upwards of one hundred and thirty fashionables'.

An anonymous account of the races entitled 'Swansea Races Over 100 Years Ago' [23] discovered in the Royal Institute of South Wales and published in 1964 highlighted just how popular the annual event was. Judging by the information given in this account, it is likely the writer is recounting a trip between 1834 and 1837, and he describes what must have been an eventful trip for many of those people who travelled from Swansea to the race track:

A RED-LETTER DAY (or days, indeed) was this to me, for when a boy, a mere child, in fact, this event was looked forward to, year after year, as one, if not the chief, of the enjoyments of my young life. A shocking commencement, Mrs Grundy, would say, for a young life! The racecourse was on Crumlyn Burrows, about halfway to Neath, as the bird flies, and the road to it, most exciting at all points, lay across the Swansea River, through St. Thomas past Danygraig, then the Colonel Cameron's residence, where the cemetery now is, and across Tenant's Canal. There were usually two days racing - flat running on the first and both flat and hurdle racing on the second, to both of which my relatives and I usually went, and the proceedings were thus;

About noon, a 'fly', having an opening and closing capacity in case of rain, a roomy machine, a kind of landau, we might now say, with a pair of good horses and an outrider or postilion in yellow jacket, appeared at the front door. The prog in sundry baskets and hampers, similar to those provided on a memorable occasion by Mr Wardle, the hospitable owner of Dingly Dell, without, however, the presence of the Fat Boy, were placed in the boot, and other convenient parts of the carriage, and we all got in. the advantage of having a post-boy was that we saved two good seats on the box, and as these flies were, as I say, roomy vehicles, there was plenty of space inside in addition.

THE FORD. The first anxiety of the day was whether or not there were much freshets in the river, as when the tide was out, the crossing of the Tawe had to be effected by a ford, situated at the extreme end of the Somerset -place, opposite the old Cambrian Hotel. This we usually succeeded in accomplishing very comfortably, though often with terrible jolts over, and amongst boulders, we could not have seen. This ford at these times was much used, and we had plenty of company on the transit. On other occasions when the tide was in, or rough weather about, or dangerous currents of stormwater were coming down the river, we had to start earlier, and drive up High Street and Greenhill on to the Neath-road, crossing the river near the Wych Tree Bridge, and thence down its left bank past the copper works, until we reached the "Red House", back indeed, to within a stone's throw from the ferry boat, and thence along the road by Danygraig House.

The ferry referred to was worked with a broad, roomy boat, capable of carrying besides pedestrians, horses, and a carriage or two, and was wound across the river by a windlass with rope or chain; but this mode of crossing was by no means a favourite one, more especially when restive quadrupeds were on board. It was, in fact, a dangerous proceeding in rough weather, and several times I remember hearing of the ferry boat and passengers breaking loose and being carried away by the heavy flood to the Pier entrance of the Harbour. It is necessary to keep in mind that there was then no North Dock, no New Cut, and no bridges to facilitate our movements, as there are now.

CRUMLYN BURROWS. Having got on to the Burrows we had yet to proceed a considerable distance before reaching the course, and I well recollect the constant alarm I felt in the travelling over mounds and tumps, one side of the carriage down one moment, next up and so on, like a ship in distress; it's true we should have fallen 'soft' had we capsized. If the post-boy instead of being in the saddle, had been handling the ribbons on the box, I used to think he would have chosen more level ways, for he would have required the freedom of both hands to hold on with; as it was, he experienced no inconvenience on the animal's back and therefore did not enter into the anxieties of his freight.

Having reached our destination, I should state that, on one side of the course, which was roped off, and near the winning post, a row of large temporary stands and booths were erected, something in the style of the Epsom arrangements, but at Swansea, there was no grandstand. On the opposite side were ranged, for a long distance, the carriages of visitors, and the earlier the arrival, the better the position attainable. On a fine day, it was really a gay and brilliant scene, many private four-in-hand drags being usually present, notably the magnificent turn-out of Mr Fredericks of Duffryn. Four of his grey pets, himself tooling them in a handsome carriage with a good, swinging top-load of ladies and gentlemen, and a couple of well-topped grooms in the rumble were worth all the money.

THE RACING. In those days many racing men from the English counties attended the Swansea Meeting when on several occasions a goodly subscription provided valuable cups and stakes - Tom Parr amongst them - there were many local men too, such as Richard Douglas Gough, Henry Lucas, Charles Henry Smith and sometimes the officers in charge of the military. Mr Gough, like Mr Parr, commonly rode his own horses, and well he did it, but his face and action in a close contest, when nearing the post was a picture to behold. His eyes protruded as though they would out-shoot the sockets, and his mouthing was fearful. It was all but momentary, however, for his features shortly resumed their usually placid form. A small black horse, called 'Pilot' ridden by himself, won many races, I remember.

As a small boy, I have a vivid recollection of Mr Henry Lucas on one occasion winning a large and valuable cup, with a horse called 'Bay Hampton' or 'Tottenham', I forget which. He had had ill luck and been constantly losing, and there was now great joy amongst his friends and the onlookers at his success, a joy not confined to them, but vastly appreciated by himself who, kind, amiable man as he was, came round to all the carriages with a servant carrying bottles of champagne, from which he from time to time filled his cup, with a request that each lady should drink his horse's health. One lady I know, said, "I drink your health, Mr Lucas", when he as once checked her, saying "no, my horse's health, if you please!"

There was with free admission to the public, food, drink and gambling vendors were charged one guinea per booth erected, and the rivalry between Swansea and Neath often turned into brawls between the men from both towns. In 1838, local brewer Evan Evans built a grandstand [24] with an adjoining booth where alcohol was served, charging between 1 shilling and a shilling and sixpence for a grandstand seat to well-to-do patrons who whilst viewing the races in comfort, could have a clear view 'of any fisticuffs between the peasantry.' For the next nine years, the Races were popular and well-attended, with the eighteen-race 1847 event [25] being regarded as the most successful event held for many years. but the event came to an abrupt halt due to a lack of commitment from those both organising and funding the proceedings.

In 1855 there was an attempt to restart the event, including the building of a new grandstand [26]:

'After an interval of eight years Swansea Races have been once more revived, and that too under auspices which promised not only for their being successful for the present year, but of being long a source of attraction to the lovers of the turf in South Wales and the West of England. The Swansea races are revived under distinguished patronage—the Earl of Jersey not only giving permission to use the race course on Crumlyn Burrows, but liberally subscribing £30 to the funds. The Stewards were the Mayor, J. T. Jenkin, Esq., and L. L. Dillwyn, Esq., M.P.. The most complete arrangements were made for the accommodation of spectators and visitors, the grandstand having been constructed for receiving 800 persons.'

Alas, the return of racing at Crymlyn Burrows had limited success, and on 31st August 1858, after the final race under official Jockey Club rules, the grandstand was put up for auction. [27] An attempt to run a one-day event in 1861 was deemed a failure, and proved to be the last race ran on the course, and facing the arrival of the new railway routes across Briton Ferry Estate land, horse racing on Crymlyn Burrows was no more.

From Fabian's Bay to the Construction of Fabian Way

Held at The Royal Institute of South Wales, an 1849 watercolour of 'Fabian's House' painted by William Butler, identifies a property that once stood close to the shore of what was to become known as Fabian's Bay, named after a West Wales farmer called Daniel Fabian who moved to Swansea from Llandrhidian c1693, and who established a farm on land previously leased to George Hutton and his family.

Daniel Fabian likely moved into the house after the death of Mrs Margaret Hutton in 1703, and whilst he died there in 1728, his son, also Daniel Fabian, was also recorded as living at the house.

Fabian's House by Williams Butler SM1989.36, Swansea Council: Swansea Museum Collection

Daniel Fabian and his son are mentioned various times in Gabriel Powell's 1764 Survey of Gower as follows:

'Salthouse Green adjoining the old salthouse held by Daniel Fabian, "with liberty to gather wood thrown up by the sea' between the mouth of the lane called Heol y Twad and St. Thomas Chapel.'

'Two pieces of land called Ty Watty Daniel and Tyr Perkin, otherwise known as Cae Sychan, both of which 'cannot now be found, but they lie in the tenement of lands of George Hutton gent. called Tyr Glan Y Bad"... Daniel Fabian paid 2 shillings and 4 pence per annum rent of Tyr Glan y Bade to George Hutton.'

'Daniel Fabian also paid six pence annually, for the 'use of a level by the salt house' in order to drain his meadow... A fishing wear on the east side of Swansea river and also another wear lying on the salt sands.'

Both Daniel Fabian Jr. and his wife Jennet Fabian are later recorded as living and working on Briton Ferry Estate land [28] [29]. and a local contemporary of both Daniel Fabian Snr. and his son was John North, who was living on or around Crymlyn Burrows at his farm at 'Tyr John North' [30].

Whilst it is the Fabian name that is remembered and still used locally today, a 1973 article by Dr Prys Morgan [31] offers an understanding of the history of both the house and the area, dating back to the 17th century. The 1686 Survey of Gower and Kilvey refers to the land adjacent to the foreshore at St. Thomas as 'Tir Glan Y Bade' alias 'Tir Jenkins ap Evan Ychan', and owned by 'Roger Morgan, Gent', who was likely the grandfather of Mrs Hutton.

Dr Morgan writes that in 1804 a Swansea solicitor called John James discovered the 1703 inventory of Mrs Hutton's house when working on the estate of the late Thomas Morgan, which confirms that the farm was officially known as Tir Glan Y Bad ('boat bank'). Glad Y Bad was one of six farms in the small hamlet of St. Thomas, and the other properties had long been 'in the families now possessed them, namely those of 'Lord Vernon and Calvert Jones'. Thomas Morgan, possibly the same man that had replaced Gabriel Powell as Steward of Gower for the Duke of Beaufort, was the last of the Morgan's of Pendderi Fawr near Penllagaer, a large 'low-level gentry' family that owned property in and around Swansea.

Thomas Morgan died a bachelor, and his estate was eventually split up amongst his extended family. 'Glan Y Bad' in St. Thomas and

'Thistleboon' in Oystermouth eventually passed to Francis Pinkney, a London bookseller and son of a Neath vicar who was related to the Morgan family via the Hutton family, and was the great-grandson of Mary Hutton. Fabian's house was demolished in c1859 when the land was cleared to construct housing to support industrial growth.

Housing in the Port Tennant area had been built and developed around the businesses brought to the area by the canal, whilst Foxhole and Pentreguinea were also developed in line with the growth of the copper industry and the businesses it spawned, but until the mid-1800s much of the rest of the Eastside remained rural. The 1841 census shows only five 'Fabian's Cottages', presumably all part of the same smallholding. However, the 1851 census showed thirty properties on Fabian's Bay, although it is not clear that they were part of the same smallholding.

Fabian St c1960 (c) Rev. R. Alan Evans Collection

A new residential housing boom began with construction between the New Cut and Port Tennant, and the 1861 census shows that a road had been built running adjacent to the shoreline that ran east from the rear of the Red House public house. The new road had three shorter blocks of buildings adjacent to it known as 'Gillian Terrace', 'Cawnpore Street' and 'Fabian Row', which included the

Fabian Inn. In the 1871 census, the same road lists Gillian Terrace and Fabian Terrace (made up of what was previously Cawnpore Street and Fabian Row), and by 1881 the census shows that Gillian Terrace was no more and that it too was now part of 'Fabian Street', which ran between the rear of the Red House and the bottom of Sebastopol Street.

Over the next seventy years or so, Fabian St became an integral part of life on the Eastside as in addition to being the main thoroughfare to Swansea, as the commercial hub of St. Thomas it was lined with shops and public houses.

Fabian Way

In the mid-1940s, the British government began rebuilding the country's war-damaged towns and cities. The Ministry of Transport put forward a plan, first mooted before the Second World War, for a major upheaval of the road network in England and Wales and the development of a modern road transport infrastructure, that included the proposal to construct a new South Wales Motorway linked to the west of England via the construction of a new road bridge over the River Severn. The new motorway system would tie into the towns of South Wales utilizing a series of feeder roads, opening up the region to industrial and commercial development.

At that time, the main route in and out of Swansea to the east was via Llansamlet and Skewen, so the opening of the new A483, linked to the new Briton Ferry Bridge, and running nearly four and a half miles west from Earlswood to the River Tawe, would make access to and from Swansea far easier, and would greatly improve trade routes whilst offering much-improved access to both the port and the town. In April 1946 the go-ahead was given for the construction of dual carriageway roads between Briton Ferry and Swansea, and after the successful acquisition of land from the Estate of Lord Jersey, work began on the first section of what was first called The East Side Road, which had seen an over 50% rise in traffic volume since the construction and opening of the Briton Ferry Bridge in the early-1950s.

The proposed new highway ran parallel with the sand dunes between Earlswood and the Swansea-Neath boundary at Jersey Marine and was completed in 1950. On the Swansea side of the boundary, the new road was to run through an area of land owned by the British Transport Commission that sat between Port Tennant and Swansea Docks and was predominantly utilized by the canal and railway companies before connecting to a section of the old B4290 road that ran from the bottom of Maes St along Fabian St to the Swing Bridge near Thomas St (the original B4290 ran between Fabian St and Neath Abbey).

According to government figures, in 1951 around 15% of households in the UK owned cars, however, a 1966 census of the new Borough of Swansea showed that the number had tripled over a period of fifteen years, which also meant a substantial jump in car travel, whilst at the same time rail companies noted a decline in both journeys and passenger numbers. In late 1951 the Swansea Borough Council gained approval from the Minister of Transport for its plans to construct new dual carriageways running from the Swansea - Neath boundary to Wind St at an estimated cost of nearly £1.3 million. [32]

The work was to be completed over a seven-year period, with construction broken down into six sections, the first of which was to run from the county boundary to the canal bridge adjacent to the Vale of Neath pub. The development of the new road threw up many challenges as the area on the Swansea side of the boundary was threaded with railway lines, service and support buildings, a canal, dock access roads, as well as various commercial and residential properties.

In order to complete this project as planned the Swansea Corporation needed to make compulsory purchases on properties on Fabian St, as well as nearby corner properties on Miers St, Inkerman St, Balaclava St, Sebastopol St, Lewis St. and Maes St. In addition, they had to carry out alterations to Morriston Terrace in order to improve the junction between Port Tennant Rd and the new Fabian Way.

Junction of Morriston Terrace (left) and the East Road (right) (c) Rev. R. Alan Evans Collection

The road between the county boundary and Kings Dock Level Crossing was completed in February 1953 [33] but whilst the road between the Level Crossing and the Vale of Neath pub was completed in September the same year, work on the Kings Dock Level Crossing was delayed until September 1955. Work on both the Kings Dock Level Crossing Bridge and the new Vale of Neath Bridge was further delayed before the south carriageway was opened to traffic in January 1958.

The next short section ran between the Vale of Neath pub to Danygraig Bridge and involved the alteration of railway sidings and sewers, the culverting of the Tennant Canal, as well as the demolition of the Burrows Inn, and the removal of two steel bridges.

Work was finally completed in March 1958, quickly followed by the section of road between Danygraig Bridge to East Dock Station, parallel to Port Tennant Road, and built on land that was previously owned by the British Transport Commission. [34]

In June 1958 the Vicar of All Saints, Newbridge-On-Wye, in Radnorshire, the Reverend R. Alan Evans, took over as Vicar of St. Thomas Church. A keen photographer, he managed to capture many images of St. Thomas and Swansea, some of which are included in this book. Much loved in his parish, Reverend Evans officiated in the vast majority of weddings, christenings and funerals on the Eastside for over 22 years, touching literally every family in one way or another. He retired in November 1980, and passed away aged 78 in December 1993.

The Reverend R. Alan Evans

Construction of a dual carriageway between East Dock Station and the New Cut Bridge followed, and with compulsory purchase orders issued on the various residential and commercial properties on Fabian St [35] the commercial and residential shape of St. Thomas was completely altered, and a small area at Pinkney St was cleared and made available to displaced traders to erect temporary shops. Five pubs were demolished on Fabian St; the Station Inn, the Cyprus Hotel, the Railway Inn, the Red House and the Bridge Inn.

There were also major changes made at the junction of the main Docks entrance and Thomas Street that included a compulsory purchase of the Ivy Bush Inn. In early 1960 it was agreed that two new pubs could be built to replace the five pubs that had been demolished on Fabian St but only one, the Cape Horner Hotel, was actually constructed, although in December 1966 The Swansea Dockers Club relocated from Victoria St, opposite the Royal Institution of South Wales (aka Swansea Museum) to newly-built premises on the corner of Delhi St and Thomas St.

Work on the final section between Thomas Street to Wind St, to be known as Quay Parade, was carried out between 1961 and 1965 at an estimated cost of £678,000 [36] and saw the demolition of the Docks Entrance Bridge, the Cuba Hotel, the Cuba Bridge, the Strand Bridge, and the Sailors Home. The New Cut swing bridge, in operation since 1897, was replaced with the new 200ft span New Cut Road Bridge, while a pedestrian subway was built from Somerset Place to Wind St.

Nearly 140 years after the 1827 Parliamentary bill amendment to the Glamorgan Turnpike Act of 1823 gave the go-ahead for its construction, the road from Briton Ferry to Swansea town centre was completed, and the Eastside, its commercial heart removed, was the home of a major road artery called Fabian Way, a thoroughfare that, whilst separating its residential districts from the docks, would carry thousands of road vehicles a day in and out of Swansea.

The Carbon Black - How the East Was Won

Many of today's Eastsiders are descendants of the coppermen, mariners, dockers, railwaymen and many other trades and labourers that came to Swansea in the mid-1800s and who established their families on the east side of the Tawe. In a time of huge change driven by the industrial revolution, pollution from the many surrounding industrial plants was a part of everyday life; infant mortality was high, and working-class men and women seldom lived past their 50th birthday.

In the early twenty century, the Eastside and in particular the docks continued to develop as the centre of Swansea's industry, and in 1935 when the Strand Power Station was deemed no longer capable of handling the town's power requirements, Swansea Corporation again looked to the Eastside and commissioned and built the 150-megawatt Tir John North Power Station on Crymlyn Bog close to Danygraig.

Tir John North Power Station (author's collection)

At the time, 'Tir John' was the biggest power station in Britain and was in operation from 1936. It ran on anthracite duff, a cheap coal waste that left a sulphur dioxide residue that billowed and belched out of its three chimney stacks either over the Eastside or towards Neath, depending on which way the wind blew. This discharge continued until Tir John converted to oil burning in 1970 when it was linked directly to BP Llandarcy Refinery. Six years later, it was decommissioned as a result of the 1973 OPEC oil embargo. [37]

In 1948, on the other side of Crymlyn Bog, the US-owned Anchor Chemicals Ltd opened a new chemical plant in Port Tennant that via the partial burning and pyrolysis of low-value oil residues at high temperatures, produced 'Dixie' and 'Kosmos' grades of 'carbon black. [38] Carbon Black is a fine black powder used to strengthen rubber in tyres, hoses, conveyor belts, and other rubber products, as well as a pigment in printing inks and automotive coatings. The discharge from this plant was far more visible to the eye than the pollution that poured out of the Tir John stacks, and it produced black clouds of soot-like residue that fell daily on Port Tennant. It was later revealed that even short-term exposure to high concentrations of carbon black dust could be very uncomfortable to anyone unfortunate enough to breathe it in as it irritated the upper respiratory tract.

Over the next twenty years, daily clouds of black smut and dirt fell on local houses, soiling freshly washed clothes within an hour of being hung out to dry. The dust also made its way inside the houses and covered furniture and contaminated food. Some mothers complained that it was so dirty that they had to use detergents rather than soap to wash their children when they came in from playing in the local streets. [39] Throughout that time the local community pleaded with Swansea Council to act on their behalf and speak directly with the company, but without success.

In January 1966 BBC correspondent George Ashwell visited the area to interview a group of local women, led by Mrs Pamela Shadbolt, who had recently presented Swansea Council with an 800-signature petition to complain about the pollution. [40] Mrs. Shadbolt said that the problem had been ongoing for 'fifteen to sixteen years,' whilst another of the women interviewed, Annie Wing, commented that there had been numerous complaints made previously, but they had been continually ignored, and rather than filter the existing stack, the company had added a second stack to the plant. A third resident, Liza Draper, highlighted the fact that local women had to buy washing powder on a daily basis to ensure children had clean clothes for school.

Swansea Council was not oblivious to the problem, and records show that it was considering possible legal action against United Carbon Black Ltd concerning the health hazards of carbon black [41]. In January 1970, after being ignored for over two decades, a group of local women took their grievance directly to Swansea Council, and after dumping their dirty washing at the council's Guildhall offices, returned to Port Tennant and temporarily blocked the road leading to the plant, now operating and trading as United Carbon Black Ltd. but still owned by Anchor Chemicals.

"Windows and washing are all marked by the carbon," said Edgar Cutler who lived close to the plant; "If I want a clean shirt my wife has to take it to the launderette to get it dry...my wife and I have to scrub our carpets once every eight weeks and we have to redecorate three or four times for every once that other people have to do it" [42] Another resident, Mrs Jessie Cottle, said: "I suffer from asthma and the air is seriously affecting my health. I cannot even open my bedroom window at night".

In March of that year, the company's management announced that they had installed a new burner that they claimed would end the 'muck-spreading', however, the funding for this equipment would have likely already been passed as part of their business plan agreed on in the previous fiscal year, rather than as a response to the protests of local residents. By January 1971, it appeared that nothing at all had changed, and after ongoing meetings with the local health authorities and the council, and after appealing to local Members of Parliament without success, the local women decided on a more direct approach to the problem.

Upset at being continually let down, at a meeting held on January 26th 1971 the woman, with the full support of the local community, decided that the only way to end the daily downpour of dust, was to block the road leading to the factory until they had achieved their aims, irrespective of the time it might take. A committee was formed that included a representative from each street in the area, and the first task in hand was to decide when the action would take place. On February 1st, incensed on hearing that Carbon Black management had planned to increase its production output by 25% in spite of their concerns, the residents' committee decided that they would put their plan into action two days later.

The Carbon Black - West Glamorgan County Council; ref. GB 216 WGCC/EH 20/3

At 9.30 am on February 3rd workers attempting to enter the plant found that their access was blocked, not by a temporary blockade as they had used a year earlier but by a permanent obstruction, or at least one that would stay in place until the dispute was resolved to the satisfaction of the protestors. Staff vehicles and supplier's lorries were turned away, and the outraged company management had to involve the local police to escort workers on foot onto the plant, whilst protesters remained in position throughout the night.

Any thoughts by the management that things would blow over quickly were dispelled when a large tent was erected outside the works gates, chairs and tables appeared, radios played, and a large fire was set up to keep people warm in the cold February air. Local tradespeople supported the protestors and a regular supply of wood and coal kept the fire burning, whilst grocers, butchers, greengrocers and fish and chip shops ensured the protesters, who were by now cooking on-site, were well fed.

The organisational skills of the protestors were remarkable, and not something the United Carbon Black management could have possibly foreseen, as the whole community swung into action behind the protestors, many of whom were their sisters, mothers or grandmothers. Local life had changed for as long as it would take to put an end to the Carbon Black problem.

Port Tennant Women at the Blockade

Tarpaulins were erected to act as windbreaks and to stave off the sleet and rain, and attached to one was a notice reading 'We're not budging, even if we catch pneumonia' [43]. It was the turn of sons, brothers, fathers and grandfathers to get involved, and they did not disappoint. Whilst shifts made up of fifty or more women protestors were rotated on the blockade through the day, the men took over in the evenings and through the night.

The local press reported 'It is in the evenings that the comradeship is most evident. [44] Fighting spirit becomes akin to party spirit as people bring portable record players and share their food.' The plant's workers, many of them of whom lived locally, were allowed to enter and leave the plant on foot without any problems, but vehicles continued to be blocked, and after a week Carbon Black management conceded that the protest had had a negative effect on its output.

The blockade continued, and whilst Swansea Council had referred the matter to the Welsh Office, the company stated that they were meeting their legal requirements with regard to emissions and they would directly canvas the Secretary of State for Wales Peter Thomas to intervene on their behalf. Peter Thomas, who was also Chairman of the Conservative Party, was a close friend of Sir Clyde Hewlett, the Deputy Chairman of Anchor Chemicals, and it was reported that the two men had met at the National Conference of Young Conservatives on 7th February, during the first week of the blockade.

Port Tennant Women at the Blockade (2)

On 12th February a report from a Welsh Office Alkali Inspector showed that the factory was indeed meeting its legal requirements. Britain's Deputy Chief Alkali Inspector was next to visit the plant during which time it was noted that the plant had ceased production and therefore there were no emissions to measure, although he also noted that as soon as he left production had started again.

His report was issued within days and it concurred with the result of the 12th February report. When asked to comment on the findings of the second report by the local press, Edgar Cutler summed up the thoughts of the road blockers when he said "We've not been hanging around here 24 hours of the day for 17 days for nothing. We will continue our stand". [45]

Despite the cold and wet weather, the protestors remained in good spirits and held fast to their goals, and the shifts of people continued to rotate day and night. A few weeks later on Shrove Tuesday, February 21st, local families held a 'fancy dress and hot pants pancake race' near the plant, with a huge local turnout in support of the event. Many families cancelled their winter holidays to support the cause, and one man supposedly remarked "We don't normally spend our holidays on the Port Tennant Riviera".

The determined Eastside women also took their case to the doors of Parliament, when in April 1971, together with their children, they carried the various banners of 'The Port Tennant Anti-Pollution Association, Swansea' to the streets of Whitehall, London SW1 where their protest continued.

The Protest in London

After three weeks without supplies, it was impossible for the company to complete production commitments, and completed goods had to be stockpiled as they could not leave the plant. Several departments were temporarily closed down, and the plant's staff were put on maintenance work. Company management proposed a truce, something that was immediately rejected by the protestors. By the fourth week of February production at the plant was in a dire position, and the company's management called for a 26th February meeting to be held in Cardiff with both protesters and Swansea Council in an effort to remedy matters.

This time the company took a far more conciliatory position and stated that they were willing to commit to spending £35,000 (over £500k in 2022) [46] on pollution monitoring measures in an effort to curtail the daily grime that the residents had endured for 23 years. The company also agreed to plan their production levels based on wind direction, stating that they would half their production output whenever 'strong easterly winds' were prevalent, and it was also hinted that expansion plans for the plant were on hold, and may be dropped. They also agree to alter the entry route into the plant so as to minimise lorry traffic through the urban areas.

It was agreed that a Liaison Committee would be formed [47] consisting of company management, Port Tennant residents, and representatives of Swansea Council, whose collective task was to keep a continual watch on pollution levels. The concessions were considered by many as a victory for the protestors, who agreed to end what had been a 24-day blockade of the Carbon Black plant, and three days later the company announced that any plans to extend the plant had been shelved. Some residents remained sceptical however, as they felt that many questions remained unanswered. They needed further assertions as to who would measure the strength and direction of the wind and as well as how often measurements would be taken, further clarifications were needed as to when the committed expenditure would be made, and assurances that money committed would be enough to finally solve the problems. Finally and importantly residents wanted a voice in the control of local pollution levels.

One of the protestors, Howard Bevan, echoed these concerns and said: "A lot of us are not satisfied. We've heard all these promises before. Although we have taken down our shelter we have stored it near the entrance. If Carbon Black doesn't keep their promises we won't take long to erect it again. All we can do now is wait and see what the outcome will be. If we blockade again it will be on a much larger scale than during the last three weeks". [48]

What began as a local problem took on 'David and Goliath' proportions as news of the stand-off reached far and wide, and the following appeared [49] in the journal The Ecologist in June 1971:

'For anyone with a feeling for justice, it is inconceivable that the people of Port Tennant should have had to suffer for so long. Yet nothing was done because United Carbon Black Ltd could hold up their heads and say, we have done all we are required to do by the Alkali Inspectorate. Astronomical figures are frequently quoted for the cost of the effects of air pollution' writes the Chief Inspector of Alkali, 'but we see no rush by the alleged sufferers to finance the prevention of pollution at source when on the face of it, there should be a phenomenal return for the outlay.' The article's author Robert Allen vehemently disagreed with this statement and argued that 'In the cases of Anglesey's aluminium smelter and Swansea's carbon black works, the costs are gross contamination and simple human misery. The sources themselves are quite capable of meeting them.'

In their May-August 1973 issue the Liberation News Service in New York [50] reported that the Board of Trade and Industry had informed the Resident Committee in February 1973 that talks had begun to relocate the plant that should last a few weeks, but on being informed by a reporter that talks would likely go on for years rather than weeks, a statement from the committee said: 'We are not prepared to wait and live in those conditions any longer'.

On 2nd December 1973, the BBC showed a programme called 'The Carbon Black. Economics of the Real World - Pollution--A cost of growth?' followed by a report in the New Scientist magazine on 6th December [51] as follows:

'The stuff is so fine it creeps through closed windows, and once it gets into synthetic fibres it is almost impossible to remove. The programme gives a fair rundown of the factors involved. We need carbon black to make car tyres and colour things like liquorice black (is this why it tastes of rubber?). The factory is only a single blot in the great smear of heavy industry that lines Swansea bay. Those whose homes first came under its black umbrella 25 years ago, think the UCB should spend many millions of pounds to take its pollution elsewhere. The people have a strong sense of community and don't want to move away. Now they are militant - they blockaded the factory in 1971 and hired a coach to go and lobby MPs. However, around 100 locals have 'shaken hands with the devil' and found employment with UCB.

Credit is due to UCB for allowing the cameras into the factory to interview the workers and the managing director. The latter claims that his factory has a more sophisticated system for controlling emissions than any other carbon black factory in the world. It does all that the law requires, and the Alkali Inspector would be round if it didn't. Two implicit conclusions are that the law could be changed, and UCB could spend more of its annual profit of a million pounds on improving filtering and packaging techniques.

Professor Wilfred Beckermann's...solution is incentive rather than compulsion. Under the present system, if the Alkali Inspector is satisfied, his limits will not be improved. A graduated tax on pollution would encourage the continuous reduction of pollution to the point where it becomes economically unviable. The tax might increase the cost of the product but so have other social advances, such as the abolition of child labour.'

By the 1980s the company was trading as Ashland United Kingdom Chemical Ltd (Carbon Black) and still known locally as 'The Carbon Black', continued to operate on the Eastside until early 1982, at which time the plant was closed down, and the facility was demolished. However, since that time the actions of those local women that took on an American chemicals company have been a reference point for those academics and experts who champion the cause of clean air.

In 2017 a series of scientific papers called 'Progress in Planning' [52] did a case study on Crymlyn Burrows, in which the United Carbon Black plant is described as the second-most concerning source of pollution on the Eastside after Tir John Power Station, whose sulphur dioxide discharge was deemed far more damaging to the local population than the carbon that had covered the area for so long, and when Tir John Power Station was demolished in 1980 it become yet another source of pollution when it was designated as a landfill site by the local council. Supported by information supplied by from the International Agency for Research on Cancer 2010, the paper also noted that close to the Carbon Black was a tar distillery plant that until the 1970s, had operated using the partial combustion of heavy oil-based products to produce tar, a process that was, at the time of writing, 'recognised as potentially carcinogenic in humans.' The paper's authors used both Tir John Power Station and the Carbon Black as benchmarks in which to measure the effect of the placing of a waste incinerator in Crymlyn Burrows on the Swansea-Neath/Port Talbot county border in 2002, and just as in 1971, distrust in local politicians again raised its head as local people questioned why the plant was to be built so close to a residential area.

Comments from individuals A1 (from the community pressure group) and B1 (from local government), addressed the issue when interviewed in 2009 for the same paper:

"Apart from the environmental things, it is the social injustice. That's what really, really annoys me as well. More so. It's not fair. It's really not fair . . . Why are we always being dumped on?"
(A1 Interview, 2009)

"There were seven sites originally and Crymlyn Burrows was chosen I think for the potentially low political impact. It's on the border between two authorities so Swansea people in Port Tennant don't have a say in the [NPTCBC-led] planning process, and Crymlyn Burrows is literally made up of just two streets of residents. If they kicked up a fuss, well, they could be ignored." (B1 Interview, 2009)

Echoes of 1971 perhaps?

Weavers

For nearly ninety years, the imposing structure of Weavers Mill stood at the side of the Half Tide Basin between the North Dock and the River Tawe on land that was once part of the Eastside until the New Cut created an island that separated St. Thomas from the old route of the River Tawe. A building as iconic to the people of Swansea as the Eiffel Tower is to the residents of Paris, it was loved and loathed in equal measure.

Weavers (left) with overhead enclosed conveyor system linking to the ferro-concrete Provender Mill (right) c1960 (c) Rev. R. Alan Evans Collection

Founded in 1892, Weavers & Company Ltd. was a flour manufacturer that set up its business in the Duke of Beaufort's Dock on Swansea's North Dock, in warehouses that had years before housed the business of 'James Michael Flour & Corn'. The new business was to be known as 'Weavers and Company Ltd', and the 'Swansea and Worcester Flour Mills', and was set up with a share capital of £200,000 and led by Managing Director Mr William Weaver, the owner of City Flour Mills in Worcester, a business that whilst acquired and taken over by the new company, continued trading as a going concern.

The new company intended to erect a 'first-class' flour mill capable of producing 3,000 sacks of flour per week, and Mr Weaver invested £20,000 in ordinary shares of the new concern, and The

Cambrian newspaper made much of the launch of the new venture on 8th January 1892: [53]

'Swansea is undoubtedly a splendid centre for such a business as this. We have ourselves a large consuming population, and we have behind us, to the east, west and north, large and growing populations. That these people should be supplied with the materials for making the" staff of life" from Cardiff and Gloucester and such distant places as they, is ridiculous. The work can be done far more cheaply and profitably in our own town. That such a business as this, when well-conducted, is a lucrative one, is conclusively proved by the dividends which have been paid, even up to 17per cent., and by the considerable amounts carried to reserve funds, by similar companies established in Cardiff, Gloucester, and the West of England. Swansea possesses exceptional advantages as a place for importing grain cargoes, by reason of her fine position on the sea, and the moderate dock charges which are levied to cover the grand accommodation which our Harbour possesses.

Then, in addition to our advantages as a place of import, we have concurrent advantages for distribution, by reason of our railway connections with the district around us. Then again there are especially advantageous facilities offered by the position, the conveniences, and the reasonable rental of the Duke of Beaufort's Dock and Warehouses. Mr Weaver, the chief promoter, and intended managing director guarantees a minimum profit from the Worcester Branch of the Company, for the first three years, of £2,000 per annum. The fact that £40,000 has already been subscribed by the wealthiest, most enterprising, and most cautious of our local businessmen, is a sufficient indication of the opinion they hold of this new venture, which we warmly commend to the careful consideration of all persons who have money to invest, and who, patriotically, would prefer to invest it in such channels as are likely to prove not only financially advantageous to themselves, but also such as will, at the same time, prove an industrial and general benefit to Swansea.'

'The New Swansea Flour Mills' [54] opened for business in fifty-year-old warehouses built around three sides of the Duke of

Beaufort Dock, and designed by borough architect James Henry Baylis 'for the purpose they are now used, they could hardly be better arranged.' The north side of the buildings housed the receipt, storage and dispatch of wheat cargoes, whilst the south side handled corn. The various machines employed at the facility were required to sort, wash and dry grain, and included removing particles of iron by using a 'magnet machine'. A roller system then crushed the grain to various sizes, after which it goes through a number of sieving processes in order to produce the various end products. The dust produced as a result of all of these manufacturing processes is removed by a number of cyclone dust collectors. The equipment used in the facility is powered by a 350-horsepower double expansion engine.

A wholesale importer of European and North American wheat, Weavers & Co. supplied flour to their many local and regional customers, and as their business grew exponentially the company decided to invest in a new mill and grain silo, to be built adjacent to the North Dock Basin, and linked to the existing company warehouses via an overhead conveyor system that spanned both road and railway.

An update on the progress was mentioned in the company's annual shareholder meeting held on 11th August 1898 [55]:

"The new provender mill was completed and commenced running on the 7th of November last, and has fully answered the expectations of your directors. The machinery is of the very newest and best description. The quantity of corn milled, although much larger than heretofore is barely sufficient to supply our customers, and this shows that your board were acting wisely when they decided to erect the new mill. The silo granary is fast approaching completion and is hoped that it will (with the necessary machinery and grain elevator) be ready for use about the end of the year. It will have a storage capacity of 30,000 quarters.

Both these buildings are fireproof and are built by the ferro-cement process—Hennebique and Le Brun's Patent. When the silo granary is used we shall have our grain supplies close to the provender mill and there is no doubt this will be a great saving as well as much more convenient and more expeditious than having to convey grain from the East Docks to the mills. A new flour manufacturing plant, with all the latest improvements, with a capacity of ten sacks of flour per hour, is being erected, and will be ready for use in about a month's time; and your directors trust that customers will not then have any cause to complain of the want of prompt deliveries at all times.

Your Board are making a new entrance to their Beaufort Dock, and placing the same on the south side, which will affect a saving in the cost of taking small vessels into dock when large vessels are lying alongside our wharf in the North Dock. The cost at present of shifting large vessels in order to enable small craft to enter the Dock through the present opening is considerable. An electric motor and band-conveyor have been placed on the wharf for discharging grain from the ship's side in the North Dock into barges in the Beaufort Dock, and this affects a saving both of time and labour. Your Board decided after careful consideration to erect a cake mill, for the manufacture of compound feeding cake. This will have a capacity when in full work of about 70 tons of cake per week.

We believe that Swansea, from its central position, is admirably adapted for the distribution of this article. From enquiries made amongst our customers, we have every reason to believe that the demand will be equal to the capacity of the mill. The mill is being fixed in the basement of the provender mill, where there is space so that no outlay on building has been necessary.'

The Cambrian also published an interview with William Weaver [56] in which he stated that whilst the company's turnover was between £ 400,000 and £500,000 a year, and that they paid the Harbour Trustees £4,000 a year in dues, 'serious difficulties and opposition had to be contended with' when setting up the business, and that substantial amounts of money had to be invested in order to ensure the mills were among the best in the United Kingdom.

Emphasising the importance of the Weaver business to the commercial prosperity and development of the district in general, he highlighted the fact that the company had 'materially increased the imports and exports of Swansea' as the port and docks were now handling vessels that had previously no reason to come to the town before the establishment of the mills, and that after offloading their substantial cargoes of wheat, grain and maize, the vessels then 'took away cargoes of coal etc. equally as large'.

The business now consisted of substantial buildings and warehousing around the Beaufort Dock plus the new provender mill and grain silo adjacent to the North Dock Basin, and Mr Weaver indicated further extensions and alterations may be needed in the future in line with growth plans.

'The premises consist of, in the flour mill depot, eight large blocks, all communicating, which stand on three sides of our private dock. Two of these warehouses are used for the storage of wheat, the wheat-cleaning plant, a 25-sack per hour flouring plant now running, and a ten-sack plant in course of erection. The mills are equipped with Grinnell sprinklers, and other fire extinguishing appliances, and are lighted throughout by electric light.

Advert for 'Weaver & Co. Ltd'

Four buildings are taken up with the storage of flour and offal, from which material is loaded directly into ships, which lie alongside, for the coasting trade; also direct into trucks on our private sidings…. the covered way for carts…is 100 yards long, and eight wagons can be loaded simultaneously…. the wheat stores abut on to a berth in the main dock, where vessels of any draught can lie alongside, and discharged directly into these stores by a discharging plant composed of elevators, bands, &c.

The grist mill… is fitted with machinery for grinding, crushing, and mixing upwards of 10,000 sacks of corn and meal per week. Alongside is the fine-grain silo I have referred to, which will have a storage capacity of 30,000 quarters….I may mention that the machinery of the provender mill and silo house will be driven by three gas engines, of the combined force of 300 indicated hp. There is also another engine of about 80 hp. in the flour mill department. We make our own gas to drive these several gas engines.'

The company's directors were keen to utilise the latest technologies available when building the mill, and may well have been influenced by a near-miss in 1893 when a fire raged in the nearby railway arches on the North Dock that was thankfully doused before it reached the Weavers properties.

The new structure was constructed using the ''Beton Arme' (stressed reinforcing) system, which had been patented by French engineer François Hennebique, and had recently been proven successful when used in the construction of buildings in St Michel, Switzerland, and in Cairo, as well as on various contracts in northern France. Mr Weaver was particularly proud of the decision to use Hennebique's system: 'We claim - and our claim is not disputed - that it is one of the finest and most modern in the country. It is substantial, scientifically equipped, and thoroughly fire-proof...'

Hennebique's agent in the UK was Louis Mouchel who had an office in Briton Ferry, and after Mouchel had put forward the Hennebique method to Weaver's director John Aeron Thomas, they travelled together to France to visit the various completed ferro-concrete construction works, which subsequently led to the commissioning and erection of Weaver & Co.'s new provender mill.

Opened officially in August 1898, the six-storey mill was known as the Victoria Flour Mills and is believed to be the first fully framed ferro-concrete building in Britain.

After the North Dock was closed in 1928, the Half-Tide Basin remained open for vessels going to and from Weaver & Co. The provender mill survived the Blitz of World War 2, and whilst much of the area was cleared post-war in preparation for new buildings and roads, Weaver & Co. continued operating until 1963, when it finally closed its doors for the last time. The Half-Tide Basin was filled in the late 1960s and standing in isolation, the ruin of Weaver's mill was the first building visitors to Swansea saw as they travelled from the east along Fabian Way and crossed the New Cut Bridge onto Quay Parade.

Swansea Mayor Charles Thomas on demolition duty © Nigel Thomas

What many people thought was an indestructible building finally met its end after nearly ninety years of existence, when in 1984, it was demolished to make way for what is now the car park of Sainsbury's supermarket on Quay Parade, and on the wrecking ball on the first day of demolition was Swansea's Lord Mayor Charles 'Charlie' Thomas, born and bred in St. Thomas, and a long time Labour councillor who had represented the Eastside for many years.

Whether or not the building should have been preserved in some way as a part of Swansea's industrial heritage has been the subject of much debate, but nevertheless, the building was considered an important milestone in the United Kingdom's construction history, and a column from the fifth floor of the original provender mill was preserved by the Science Museum in South Kensington, London, whilst Amberley Museum in West Sussex houses another piece of the building.

In Swansea, a column section remains on a riverside path near the site of the mill, and a plaque located there commemorates Hennebique and his achievement with the words "This column was part of the old Weaver's Mill, the first reinforced concrete framed building built in Britain by French engineer Français Hennebique".

Unfortunately, his first name is spelt incorrectly on the plaque (as it should be 'François').

The Day That Buffalo Bill Came To St. Thomas

Even today the name 'Buffalo Bill' immediately throws up images of a time of cowboys, indians, gunfights and wagon trains, and whilst many if not all of the paperback 'dime novel' stories and western movies that shaped the world's perception of the 'Wild West' are fiction, William 'Buffalo Bill' Cody was not a fictional character at all, but a man who would become one of the greatest showmen the world has ever seen.

Born in 1846, legend has it that fifteen-year-old William Cody joined the short-lived Pony Express service, delivering mail across the country on horseback. During this time, using a total of 21 horses, he rode non-stop for 322 miles in 21 hours 40 mins on a two-way ride from Red Buttes Station to Rocky Ridge Station and back again [57]

In 1864 he enlisted as a teamster in the Seventh Kansas Volunteer Cavalry, and after being discharged in 1865, the following year he enlisted again, this time as a scout, and was supposedly attached to troops led by Lieutenant Colonel George Armstrong Custer and General Phillip Sheridan. In 1867 he was released to work with the Kansas Pacific Railroad as a buffalo hunter where he was reported to have killed 4280 buffalo, and after killing 69 buffalo in a day in a competition with another hunter, he gained the nickname 'Buffalo Bill'. He returned to the Army in 1868 whereas as a lone dispatch rider he was reputed to have covered 350 miles in 58 hours, the last 35 miles on foot, after which General Sheridan appointed him Chief of Scouts the Fifth Cavalry [58]. He was later appointed scout for the high-profile hunting exhibition organised in January 1872 by the Grand Duke Alexei Alexandrovich of Russia [59] who wrote about Cody in his memoirs.

In his autobiography, some of the many jobs Cody claimed he had held were that of a gold prospector, a fur trapper, and a Pony Express rider, all three before he was 20 years old, but some historians argue that on closer examination, contrary to the legends built up around him, many of the tales of adventures and brave acts attributed to Buffalo Bill were either greatly exaggerated or else not true at all [60].

It appears that he did not ride for the Pony Express, but instead was a boy messenger who worked for the transport firm of Russell, Majors and Waddell who set up the ill-fated company, and rather than riding for hundreds of miles often through hostile country, in reality, his job was to carry messages on horseback between the company's office in Leavenworth to a telegraph station three miles away. Further doubt has been placed on whom he worked for as an army scout, as whilst he did scout for General Sheridan and General Eugene Carr he did not scout for Custer, and there was no competition with another hunter to earn him his 'Buffalo Bill' name.

Whether or not the adventures attributed to Buffalo Bill were fact or fiction, it is clear William Cody was a teller of tall tales and a showman who recognised that he could create a character and make a living from it. In 1869 his Buffalo Bill persona, that of a larger-than-life hunting and fighting Western hero complete with long hair and flamboyant buckskin costume, caught the eye of dime-novel writer E.Z.C. Judson who, writing under the pen-name Ned Buntline, published 'Buffalo Bill King of the Border Men', which exaggerated Cody's exploits.

First seen on the front page of the Chicago Tribune on December 15th 1869, it became the first of over 500 titles about Buffalo Bill, whose tales were regularly serialised in the New York Weekly. By 1872 Cody was part of a stage troupe performing a Wild West show produced by Buntline called 'The Scouts of the Prairie', followed by 'The Scouts of the Plains' in which 'Wild Bill Hickock' another Western folk hero also took part. In 1874 Cody formed his own group 'The Buffalo Bill Combination', and in 1879 he released his autobiography 'The Life of Hon. William F. Cody' which told of his adventures. In 1883 he founded 'Buffalo Bill's Wild West', a circus-style touring group, and in 1887 Cody and his troupe were invited to Britain to be part of Queen Victoria's Golden Jubilee celebrations.

Advanced information sent to various British newspapers [61] offered their readers an insight into what was to come:

'**Buffalo Bill's Wild West Exhibition**... The preparations for this unique entertainment have been very extensive; they were made under the supervision of Major J.M. Burke, general manager of the Wild West. This remarkable exhibition has created a furore in America, and the reason is easy to understand. It is not a circus, nor indeed is it acting at all in a theatrical sense; but an exact reproduction of daily scenes in frontier life, as experienced and enacted by the very people who now form the Wild West Company... It could only be possible for such a remarkable undertaking to be carried out by a remarkable man; and the Hon. W.F. Cody, known as 'Buffalo Bill,' guide, scout, hunter, trapper, Indian fighter and legislator is a remarkable man. He is a perfect horseman, an unerring shot, a man of magnificent presence and physique, ignorant of the meaning of fear or fatigue; his life is a history of hairbreadth escapes, and deeds of daring, generosity, and self-sacrifice, which compare very favourably with the chivalric actions of romance, and he has not been inappropriately designated the 'Bayard of the Plains'.'

The American Exhibition opened on May 9th at Earl's Court in London, and 'Buffalo Bill's Wild West', featuring 180 horses, 18 buffalo, Texas longhorn cattle, elks, and mules, as well as numerous cowboys and American Indians, drew a crowd of over 28,000 people, including Queen Victoria herself. By the end of his stint in London over two million people had seen the show at a shilling each. Cody and his entourage stayed in Britain for over five months performing in London, Birmingham, and Manchester, and his visit to Britain was deemed a great success.

On his return to America, the second edition of his autobiography was released, now renamed 'The Autobiography of Buffalo Bill'. He returned to Britain for a second time between June 1891 and July 1892, during which time he visited fourteen towns and cities in England and Wales, including six days at Sophia Gardens in Cardiff in September 1891.

His third visit to Britain was between December 1902 and October 1903, which included two days in Swansea on the 14th and 15th of July 1903 where the show was seen in Victoria Park. After touring various cities in mainland Europe, he returned to Britain for the final time in April 1904 and toured England, Scotland and Wales until October the same year.

East Dock Station c1910 (authors digital collection)

His visit to Swansea was much anticipated not only by the town but the region as a whole, and it was the people of the Eastside who got to see him first, as described in The Cambrian on the 17th July [62] the report also describes the town on the day of the show:

'A little before two o'clock the first of the three trains bearing the Wild West Show steamed into the Burrows Sidings. At this time dawn had barely tinged the horizon, and about the only persons one would have expected to see around at this hour would be the festive clubbite. This is on normal occasions. This morning. however, there were fully a thousand people in the vicinity of the East Dock station. Presently the other train arrived, and at half past three the third and last long load of vans gladdened the eyes of St. Thomas (and all St. Thomas was awake). By this time the crowd had swelled to some two thousand. There was no move from the vans until after four o'clock, and then to the suppressed excitement of the assemblage, a real live cowboy emerged from one of the carriages.

This started the exodus. In ten minutes men swarmed the sidings, sturdy draught horses pawed the ground, and in almost less time than it takes to write, the first of the vans was rattling over the New Cut Bridge. The third nearly came to grief after a valiant attempt to knock over one of GWR Co's posts. But for this everything was as clockwork. Each man knew his work and did it smartly too. A posse of police shut out the boy peris from the paradise of their dreams - only pressmen and yawning tradesmen were allowed to enter the charmed precincts of the yard. One long train stood next to the station platform. Its coaches were undeniably American in style, and while one was admiring them, the doors flew open and the Red Indian of Fenimore Cooper and Aimard popped out in all the grotesque brilliancy of redskin fancy in colour. The real article this, and plenty of it. And not quite the imperturbable being of tradition. On the contrary, they chattered volubly and smiled to each other while they saddled their wiry mounts.

Then the cowboys emerged, and the subsequent scene was a lively one. The manner in which the frisky mustangs and fiery broncos kicked around made the solitary pressman there mount some trucks hurriedly. Here also is the real article - very real. This is indeed the man and horse of the plains. Laughing Gauchos, stolid Arabs, grinning negroes, natty cavalrymen, in turn, mounted their steeds, and a procession like a leaf out of romance made its way through the prosaic streets of St. Thomas. Last of all to turn on were the quaint-attired Cossacks, in sugarloaf hat and short gaberdine.

The great Buffalo Bill paid them the compliment of a few short words. A great head of white hair emerged from a sleeping carriage window, and as the first of the Caucus warriors ambled slowly past, Colonel Cody observed "You're a nice fellow!" The inevitable drawl, the grimly-bantering expression, had a wonderful effect upon the pace of the culprit, as upon another sleepy-headed squad. As each trotted past, "Scurry, you!" and "You're a nice fellow!" greeted their ears and quickened their footsteps. The great "William" glanced prospectively at the sky - it was brilliant - and disappeared. He is getting on in years is "Buffalo", but he is very much alive.

By six o'clock the last of the vans was away, and the squaws and papooses - black-eyed, berry-cheeked mites - were tucked away in the overland coach. The great feature of the work was the silent manner in which it was done. A foreman did let out once: "That dumpety-dashed driver ought to be punched I guess", but as the driver deserved it, it doesn't much matter. On all hands it was generally agreed, however, the Wild West is a big show - about the biggest that has struck Swansea.'

Victoria Park was soon transformed by Buffalo Bill's 'tent gang' whose job it was to first stake out and set up the show field. After first setting up a number of Indian tepees, a huge mess tent was erected in order to feed Cody's team, who throughout the day carried on with the erection of the various structures need for the show. Large crowds were already gathering, and the Cambrian noted the 'hum of anticipation and laughter of the multitudes who flocked to the enclosure combined to exhilarating effect.'

On Wednesday 14th July, Swansea's streets were packed with people keen to see the Wild West Show, and The Rhondda and Swansea Bay Company ran several additional early morning trains to accommodate the thousands of visitors from the Swansea Valley, where many of the works were on shorter hours or else had closed for the day to allow their staff to come to town. The Great Western Railway Company ran relief trains from Port Talbot to Swansea, and the Midland Rail Company also ran 'specials' into St. Thomas Railway Station, each train full of people wanting to see the show.

Fact or fiction, the exploits of Buffalo Bill Cody's version of the Wild West have played a huge part in influencing both literature and film depicting America of that time, and have undoubtedly sparked the imagination of every young boy ever since.

I wonder if 'Cowboy Rock' on Kilvey Hill got its name as a result of Buffalo Bill's visit?

The Eastside Comedy Bands

In 1952, when working on the content and logistics of the upcoming Eastside Carnival, the Carnival Committee Organising Secretary Bill Hughes decided that a local comedy band was needed [63]. After first rounding up Jack and Charlie Thomas, the sons of local councillor Charles H. Thomas Snr, he set about recruiting other willing local men to play a part in what would become a central part of the Eastside Carnival for many years, and soon there were over twenty men rehearsing three evenings a week at the reservoir above Grenfell Park Road, in anticipation of their first public appearance as a comedy troupe.

The 'St. Thomas Comedy Band' appeared for the first time on July 12th 1952 and was a huge success. Their antics in the carnival procession gained them the immediate attention of local children who followed them around the streets of the Eastside and onto the carnival ground at Maesteg Park, where their hilarious performance ensured they would be a much-loved fixture for years to come. They were so impressive that they soon had offers to take part in various other carnivals around the town, and their first excursion 'over the bridge' was to take part in the Townhill & Mayhill Carnival, although due to the fact that many of the St. Thomas troupe were keen cricketers and committed to the local league calendar, some of the offers had to be turned down.

They did not however turn down Swansea's biggest Fete & Gala, held at Singleton Park on August Bank Holiday Monday, where their madcap performance was witnessed by nearly 19,000 attendees, and from which point they gained a worthy reputation as the town's finest comedy band. On the final weekend of that year's summer season, they performed on the other side of Kilvey Hill and Bonymaen residents witnessed another hilarious performance at the local community centre.

The following year the comedy band was in great demand, and it took part in many carnivals around the town. On June 2nd 1953 they had multiple bookings for Coronation Day streets parties followed up by taking part in the official Swansea Coronation Fete & Gala at

Singleton Park held only four days later. July saw their triumphant return to the Eastside Carnival, and the same month they played a key part in the success of the British Legion Carnival in Mumbles.

Members of Bill Hughes' original troupe included Tommy Lloyd, Haydn Sparkes, John Dewsbury, Herbie Hughes, George Daniels, Alan Leaker, Frank Morris, Jimmy Aspell, John Miller, John Bennett, Jack Thomas, and the band's leader Charlie Thomas (my apologies to the families of any others I may have omitted).

The St. Thomas Comedy Band © Nigel Thomas

The Eastside Carnival, together with the St. Thomas Comedy Band, was a regular feature of local life in the 1950s, but by the mid-1960s the popularity of the carnival had waned and for a number of years there was no Eastside Carnival. However, in the early 1970s now-councillor Charlie Thomas, together with a local carnival committee of like-minded individuals that included his brother Jack, Jean Matthews, Susan Leonard, Rita Davies, Leah Rose Goss, Rona Powell, Glenys Morris and Danny Flavin, set about the resurrection of the Eastside Carnival (again, my apologies to the families of any others I may have omitted).

Ron Tovey recognised that a new local carnival was also an opportunity for the re-emergence of the local comedy band that he had loved as a young lad, and suggested to Brin Bidder and Colin Warlow that they put a new comedy troupe together. The three men agreed it was a good idea, and realising they needed a percussion section, drove to Llanelli to purchase a second-hand bass drum that Tovey had seen advertised in the Evening Post. They then sort out the knowledge and input of Jack Thomas, a member of the original comedy band, who loved the thought of a new comedy band parading through Eastside streets. Secret practice sessions were held on the 'Tip Field' led by Jack Thomas who, according to Ron Tovey, "rigorously coached us to perfection" in preparation for the upcoming and eagerly anticipated Eastside Carnival.

Many of the new band's members were involved with Port Tennant Colts Football Club or else were regulars in the Windsor Arms, and it was soon decided that Colin Warlow would lead the band, supported by a three-man percussion section made up of Ron Tovey on his newly acquired bass drum, Malcolm Davies and Dai Ashford, as the trio had previously 'served their time' together in the Eastside Jazz Band. This made training the comedy band much easier for all concerned. Other original band members included Alan Mahoney, Ted Johnson, Brian Salmon, Alfie Hambly, Freddie Edwards, Robert Stevenson, Stuart Williams, Robert Harrison, John Randall, John Davies, Tony Kelleher, John Smith, Steve Meyrick, Roy 'Coco' Jones and Swansea RFC, Wales and British Lion Geoff Wheel (my apologies to the families of any others I may have omitted).

The men discussed a new name for the band, and given that most men had either played on or regularly visited the local bog as children, decided on 'The Crymlyn Bogside Band', Whilst the name was readily accepted locally, the troupe did run into a problem in a carnival held in Baglan, where some people felt the name showed a reference to the ongoing 'Troubles' in Northern Ireland.

The months of preparation by the local carnival committee to produce a successful event were matched by the efforts of the residents of those streets that had entered a themed 'float' - essentially a dressed-up flatbed lorry that was often supplied free of charge by local companies. The carnival parade always ran without a hitch, or if there was a problem, the public was never made aware of it.

The Crymlyn Bogside Band (c) Ron Tovey

Throughout that period, on the day of the carnival the streets of the Eastside were filled with locals and visitors alike, all waiting patiently for what seemed like an endless line of themed floats of all shapes and descriptions, as well as a multitude of marching bands from all over Swansea and beyond that including the Swansea Eastside Carnival Band, founded in 1951 by Mr Jess Tanner, and at this time known as Swansea East Jazz Band and run by Percy Gilbert.

The unofficial title of 'carnival favourites' was always given to the Eastside's own comedy band, whose antics along the route had adults and children in fits of laughter. The carnival parade travelled from the terminus end of Danygraig Road and eventually ended at Maesteg Park, where the afternoon continued with a packed-out funfair for the families as well as a beer tent for the dads.

The next five years or so are thought by many to be the peak period in the history of the Eastside Carnival, which was normally held one

Saturday in July, and it was regarded as one of the very best carnivals seen in Swansea, if not the best.

Unfortunately, by the early 1980s, a combination of work and family commitments saw the demise of first the comedy band, and then of the carnival itself, as the ushering in of new Health & Safety rules and the subsequent changes in insurances costs meant the use of flat-bed lorries for floats became far too expensive for companies to donate their use, or for local residents to even contemplate hiring a vehicle.

Eastside Etymology

Whilst I have included this listing in this book, it should be considered a **'Work in Progress'** and I welcome any additional info to amend or update it.

Part 1 - 'The Terminus' end of Danygraig Rd to Ysgol St.

Gelli-Grafog Road – Rowanberry Grove (Gelli = Grove and Grafog = Rowan Berry)

Danygraig Road - 'Dan-y-Graig is Welsh for 'under the rock'

Bevans Row: In 1868, Neath Brewer Evan Evans was given a leasehold by Briton Ferry Estate to build "five houses with gardens" on land previously occupied by Swansea Zinc Company, adjacent to Tennant Canal. Given that his grandson was Bevan Evan Evans, it is likely that 'Bevan's Row' bears his name, although they may have been originally known as Canal Cottages. The row was extended by The Swansea Harbour Trust extended in 1906.

Crymlyn St - previously considered part of Gelligrafog Rd, it began as a row of houses called Shackleford Cottages built for workers employed by Shackleford & Ford, who owned the Crown Spelter Works in Port Tennant. Crymlyn St was named after the nearby Crymlyn Marsh or Bog; 'Crymlyn' meaning a Druid place of worship.

Hoo St –built for workers employed by Shackleford & Ford, who owned the Crown Spelter Works in Port Tennant, and named after a title held by the first 'The Earl of Jersey' (created in 1697) who had already been created Baron Villiers of Hoo, in the County of Kent in 1691.

Wern Fawr Rd – Big (or Great) Marsh

Wern Terrace – Welsh for Marsh

Robert Owen Gardens - named after an 18th-century philanthropist and social reformer often regarded as 'the Father of British Socialism.'

William Morris Gardens - named after a 19th-century socialist

David Williams Terrace - named after a prominent Labour Party stalwart of the 1920s and 30s, David Williams was at one time the MP for Swansea East.

Grafog St – Welsh for Rowan Berry

Gelli St – – Welsh for Grove

Tymawr St – 'Big (or Great) House', the approximate location of Danygraig House

Pant St - a hollow or dip

Ysgol St – 'Ysgol' is Welsh for 'school', but it was previously known as Cemetery Terrace and Cemetery Rd, and prior to that it was the drive to Danygraig House.

Part 2 - Jersey Terrace to the beginning of Port Tennant Rd.

Jersey Terrace – named after the Earl of Jersey, who owned large tracts of land in Swansea, and in the Eastside in particular

Baglan St – likely named after Baglan where the Welsh seat of the Earl of Jersey was located.

Bay St – presumably because there was a great view of the bay!

Reginald St – possibly after Edward Reginald Child-Villiers, the brother of the 7th Earl of Jersey

Ormsby Terrace – Once part of Baglan St. Possibly named after the builder of the houses there?

Monton Terrace - Possibly named after the builder of the houses there?

Port Tennant Rd – named after the port built at the end of the Tennant Canal, which was named after its owner, George Tennant.

St Illtyd's Crescent – named after the original mission house which became St. Illtyd's School (the church was built some years later)

Jersey Park – the ground was gifted by the 7th Earl of Jersey

Longford Crescent –named after Lord Longford, one of the children of Margaret, Lady Jersey (wife of the 7th Earl)

Upton Terrace – named after Upton House in Warwickshire, the home of the 5th Earl of Jersey.

Harbour View Rd - presumably because it has a view of the harbour.

Gwynne Terrace - likely named after the headteacher of the Kilvey school, Richard Gwynne.

Margaret St – named after Margaret Elizabeth Leigh Childs, wife of the 7th Earl of Jersey

Osterley St – named after the Jersey family seat 'Osterley Park' in Middlesex, where the 7th Earl died.

Middleton St – named after another Jersey family house, Middleton Park in Oxford, where Margaret Elizabeth Leigh Childs died.

Lee St - Originally called Short St, it was renamed after Councillor John Henry Lee

Kinley St –. Originally the site of 'Ffynon Hyssop' (The Well of Hyssop'), it would be later called Farm Lane. Kinley Terrace was at one time part of Farm Lane, which later become Kinley St, possibly named after local builder Thomas Kinley who lived at Bay View, in St. Thomas.

Part 3 - Wallace Rd to Windmill Terrace

Whilst Grenfell & Sons built few if any houses I this area, they did build workers housing further north in Pentrechwyth, naming the roads and streets thereafter their family. However the name Grenfell was also attached to a new 1920s council housing project built on the family's local seat Maesteg House which was demolished and the new housing built on its grounds. The land was owned by the Briton Ferry Estate, and the land and building leases held by the Grenfells were sold off as part of a bankruptcy case in the 1890s.

Wallace Rd - named after Field Marshal Francis Wallace Grenfell (1841-1925), 1st Baron Grenfell of Kilvey, son of Pascoe St. Leger Grenfell

Dupre Rd - named after the family of Pascoe St. Leger Grenfell's second wife, Catherine Anne Dupre, her family name also passed to one of their sons, Pascoe Du Pre Grenfell (1828 - 1896).

Grenfell Park Rd - named after the Grenfell family who lived at Maesteg House, which stood above what we now know as Grenfell Park Rd.

St Leger Crescent - named after Pascoe St. Leger (1798-1879), the name passed on from his mother (Georgina St. Leger), who was his father's (Pascoe Grenfell) second wife.

Pen Isa Coed - Welsh for 'the lower end of the trees.'

Maes St - Welsh for 'field', it was originally called Church St.

Lewis St - possibly named after local builder Samuel Lewis who built some houses on Morris Lane and it is very likely that he also built Lewis St.

Sebastopol St - named after the Crimean Siege of Sebastopol, fought between October 1854 and September 1855

Balaclava St - named after The Battle of Balaclava, fought on 25th October 1854 during the Crimean War and was part of the Siege of Sebastopol (1854–55)

Inkerman St - named after The Battle of Inkerman was fought during the Crimean War on 5th November 1854 and was followed by the Siege of Sebastopol.

Miers St - named after Mary Anne 'Molly' Miers, who was the wife of Sir Robert Mackworth, who had owned much of the land in this area. The lower half of the street was originally called Alma St, after The Battle of Alma, the first battle of the Crimean War fought on 20th September 1854, whilst the upper half was called Miers Terrace. After Sir Robert Mackworth died in 1794, his widow married Capel Hanbury Leigh of Pontypool in 1797, and it was he that named the streets after Crimean battles. A few years later Alma St and Miers Terrace became one street, under the new name of Miers St.

Delhi St - named after the Siege of Delhi (June-Sept. 1857), where the British Army put an end to an Indian Mutiny against British rule.

Pinkney St - once known as Benson St, after landowner Starling Benson, Pinkney St is named after the Pinkney family who had previously owned the land. It is currently a street in name only, as it has no houses on it, and is the access road to the car park behind the Swansea Dockers Club.

Mackworth Terrace - named after Neath industrialist Sir Robert Mackworth, who owned much of the land in this area.

Roseland Terrace - presumably because of an abundance of roses?

Thomas St - shown as 'St. Thomas St.' on a Swansea Harbour layout map of 1857 as well as being listed as such in the 1871 census, this suggests that the original name was shortened at a later date. Likely named after 'The Hamlet of St. Thomas', which itself was named after the original St. Thomas Chapel.

Morris Lane - possibly named as an extension of Morris Lane between High St and The Strand (now Lower King's Lane) which was named after industrialist Robert Morris, father of John Morris (whom Morriston is named after). At the top it connects to the trail over Kilvey Hill, known in Welsh as 'Heol Meurig'. However, the 1919 notes of WH Jones suggest that it was named after 'one William Morris, guard of the mail-coach from Swansea to London, having built some houses in the lane, in which one he himself lived.'

Benthall Place - named after the Benthall family of Shropshire who via marriage inherited land locally from St. Thomas landowner Elias Jenkins of Tyr Gwl. The family also built a schoolhouse on Morris Lane in 1862 (opened in 1863), and when the lease lapsed in 1945, the Benthall family gifted the building to the local community.

Kilvey Terrace - presumably once a trail that led to Kilvey Hill, 'Kilvey' is an anglicisation of 'Cilfai'. 'Cil' comes from the Latin word 'cella' which originally meant a small room, and used in the sense of a monastic cell, which in Gaelic was known as 'a Keeiil'. Legend has it that an Irish Culdee (monk) once lived and prayed in solitude on Kilvey Hill. In Welsh 'Cil' means 'a little nook, a corner, a retreat, whilst 'Fai' is the mutated form of 'Mai' (a version of the name 'May' or 'Mary'), so 'Cilfai' may mean 'Mary's Retreat', after a place of worship.

Dring St - 'Dring' is likely a shortened version of 'the Welsh 'dringfa' which means 'climb' or 'ascent', and it is notable for having no houses on it.

Bay View - likely so-named as it had a wonderful view of Swansea Bay.

Vicarage Terrace - so named as it fronted Kilvey Vicarage.

Windmill Terrace - so named as it leads to the trail up and over Kilvey Hill called 'Heol Meurig' that once led to and from a nearby Windmill.

Pentreguinea Rd - on first look this name appears to be a combination of the Welsh 'Pentre' or 'village', and 'guinea' a monetary measurement of £1 and 1 shilling, however, Colonel Morgan William Llewelyn (1847-1927), then President of the Royal Institute of South Wales, theorised that the name 'Pentre-guinea' likely evolved from Pentre-Cennydd'. 'Cennydd' is 'Kenneth' in Welsh, (as can be seen in the word 'Llangennith') so supposedly the Village of St. Kenneth, although there is no documented proof of this.

Part 4 - Foxhole and Kilvey

Whilst the Manor of Kilvey is first mentioned in King John's 1215 Charter of Swansea, to all intents and purposes, at that time it was forest and pasture land. The Manor of Kilvey reached from Swansea Bay to Glais. The earliest recorded residential area on the Eastside was a number of streets and roads built in Foxhole by Freeman & Co., later known in official documents as 'The White Rock Estate' that included Freeman's Row and Owen's Row. The residential area we now refer to as Kilvey was first recognised as an ecclesiastical parish in 1881, from which time the area of Foxhole became less known.

Foxhole Rd: The origins of this are unknown, but may well have been a natural habitat for foxes at one time. It is likely that the name predates most if not all of the surrounding streets, as it was the most heavily populated in the first census of the area in 1841.

Kilvey Rd: - see Kilvey Terrace.

Jericho Rd: Jericho was a small prominent city of the Canaan region (now part of the West Bank of Palestine), and the name Jericho' is often used in relation to Methodist churches. Given its close proximity to the old Canaan Chapel on Foxhole Rd, it construction was likely connected to the chapel.

Maesteg St: 'Maesteg' means 'Fair field' in Welsh, and it is possible that at one time it may have been a pathway to the Grenfell family home Maesteg House.

Granville Rd: named after Pascoe Grenfell's first wife Charlotte Granville (1765–1790)

Headland Rd: one definition of a headland is 'the area of land that is high, steep and extends over a body of water', so it may well be the logic used in naming this road.

Grenfell Park Estate Addresses

A private housing estate built on land that had nothing to do with the Grenfell family, I am somewhat perplexed by the names of the streets of private housing known as Grenfell Park Estate, built c 1928 onwards on the grounds of Ty-Gwl above Windmill Terrace, land leased by Freeman & Co. from Briton Ferry Estate It has been suggested that they may have been named after steamships, or after locations in Devon, but I am yet to find any concrete evidence of either of these suggestions.

Lydford Avenue: ?

Glenroy Avenue: ?

St. Elmo's Avenue: ?

Elmhurst Crescent: ?

Beaumont Crescent: ?

WWII Bombing of the Eastside

The bombing of Swansea during the Second World War is probably the biggest single series of events to shape the town's history. There were forty-four attacks made on the town between June 1940 and February 1943, most involving a small number of aircraft, however, it is the terror of the 'Three Night Blitz' over the 19th, 20th and 21st February 1941 that flattened the town centre and had a huge effect on the shaping of the town from the 1950s onwards, as bombed structures were cleared to make space for the new town layout that replaced the destruction and devastation that went before it.

At the beginning of WW2 Swansea, like the rest of the west coast of Britain, was thought of as out of reach of the German air force, as it was not possible to fly from Germany carrying bombs and then return again due to limitations on distances covered as well as fuel requirements needed, but after Germany's occupation of France, this dynamic changed.

France had a relatively large network of airfields and support facilities across the country and was developing more sites in the northeast of France when in 1940, it capitulated to Germany, who immediately utilised France's airfields, as well as built additional airfields facing the Channel coast from where they intended to launch their air offensive against Britain.

The first attacks on Swansea involved the Eastside when on the 27th of June 1940 properties on Danygraig Road suffered damage but there were no casualties. The third raid, carried out on July 10th by a single aircraft whose objective was to bomb the King's Dock, killed twelve people and twenty-six others were wounded. Between the first bombing raid in June 1940 and the last in February 1943, 802 premises were completely destroyed, and over 27,000 were either seriously damaged or slightly damaged, with the loss of 230 people, plus another 409 people injured, much of which happening during the Three Nights Blitz.

Outside of Swansea's town centre, the Eastside of Swansea suffered more than any other district because of its proximity to BP Llandarcy and Swansea Docks.

The bombs dropped on the Eastside are listed below using the following codes:

HE (High Explosive) **IB (**Incendiary Bomb) **PhIB** (Phosphorus incendiary Bomb) **PM** (Parachute Mine)

27th June 1940
6No. HE bombs fell near Danygraig Road
2No. HE bombs fell adjacent to King's Dock

10th July 1940
4No. HE bombs fell west of King's Dock and caused significant damage to several goods sheds.

24th August 1940
IBs fell across the districts of Port Tennant and St Thomas, no significant fires were subsequently recorded.

1st September 1940
251 No. HE bombs and 1,000 No. IBs fell across Swansea, which was concentrated in the town centre, the exact locations for most of these incidents were not recorded.

24th September 1940
1No. HE bomb fell in King's Dock.

9th October 1940
1No. HE bomb fell on Prince of Wales Dock

5th January 1941
Several HE bombs and IBs fell across the district of St Thomas.

13th January 1941
2No. HE bombs fell north of King's Dock.

17th January 1941
178No. HE bombs and 7,000No. IBs fell across Swansea.
HE bombs and IBs fell across Jersey Terrace, causing significant damage to Danygraig School.
HE bombs and IBs fell across Port Tennant Road, demolishing 4No. houses.
Several HE bombs (number unspecified) fell on 'D' Shed, King's Dock.

19th – 21st February 1941
The Swansea 'Three Night Blitz' took place. During these raids, 896 HE bombs and more than 30,000 IBs fell on the town. Approximately 112,000 properties were damaged or destroyed, mostly located in the city centre and adjacent residential districts. Due to the large numbers of bombs that fell during this raid, and the widespread fires caused by IBs, many incidents went unrecorded by the ARP wardens.
1No. HE bomb fell on and demolished 129 Port Tennant Road.

28th November 1941
1No. PM fell in the vicinity of the Burrows Inn, causing blast damage to structures.

16th February 1943
In the final raid to occur over Swansea, 32No. HE bombs, in addition to Firepots, PhIBs and 1kg IBs, fell across Swansea town centre.

More info at this link...http://zeticauxo.com/downloads-and.../ordnance-data-sheets/

Eastside Pubs - Past and Present

This list covers pubs that have been opened since 1800 between Port Tennant and Kilvey inclusive, and does not include any bars that may have opened and closed on the SA1 residential and commercial development. Only three pubs still exist from a list of over fifty; the Union Inn in Port Tennant, mentioned in Swansea's first census documents of 1841, the Mile End Inn in Port Tennant, mentioned in the 1851 census documents, and the Ship Inn, built in 1989-90 on the site of the 'Bottom' Ship Inn in St. Thomas, with part of the old building retained within the new pub. Note: The Swansea Dockers Club is not included below as it is a Social Club rather than a Public House.

During the 1800s, in addition to the official pubs, there were also many unofficial 'pubs' serving alcohol in the area, where people sold homebrewed beer from their houses; such a 'pub' was called a 'cwrw bach' (literally 'small beer'.

1. Vale of Neath
2. Mile End Inn (105 Golden Row)
3. Mermaid Inn (92 Golden Row)
4. Naval & Military Club (Ysgol St, a pub)
5. Port Tennant Inn (on Langdon Rd)
6. Union Inn (100/223 PT Rd)
7. Burrows Inn (The East Rd)
8. Station Inn (36 Fabian St)
9. Cyprus Hotel/Inn (Fabian St)
10. The Ship Inn (replaced 'Bottom' Ship)
11. Fabian Inn (Fabian St)
12. Railway Hotel/Inn (Balaclava St)
13. Inkerman Inn (50 Delhi St)
14. Volunteer Arms (18 Delhi St)
15. Miers Arms (10 Fabian St)
16. Windsor Arms/City Bar (Delhi St)
17. Coquimbo Inn (Cawnpore St)
18. Cape Horner (Miers St)
19. Chili Arms (Fabian St)
20. Hamlet Inn (27 Fabian St)
21. Ship & Castle (Fabian St)
22. Golden Cross (Fabian St)
23. Bridge Inn (Bridge St)
24. Midland Vaults (3 Fabian St)
25. Red House Inn (1 Fabian St)
26. Ivy Bush Inn (Thomas St)
27. Benson Arms (Thomas St)
28. Horse & Groom (Thomas St 1870s)
29. Farmers Arms (Fabian St)
30. Red Lion Ferry House and Inn
31. Masons Arms (Bridge St)
32. 'Bottom' Ship Inn (Pentreguinea Rd)
33. White Lion (New Cut 1850s)
34. Globe (Foxhole Rd)
35. Fuel Inn (New Cut 1858)
36. Ship & Anchor (Foxhole)
37. Malsters Arms (Pentreguinea Rd)
38. Copperman's Arms (Kilvey Tce)
39. Volunteers Arms (Pentreguinea Rd)
40. Joiners Arms (Foxhole 1854)
41. Lamb (Foxhole)
42. Lamb & Flag (Foxhole Rd 1870s)
43. Swan Inn (Foxhole Rd 1870s)
44. 'Top' Ship Inn (151 Foxhole Rd)
45. Smith's Arms (53 Foxhole Rd 1854)
46. Golden Lion (Foxhole)
47. Fox (Foxhole 1858)
48. Tap Inn (Foxhole)
49. The Sun Inn (107 Foxhole Rd)
50. Tiger Inn (Foxhole)
51. Rifleman's Arms (Kilvey)

Bibliography

[1] The Duke of Beaufort's Survey of Gower and Kilvey 1688.

[2] T. Cambrian, "The Kilvey Windmill," *The Cambrian,* p. 8, 22 October 1875.

[3] T. Cambrian, "To the Editor of The Cambrian," *The Cambrian,* 29 October 1875.

[4] T. Cambrian, "The Old Windmill of Kilvey," *The Cambrian,* p. 8, 18 January 1878.

[5] T. Cambrian, "The "Old Windmill" on Kilvey," *The Cambrian,* p. 8, 8 February 1878.

[6] T. Cambrian, "The Old Windmill on Kilvey," *The Cambrian,* 15 February 1878.

[7] T. Cambrian, "The Llansamlet Windmills," *The Cambrian,* p. 8, 22 February 1878.

[8] T. Cambrian, "Kilvey Old Windmill," *The Cambrian,* p. 8, 8 March 1878.

[9] T. Cambrian, "History of Llysnewydd...and a word or two on the Windmills," *The Cambrian,* p. 8, 8 March 1878.

[10] T. Cambrian, "To the Editor of 'The Cambrian'," *The Cambrian,* p. 8, 8 March 1878.

[11] T. Cambrian, "The Jubilee Beacons.," *The Cambrian,* p. 5, 25 June 1897.

[12] W. Rodgers, "The Windmills of Kilvey," *Gower journal of the Gower Society. 1966 -* , vol. 17, pp. 8-11, 1966.

[13] J. J. F. Melin, "The Windmills of Glamorgan - Melin 2 (p8-26).," 1986. [Online]. Available: https://welshmills.org/wp-content/uploads/2020/11/Jane-Jo-F-Roberts-The-Windmills-of-Glamorgan-Melin-2.pdf.

[14] Unknown, "Swansea from Kilvey Hill - Swansea Museum Collection," [Online]. Available: https://artuk.org/discover/artworks/swansea-from-kilvey-hill-224888. [Accessed 13 July 2022].

[15] J. G. Wood, Principle Rivers in Wales Illustrated, London, 1814.

[16] K. Wood, Artist, *no. 77.1458.* [Art]. Usher Gallery Lincoln, .

[17] T. Quirk, 'Memories' Swansea Eastside, 1995.

[18] T. C. D. Leader, "A Tower With A Tale," *The Cambrian Daily Leader,* p. 1, 29 August 1913.

[19] T. C. D. Leader, "Kilvey's Crown of Snow," *The Cambria Daily Leader,* p. 6, 13 November 1919.

[20] R. Campbell, All Bets Are Off - Racing in Swansea, Gomer, 2004, p. 23.

[21] T. Cambrian, "The. Swansea Races," *The Cambrian,* p. 3, 30 June 1804.

[22] T. Cambrian, "Swansea and Neath Races.," *The Cambrian,* p. 3, 9 August 1834.

[23] Unknown, "Swansea Races Over 100 Years Ago," *Gower Journal of the Gower Society.,* vol. 16, pp. 56-59, 1964.

[24] R. Campbell, All Bets Are Off - Horse Racing In Swansea., Gomer, 2004, pp. 34-35.

[25] T. Welshman, "Swansea Races - Yesterday.," *The Welshman,* p. 3, 20 August 1847.

[26] T. Welshman, "Swansea Races," *The Welshman,* p. 3, 24 August 1855.

[27] R. Campbell, All Bets Are Off - Racing In Swansea, Gomer, 2004, pp. 40-43.

[28] B. F. Estate, "Lease (Counterpart), for lives of Thomas Edward of Trallwng and Daniel Fabian jun.GB 216 D/D BF 256," 1 January 1767. [Online].

[29] B. F. Estate, "Lease for lives of Richard Jenkins and John Borlase Jenkins, subject to a life interest of Jennet Fabian...GB 216 D/D BF 373.," 25 July 1810. [Online].

[30] B. F. Estate, "Lease for lives of Luce Williams, and nephew Thomas Roberts...enement and lands (20a.) called Tyr John North with adj. house late in occ. of John North...GB 216 D/D BF 235," 18 August 1758. [Online].

[31] D. P. Morgan, "A Swansea farm in 1703.," *The Journal of the Gower Society,* 1973.

[32] C. Archivist, "Annual Report of the County Archivist - Fabian Way: the building of Swansea's eastern gateway p32. .," 2014-2015. [Online].

[33] C. Archivist, "Annual Report of the County Archivist - Fabian Way: the building of Swansea's eastern gateway p33.," 2014-15. [Online].

[34] C. Archivist, "Annual Report of the County Archivist - Fabian Way: the building of Swansea's eastern gateway p33.," 2014-2015. [Online].

[35] C. Archivist, "Annual Report of the County Archivist - Fabian Way: the building of Swansea's eastern gateway p34," 2014-2015. [Online].

[36] C. Archivist, "Annual Report of the County Archivist - Fabian Way: the building of Swansea's eastern gateway p34," 2014-2015. [Online].

[37] S. W. E. Post, "Pioneering Power Plant," *South Wales Evening Post,* 25 February 2012.

[38] A. F. Nick Hacking, "Progress in Planning: Networks, power and knowledge in the planning system: A case study of energy from waste.," *Elsevier,* p. 10, 2015.

[39] R. Allen, "Ecopolitics - Fresh Air Squandered.," *The Ecologist,* pp. 33-34, 1971.

[40] B. Rewind, "Wales Today: Port Tennant Pollution.," 26 July 1966. [Online]. Available: https://bbcrewind.co.uk/asset/618e6025e158480022eeb1c8?q=Swansea&size=90..

[41] C. o. Swansea, "Possible legal action by the City of Swansea against United Carbon Black Ltd concerning health hazards of carbon black: correspondence and papers FD9/1396," 1970-1971. [Online]. Available: https://discovery.nationalarchives.gov.uk/details/r/C1338724.

[42] R. Allen, "Ecopolitics - Fresh Air Squandered," *The Ecologist,* pp. 33-34, 1971.

[43] I. Bone, " Carbon Black," *Solidarity: For Workers Power ,* vol. 6, no. 10, 1971.

[44] I. Bone, "Carbon Black," *Solidarity: For Workers Power* , vol. 6, no. 10, 1971.

[45] I. Bone, "Carbon Black," *Solidarity: For Workers Power* , vol. 6, no. 10, 1971.

[46] I. Bone, "Carbon Black," *Solidarity: For Workers Power* , vol. 6, no. 19, 1971.

[47] I. Bone, "Carbon Black," *Solidarity: For Workers Power* , vol. 6, no. 10, 1971.

[48] I. Bone, "Carbon Black," *Solidarity: For Workers Power* , vol. 6, no. 10, 1971.

[49] R. Allen, "Ecopolitics: Fresh Air Squandered," *The Ecologist,* pp. 33-34, 1971.

[50] L. N. Service, "Liberation News Service (New York, New York) p3-4.," 1964-1977. [Online]. Available: https://content.wisconsinhistory.org/digital/collection/p15932coll8/id/75568..

[51] N. Scientist, "Ecomonics of the Real World - Pollution - A Cost of Growth?," *New Scientist* , p. 723, 6 December 1973.

[52] A. F. Nick Hacking, "Networks, power and knowledge in the planning system: A case study of energy from waste.Vol. 113 p3-37," [Online]. Available: https://www.sciencedirect.com/science/article/pii/S0305900615300015?via%3Dihub..

[53] T. Cambrian, "A Grand Flour and Grain Business for Swansea," *The Cambrian,* p. 5, 8 January 1892.

[54] T. Cambrian, "The New Industry that is to Supply Swansea District With Food Stuffs," *The Cambrian,* p. 7, 1 July 1892.

[55] T. Cambrian, "A Prosperous and Growing Industry.," *The Cambrian,* p. 5, 11 August 1899.

[56] T. Cambrian, "A Grand Flour and Grain Business for Swansea - Interview with Mr. W. Weaver.," *The Cambrian,* p. 5, 11 August 1899.

[57] M. S. Raymond Settle, Saddles and Spurs: The Pony Express Saga., Bison Books, 1972, p. 113.

[58] U. S. P. Service, "The Pony Express Rides Into History.," 1970. [Online]. Available:

https://web.archive.org/web/20130411065213/http://www.buffalobilldays.org/index.htm..

[59] D. Duncan, Miles from Nowhere: Tales from America's Contemporary Frontier., University of Nebraska, 2000.

[60] D. Russell, The Lives and Legends of Buffalo Bill., 1979.

[61] A. Gallop, "The History Press - extracted from Buffalo Bill's British Wild West," 2009. [Online]. Available: https://www.thehistorypress.co.uk/articles/buffalo-bill-s-british-wild-west/.

[62] T. Cambrian, "Buffalo Bill's Visit - Great Wild West Show at Swansea.," *The Cambrian,* p. 8, 17 July 1903.

[63] S. T. C. Centre, St. Thomas Community Centre Coronation Magazine, - Comedy Band, 1953.

[64] D. Duncan, Miles from Nowhere: Tales from America's Contemporary Frontier., University of Nebraska Press, 2000.

Lightning Source UK Ltd.
Milton Keynes UK
UKHW020019061222
413441UK00008B/100